I0039349

Judgment Records of Dorchester, Queen Anne's, and Talbot Counties

[Maryland]

F. Edward Wright

HERITAGE BOOKS
2020

HERITAGE BOOKS

AN IMPRINT OF HERITAGE BOOKS, INC.

Books, CDs, and more—Worldwide

For our listing of thousands of titles see our website
at
www.HeritageBooks.com

Published 2020 by
HERITAGE BOOKS, INC.
Publishing Division
5810 Ruatan Street
Berwyn Heights, Md. 20740

Copyright © 2001 Delmarva Roots

All rights reserved. No part of this book may be reproduced or
transmitted in any form or by any means, electronic or mechanical,
including photocopying, recording or by any information storage
and retrieval system without written permission from the author,
except for the inclusion of brief quotations in a review.

International Standard Book Number
Paperbound: 978-1-68034-485-1

CONTENTS

ACKNOWLEDGMENT

I am especially grateful for the assistance provided by Katherine G. Hohmann in interpreting of the records at the Maryland State Archives. Mrs. Hohmann assisted me greatly in abstracting the Judgment Records of Dorchester County.

INTRODUCTION

The Judgment Records of the County Court cover a wide range of human endeavor. We have concentrated on criminal cases, welfare cases to support the infirm and orphans, and transportation. Of special interest to genealogists will be cases involving orphans and illegitimate children.

The criminal cases included felonies that came before the Justices such as theft, assault, and in my opinion, a large number of bastardy cases (as they were then called) - 64 cases in the period, 1742-1745. There were a few cases of adultery. Punishment seemed to be fairly consistent. Theft usually called for time in the pillory and/or whippings along with a four-fold payment of the estimated cost of the stolen property - to paid to the injured party. One who was found guilty of assault was usually fined 5 shillings. The Court was concerned as to the support of illegitimate children and sought to indemnify the county from maintaining the child. Punishment of the woman was usually 30 shillings; those who were "whipt" were usually those who could not afford the fines or repeat offenders.

Petitions usually pertained to individual welfare, i.e., relief from taxes or levies; requests for allowances to support the infirm, insane, or aged; appointment of commissions to "perpetuate the memory of the bounders" of land tracts wherein the bounders such as trees, rocks, etc., had decayed and disappeared. Runaway servants were called into court to have their servitude lengthened to cover the runaway time and the costs in capturing them.

Transportation was a major concern of the Court which included the maintenance of roads, taverns or ordinaries, and ferries. The Court approved the clearing of new roads and adjusting the routes of old ones; appointed road overseers and fined those who failed to provide labor to the overseer for road maintenance. By associating the names of petitioners with the location of these roads as shown in the court records one is aided in pinpointing the area where an ancestor lived.

Taverns and ordinaries were licensed by the Court, and ferry operators were appointed after being bonded.

Because the county or parish was responsible for the welfare of its citizens the Justices took a keen interest in orphans. Those who had sizeable estates left to them by their father were guaranteed their estate by three person bound to the Court to hold the estate until the orphan reached his majority. Those orphans without sufficient estate were bound into apprenticeship by the Court which determined the age of the orphan so that a date could be established when he or she reached the required age.

A major portion of the cases involved debt resolution and for the most part are not covered in this work because of their limited value in genealogical research. Nevertheless the researcher may wish to examine these records. Likewise we have given limited coverage to actions of trespass in which one party sues another for recovery of damages or injury to his person, property or rights.

This volume encompasses selected data from the following records:

DORCHESTER COUNTY
1690-1692. Liber Old 4 1/2. Microfilm CR49,048-4,
1728-1729 MSA No. C704-2. HdHR 8907-2. (There is no microfilm copy despite the statement of existing indexes.}
1733-1734 Not on microfilm. MSA No. C704-3
1742-1743 Liber Old 11, reverse. Microfilm CR 49,052-1.
1742-1743 Liber Old 12, reverse. Microfilm CR49,053
1742-1743 Liber Old 13, pp. 483-529. Microfilm CR 49,052-2
1744-1745 Liber Old 13, pp. 1-479. Microfilm CR 49,052-2

QUEEN ANNE'S COUNTY
1709-1716 Liber ETB. Microfilm CR 6397-2

TALBOT COUNTY
1662-1674 Liber BB2. Microfilm WK 1392-1393-2
1686-1689 Liber NN6. Microfilm WK 1394-2
1692 Liber NN6. Microfilm WK 1394-2
1692-1696 Liber LL7. Microfilm WK 605-606
1696-1698 Liber AB8. Microfilm WK 606-607
1705-1706 Liber RF10. Microfilm WK 607-608-2
1706-1708 Microfilm CR6399-1
1714-1717 Liber FT1. Microfilm CR 6399-2

Some of the Queen Anne's County Judgment Records have also been abstracted by Irma S. Harper and published in *Chesapeake Cousins* (periodical of the Upper Shore Genealogical Society of Maryland) for the following periods: 1710-1729 (Vol. 24#1), 1730-37 (Vol 24#2, 1737-41 (Vol. 25#1), 1741-46 (Vol. 26#1), 1746-51 (Vol. 26#2), 1751-56 (Vol. 27#1), 1756-60 (Vol. 27#2).

F. Edward Wright
Lewes, Delaware
2001

DORCHESTER COUNTY JUDGMENT RECORDS

1690-1692
Microfilm: CR49048

August Court 1690

The fine of last June Court on Robert Thornwell, ordered for not answering to serve on the grand jury being summoned, was remitted, he having now shown good and sufficient reasons to the Court for his absence. Thomas Flowers who had been also fined was also relieved.

Upon the complaint of John Makeele, jun., overseer of the highways in Fishing Creek Hundred that William Mills, Mr. Pollard's man, David Jones, Mr. Clark's Edward, Thomas Nooner, Cornelius his Negro, William Hill, planter, John King servt to John Branock, Walter at Mrs. Woodwards and Rice Thomas would not attend the clearing of the highways - [having been] summoned by the said overseer.

Complaint of John Lecompt overseer of the highways in Little Choptank Hundred that Mr. Thomas Cooke, Mr. Edward Cooke, William Willoby, Thomas Killman, Henry Wheeler, Junr., Cornelius Herrington, William Warener, Junr. Henry Trippe, Henry Beckwith, would not attend the clearing of the high ways.

Ordered that the bastard child born of Katherine Baggett, Mr. John Brooks woman servant, shall serve Mr. John Brook until it arrives to the age of 21 or the time of marriage. Katherine Baggott was fined 500 lbs. of tobacco for having born a bastard child. Thomas Wells paid the fine.

Ordered that Mary Bradston be whipt 15 lashes for having borne a bastard child.

The fine of Andrew Parker remitted (for not serving at a jury).

Ordered that Mathew Carry be fined 500 lbs. of tobacco for not obeying the sheriff.

Aaron Tunes was ordered to bring or send to next Court, a gun that he formerly bought of an Indian called Cut Wilson Jack, supposed to be a gun belonging to John Dryson.

Upon her petition Francis Twyford, being fined last June Court for not appearing to serve on the grand jury, the fine is remitted.

Ordered that Katherine Fielding be whipt 10 lashes for contempt of the court.

Katherine Kenedy otherwise called Katherine Fielding, wife of James Fielding presented in that sometime in June 1690 and before and after did adulterately associate herself and keep company with one Mr. Edward Cooke of

Cooks Point. To be whipt and fined [numbers obliterated].

Upon the petition of Thomas Gray his fine is remitted for his contempt of Doctor. John Brook.

Matthew Carry to be whipt with 10 lashes for giving false reports against John Brooke, one of the Justices of the Court.

The Court ordered that James Nowells be fined 500 lbs. of tobacco for his wife Margaret Nowells abusing Mr. Wm. Hill and our Burgesses biding them be damned.

8 Aug 1690

John Branock's who failed to serve on the petty jury last June Court, petitions to have his fine remitted. Remitted.

Witnesses in the case of Katherine Fielding: William Trigoe, John Rue, James Vaulx, William Watson.

Presented that Edward Willowby of this co., son of William Willowby of Cooks Point, on or about Nov last past together with other accomplices, stole 6 unmarked shoats, less than one year old, and four hoggs of about the age of one year and one-half or two years. Not guilty.

Presented that William Willowby and his wife Hannah about 4 years since at the plantation of Cooks Point killed and feloneously killed a boar and carried away of Edward Cooke. Not guilty.

Petition Margaret Nowell prays to remit to her husband the fine for her contempt in giving unseemly words to Mr. William Hill, sub sheriff. Remitted.

Presented that John Standford of Nanticoke Hundred stole corn from the corn house of Benj. Hunt. Not guilty.

Witnesses in the case against John Standford: Benja. Hunt, Thomas Harris.

John Sharpe indicted that he on 7 March 1689 assaulted John Richards. Fined 200 lbs. of tobacco.

John Taylor having refused in open court to take the oathes of allegiance and supremacy to our sovereigne Lord Lady by the grace of God, William and Mary, is committed to the Sheriff's custody until he does give good security for his good behavior.

Witnesses in the case against John Sharp: Jane Sumpter, John Kirke.

Presented that John Dowdale of the freshes of Great Choptank on or about 16 June last past did milke one red cow of John Richards. He to pay to John Richards 100 lbs. of tobacco.

Presented that Thomas Norcome of Hunting Creeke in Greate Choptank Hundred on 17 Sep 1689 last past at the town of Cambridge in company with several other persons asked whether he would drinke the kings health: damanded what king. The said persons so asked afsd. replyed King William. The said Thomas Norcome there upon treasonally, seditiously and with a wicked intent not only to degrade the Royall person of our said sovereigne Lord the king but allso with an evill and wicked purpose to with.... answered I will drinke his damnation and all his posterity meaning the damnation of our soveraigne Lord. Not guilty.

Witnesses in the case of Thomas Norcome: Thomas Wells.

Witness in the case against John Dowdall: Thomas Norcome.

Presented that Francis Bullock and William Pritchett of Blackwater within the jurisdiction of the hundred of Fishing Creek stole two barrels of Thomas Cook in April 1687. Francis Bullock guilty, William Pritchett not guilty. Following a petition of Francis Bullock, the Court remits the corporal punishment but he is to pay 4 times the cost of the two barrels.

Witness against Francis Bullock: John Vincent.

Presented that John Alford on or about last of June 1689 stole property of William Spencer of Cabbin Creek one mouse coulored coat. guilty. fined 1000 lbs. of tobacco.

Upon the petition of Christopher Short and his wife Anne, it was ordered that they shall have and recover of Joane Basley the sum of 240 lbs. of tobacco.

Witnesses against John Alford: Thomas Wells, John Dyer, Joseph Smith, Thomas Norcombe, William Shepherd.

Susannah Richardson wife of John Richardson to answer unto Jeane Bassy, extx. of Michaell Bassy. The jury found for the plaintiff.

Witnesses in the Bassy case: Christopher Short, Obadiah King, Robert Cromwell, John Stoker

September 1690

The court this day ordered that Elizabeth Roe an orphan now in the tuition of Francis Howard shall serve him the said Francis Howard until she be 21 years of age or until she be married.

Ordered that Honnorah Pendergrass shall be whipt with 20 lashes for having borne a bastard child by John Buely.

Fine against William Covey for not attending court is remitted

William Fisher stands indicted that he on common fame and the general report of all his neighbours doth familiarly associate himself and inordinately keep company with a strange woman named Thomasin he the said William Fisher having a wife of his own. Not guilty.

Petition of Harry Will Tom one of the Ababcoes Indians. Being at the house of Edmond Branock in Fishing Creek found several English men drinking of sider and other drink and amongst the rest gave the petr. Some of the drink that they themselves was a drinking, soe that your petitioner became fuddled; and in that condition John Branock would have your petitioner to goe to John Button's to fetch a flitch or two of bacon for the said John Branock, and had a small payr of still-yards to weigh the said bacon and as he was goeing along the drink overcame him so much that he lay down in the woods to sleepe and by that means lost the said John Branock's still-yards and cannot find them; whereupon the said John Branock detains one of his guns, a quantity of peake and a match coat.

Petition of John Fleaharty states he was overtaken in drink. Remitted.

Petition of Robert Webster who was transported into this Province into the good ship called ----blank--- Daniell Powers [or Towers or Pouros?], commander, and sold to Mr. William Dorrington for the custome of the country which may please worships was judged by the court to serve the space of 6 years which time of service yr petioner hath honestly served. Yet his master still detaines him. Robert Webster is judged to be 16 years of age and will continue to serve??

November 1690

The court ordered that Mr. Philip Pitt shall deliver to the clk all papers he hath in his custody belonging to the court.

The court fined Mr. Philip Pitt for swearing in open court.

Honorah Pendergrass petitioned the court, stating that she had served her time and had only been awarded part of her promised 1000 lbs. of tobacco by Gournay Crow. The Court ordered the remaining 450 lbs. of tobacco to be paid to her along with a suite of clothes.

Presented that Jonathan Waters, Sebastian Mason and Ralph Hurleston of TA Co. on 23 Oct last past gathered together in the dwelling house of Richard Holland of the freshes of Great Choptank Hundred and stole one new black hood, one new Scotch cloath, two Scotch cloath handkerchieffs, 2 Scotch cloath caps, 1 piece of blue page, ½ piece of red page, 3000 pinns, 3 new knives, 1 ½ lbs. of thread, etc. The jury found Sebastian Mason and Ralph Hurleston found guilty and Jonathan Waters not guilty. The Court found Jonathan Waters also guilty. Each fined 40 shillings. Witnesses in this case: John Barton, John Richards, William Lowe, Edward Piner, Elizabeth Wansey.

Charles Powell is admitted as one of the attorneys of the court.

Petition of Francis Bullock, stating that the bastard child born to Katherine Raggett was formerly bound by the Court to John Brooks and agreed by John Brooks that said child shall serve Francis Bullock until 18 years of age or when he marries whichever is first. Francis Bullock is to be fined £20 if he does not keep said child.

Robert Buchoxy (?), a Negro, did promise to pay unto Andrew Gray the full sum of 800 lbs. of tobacco for the raising of the bastard child of his woman servant Katherine Raggett.

Robert Buchoxy (X), Negro, appeared in court with £—, if he does not indemnify the county from the charge of keeping a bastard child borne of Elizabeth Cobham, servant to Andrew Gray.

The following persons received a bounty for wolves heads: William Kirke, John Pollard, Jacob Loockermann, Coll. Charles Huchens, Capt. Thomas Ennalls, Mr. Edward White, Mr. Thomas Hicks, John Williams, Henry Swigget, John Willson, Mr. William Mishew, Richard Hooper, John Winsmore, John Dyer, John Makeele, Junr., William Makeele, John Alford, Senr.

Owen Morgan, for attending the delegates over the Bay

George Davenport, for the same

Robert Bromwell, for the same

Richard Watts for his mare being prest 6 days

Henry Beckwith for 2 horses prest for the county's service

Coll. Charles Huchens for 171 yards of wollen cloath

James Peterkin for 25 yards of linen cloath

John Foster for 40 yards of linen

James Peterkin for .... linen cloath

Mr. Thomas Cooke per accompt

John Winsmore for himselfe and horse 7 days ... in the service of the county

Edward Poole for himselfe and horse for same

Obadiah King on the same

Mr. Edward Pindar ... [housing the prisoners?] Sebastian Mason, Ralph Hurleston and Jonathan Waters

Mr. Edward Pinder for Higgins? and fees Mr. Denton's servant

John Russell for serving the county in ferrying ...?

To the Justices expenses in laying the ...?

John Haslewood for himselfe and boat attending the burgesses several times

James Dun for serving the county

William Davise for serving the county

Nicholas Parsons for serving the county

William Covey for serving the county

John Rice for serving the county

Mr. John Haslewood, Coroner for two inquests

Samll Crayher?? pr order of August Court

Mr. Edward Pinder sheriff for oxen bridges fees???

Thomas Pattison clk for fees on Oxen Bridges tryall

John Ross, Cryer

Thomas Victor??, door keeper

The Justices

Mr. William Hart sub sheriff

The Jury to view the body of Jane Howard [Herard?] "presuming to pass the creek on the back of Jacob a Negro and was accidentally drowned." John Haslewood, coronor: Thomas Colton, John Richards, Thomas Norcome, Robert Carter, Anthony Squire, Solomon Ro...???, Robert Wells, Mathias Shicklett, John Hunter??, Thomas Burckett, Symon Richardson.

The Jury to view the body of Negro Jacob. Same jury, same verdict.

... *[Blurred and faint]* ....

January Court 1690/91

Jan 7th

The court ordered that Mabella Kelley shall be whipt 6 lashes having born a bastard child.

Jan 8th 1690/91

Complaint of Daniel Clark and Katherin Fielding and Capt. John Makeel against John Alford Senr, and Elizabeth his wife and one Elinor servant to the said John Allford. who are charged with the murder of a bastard child last summer born to the said Elinor.

Petitions of Nicholas Massey and Jacob Taylor to remit fines for his not attending jury.

... *[Blurred and faint]* ....

March Court 1690/91

David Murphy of this county, servant unto Humphrey Hubbart stands indicted that he on 5 Dec 1690 assaulted Aron Tunisey

Elizabeth Causby bound her son Benjamin to Thomas Wells and his wife until he arrives at the age of 21 he being born on 4 Dec 1682.

Came into court Mrs. Katherine Clarke and did swear that her husband Mr. Danell Clarke will kill or doe her some other boddyly harme. He is to be apprehended.

John Yonge to be fined for not appearing to serve on the petty jury.

Indictment of John Harwood and Margaret Howell, wife of James Howell of Little Choptank Hundred for living in adultery. The jury finds for the defendants.

Came John Nichols and did assume to pay 500 lbs. of tobacco for a fine for his woman servant Doysey for having borne a bastard child.

Andrew Insly shall pay Elenor Stafford the sum of 100 lbs. of tobacco and to allow to take all her cattle belonging to her husband Will: Staford's estate.

August Court 1691

Presented that John Harrod of Little Choptank Hundred on 18 June 1691 did enter and in and upon the body of Magdalin Coarner, wife of William Corner in a ... manner being an assault did make and her the said Magdalin Coarner ... and she miscarried of the burden she the said Magdalin was bigg with ...???

The Court ordered that a special warrant issue to apprehend Daniel Clark and Katherine Fielding for living in adultery.

The court his day ordered that a speciall warrant issue to apprehend Jane Pollard for having borne a bastard child.

Petition of John Williams that whereas Elinor Williams, wife to the petitioner, had formerly a son by her former husband which child Humphery Mould now hath in keeping and your petitioner's in behalfe of his wife the mother of the said child did demand the bringing up of said child as in right ought to have: but the said Mould is grandfather to the said child still keeps the said child to the mother yr. petitioner's wives [wife's] great griefe and vexation of spiritt. The court ordered that Humphery Mould do deliver unto above named John Williams his said wives child he making such satisfaction to the said Humphery Mould for the time that he hath kept the said child.

Upon the petition of Johanah Pritchett the court ordered that she shall have and recover of Edward Cooke the sum of 60 lbs. of tobacco.

Petition of Richard Foster for some years an inhabitant of this co. He has lost the use of one of his limbs. Exempted from tax or levy.

Ordered that letters of administration be issued to Thomas Wells on the estate of Thomas Lang.

Petition of Stephen Seaton who is above 60 years of age, weak and lame. Freed from paying tax or levy.

Thomas Gibbins, servant to Mr. Edward Pindar, being brought before the court for begetting a bastard child on the body of Mary Oneale, servant to Mr. Thomas ...

September Court 1691

Ordered that Jone Hamilton shall receive 20 lashes for having borne a bastard child.

John Gladstones and John Dyer to be overseers of highways in Great Choptank Hundred. John Foster and Daniel Fox ...Nanticoke. William Canerly and Phillip Tall in Fishing Creek Hundred. Moris Mathews and Henry Willmott in Little Choptank Hundred. John Phillips and Henry Symons in Armitage Hundred

Deposition of Thomas Vietch, aged about 64 years, saith that about 6 years since being at the house of Thomas Wall in company with him and Capt. George Cowley the deponent heard the said Capt. George Cowly say and promise the said Thomas Wall to deliver a bill? he had of him the said Thomas Wall the first opportunity.

John Kirke prays to have a license for an ordinary at Cabin Creek. Approved.

Thomas Pattison prays to have a license for an ordinary at Oyster Creek.

Petition of Thomas Cook to keep an ordinary at the town of Cambridge upon his passing a bond for the sum of 1200 lbs. of tobacco .

November Court 1691

Charles Booth orphan child of John Booth is bound to Humphry Mould til he comes to the age of 21 he being 5 years of age the 25th day of April next.

The court his day bound John Orithason? to Will Marchant til his is to the age of 21.

Came Martha Woodward and made oath that Joan Tomkin had run away and deserted her service 63 days and it was ordered that she serve for the same time according to the Act of Assembly.

Joane Hambleton to receive 6 lashes for having borne a bastard child. She asked for forgiveness and prayed that she might be released from punishment which was granted.

The following persons received credit for wolves heads: John Gladstone, John Pyar, Thomas Vickars, John Pollard, James Pattison, Mr.? Jacob Lockerman, Thomas Newton, Arthur Whiteley, John Peirce, John Nutter, William Travers, William Shinton, Mr. John Hodson, John Luon?, Samuel Millington, Mr. Thomas Hicks, William Stevens of Dumplin Poynt.

[Payment for other services:]
John Haynes for interpreting with the Indians
James Buswick for going over the Bay
John Newton [no reason given]
William Dwyar for attending the Burgesses
Mordant Thacher for attending the Burgesses
John Phillips [reason not given]
Robt. Taylor for his servant Tho: Shawne attending Burgesses
To John Rowlings [reason not given]
James Nowell [reason not given]
Thomas Booth the door keeper
Nicolas Browne towards his reliefe
Robert Screech? for maintaining Martha Edwards and keeping the county harmless for a year her corne and cloaths due to her, for her time of service.
John Hasselwood for inquests including one jury of inquest on John Gripple and aiso on a Negro and woman servant of Mr. John Alfords
John Hasselwood for one jury of inquest on John Dawson.
John Harwood that the Delegates expended
John Harwood for keeping the ferry over Choptank til Jan next
Mr. Thomas Fookes amount
Patrick Marlow for attending the Burgesses

John Browne for attending the Burgesses
William Trotter for attending the Burgesses
Robt. Screech for a saddle that was prest for the ...? and cost
Tho. Pattison ...?
Humphry Hubbert for fetching the armor from Majr. Trippe
His Justices expences this court
Mr. Tho. Hicks for maintaining Chickaacomoco 2 years
The Justices ...?
Mr. Tho: Fooks for collecting 2647 lbs. of tob: at 10 lbs. per 100

Ordered that Edward White shall two levies free and Benjamin Palmer one levy for ???

Honour Fitzgerald was brought before the court by John Button, constable, for having of her body a bastard child [and] by her oath layd this child to Bryan Fitzpatrick.

Mary Pitchford presented for having one bastard child at the hosue of one Richard Holland.

John LeCompt of Little Choptank Hundred was indicted on presentment by the grand jury that he on 26 Oct 1691 at the house of John Winsmore and being required and demanded by Mr. Thomas Cooke, high sheriff, to be aiding and assisting unto him the sayd Thomas Cooke and in the conveying of one Moses LeCompt unto the prison of this county of Dorchester County and for not giving in bayle to a certain action against him the sayd Moses commanded by one Richard Owing and being so commanded by the sayd Thomas Cooke in their Majesties names to be aiding and assisting as aforesayd he the sayd John LeCompt contempuously and in resistance of their Majesties power and authority as aforesayd: made reply unto him the sayd Thomas Cooke that he the sayd John LeCompt in their Majesties names would not obay the sayd command and sayd a turd for your or your power and also further replyed unto him the sayd Thomas Cooke that if he the sayd Thomas Cooke would touch him he would knock him down and other contempts did shew and their offer contrary to the peace of our Sovereigne Lord and Lady the King and Queen and the statue in that case made and provided. Pleads not guilty.

John Nicolls of the county, constable of Great Choptank Hundred is indicted for having a warrant directed to him for the apprehending of John Attkey of Calvert Co. on complaint of John Brannock of this co. against said Attkey for a perjury supposed to be committed by him the sayd Attkey notwithstanding the strictness of their majesties command, after he had apprehended the sayd John Attkey contemptuously and in resistance of their Majesties Command, lett the sayd John Attkey goe at large. Fined 200 lbs. of tobacco.

Rachel Anderson, servant to Nicolas Phillips imported in the *Edward and Sarah*, John Tench, master. adjudged to be 8 years old and to serve accordingly.

Came Cornelius Macknamarra and faithfully promised to pay Honour Fitzgerald's fine of 500 lbs. of tobacco.

Arthur Whiteley stands attached to answer unto Walter Campbell, adm of all and singular the goods and chattels of Luis Page late of this co. dec'd.

Came Thomas Cooke and sett Mary Martin free from all service due him.

Fined 500 lbs. of tobacco for not appearing on the petty jury: John Branock, Thomas Wells.

Benjamin Hunt to have a licence to keep ordinary in this county, he passing his bond for the sume of 1200 lbs. of tobacco.

The constable of Fishing Creek Hundred is ordered to apprehend William Dossey and his wife Mary on suspition of murder.

John Harwood shall keep the ferry over Greate Choptanke and be allowed as he was last year, viz. 4250 lbs. of tobacco.

Hugh Eccleston promises to pay 500 lbs. of tobacco being for the fine for Mary Pickford having borne a bastard child.

February Court 1691

Gourny Crow allowed 800 lbs. of tobacco for looking after and maintaining Elizabeth Dicks, orphan child of Robert Dicks, dec'd.

The petition of Ann Browne that she was transported into this country in the good ship *Thomas and John*, Capt. John Browne, commander, for the time and space of 4 years which time she has compleated but in the time of her service she lost her indenture and has served 5 years. She was in the service of Robt. Anderson, William Walker and Walter Campbell. Freedom granted.

Presented that Robert Butcher sometime in Aug 1691 last past, he stole 9 ..., 3 new matchcoats, a remnant of kersey, about 4 yards of 18 muskratt skins to the value of 900 lbs. of tobacco, property of Thomas Wells in Cabbin Creeke.

Thomas Norcome of Great Choptanke Hundred indicted in that he sometime in March or Aprill 1691 last drove and carried away one whiteish coloured mare bigg with foal about 3 years old being wild and unbranded or anyway marked did take up and into the pasture of William Norcome. Not guilty.

Thomas Norcome of Great Choptank Hundred indicted for that he on or about 14 Nov 1691 did lead 16 young shoates of about 5 mos. old on into a penn of the plantation of Thomas Norcome in Hunting Creek. Guilty. Put into the pillory for 4 hours for a second offense for hogg stealing and fined 600 lbs. of tobacco.

Gourny Crow one of the attorneys of the court fined 100 lbs. of tobacco for not giving the attendance of the court.

John Alford, Jr. fined for not appearing and attending petty jury.

Jane Stinson, wife of Alexander Stinson of Nanticoake Hundred indicted for that she on or about 3 Jan 1691/2 assaulted Edmund Branock. Not guilty.

Presented that John Ryon of Little Choptanke Hundred on or about 1 Feb last past stole 400 to 500 lbs. of tobacco of John Pope. Verdict: ignoramus.

Presented that William Dossey of Fishing Creeke Hundred and his wife Mary on or about 21 Dec 1691 assaulted Elizabeth Nowland [apparently placed her] into the woods an obscure place where she died from lack of food and rayment and other sustenance. The jury found ignoramus.

Daniel Clarke of Little Choptanke Hundred indicted several times past and doth live in adultery and evil conversation with one Katherine Feilding the wife of James Feilding. Not guilty.

William Heather delivered to the Justices a piece of gold that he took from a dead corpse at his landing and it was ordered that William Heather keep the said piece of gould for trouble and labour of securing the said corpse, sending for the coroner and buriall of him.

Petition of Thomas Long and his wife Mary being summoned to the court in a difference between Edmund Branock and Jane Stinson deft. your petitioner craves order for 4 days each.

March Court 1692
Presented that Thomas Norcome of Great Choptane Hundred on or about 16 Feb last stole about 13 shoates of Wm. Emmory and remarked them. The Grand jury finds Ignoramus.

Isaac Hill brought before the court upon the complaint of his master John Duckworth. Ordered that the said Isaac Hill shall return and serve his said master the remaining part of his time faithfully; otherwise his master upon his next just complaint shall carry him before some one of their Majesties Justices for this county and there receive 20 lashes.

The court ordered that warrant issue out against Walter Kinnins for begetting a bastard child upon the body of Joane Tomkin.

Ordered by the court that a warrant issued to the constable of Greate Choptank Hundred to apprehend Eliz: Cobham for having borne a bastard child.

Arthur Hart to be constable of Armitage Hundred in room of Timothy Macknamarra.

On 10 Feb 1691/2 David Estradling aged about 46 saith that sometime in Sep last past he heard Turlogh Sweeny tell a slave of Mr. Thomas Ennalls that he would provide a boate to carry the said slave over the Bay. Turlogh to receive 30 lashes for bartering with a slave of Capt. Thomas Ennalls.

Ordered that Gorney Crow shall be allowed 1000 lbs. of tobacco for keeping Grace the bastard child of Joane Tompkins for one year.

Ordered that a ferry be kept by John Russell over Nanticoke River and that

Capt. Thomas Ennalls and Mr. Thomas Hicks doe treat with the Justices of SO Co. to know what they will contribute.

Robert Butcherly and his wife Hannah stand attached to answer unto Ellis Thomas in a plea of trespass.

The fine of 400 lbs. of tobacco on Philip Pitt for failure to the calling of the court is remitted.

Jury summoned by Richard Owin, coroner, to enquire into the death of Joseph Shelly being found on the main road of Dorchester Co. the 3rd instant Oct 1691 finds that he perished for want of reliefe - Richard Teate, Charles Powell, Willm. Wattson, John Franks, Edward Gould, Jervis Cuttler, Henry Willmott, William Fisher, William Covey, Edward Poole, John Bolton, Tho: Burnell.

Jury summoned by John Hassellwood, coroner, on the view of the body of John Davison, finding he was accidently killed by falling between the ship and long boate - John Davis, Symon Richardson, Thomas Crumpton, Richard Holland, Thomas Early, Robt. Weling, Samuell Brooke, William Heather, William Bryan, John Lakay, John Richardson, James Richardson.

Jury summoned to enquire into the death of John Gripple find that he was accidentally drowned by the over setting of the canoe - Andrew Insloe, John Jones, Thomas Wraughton, Willm. Wraughton, John Lunn, Tho: Raglin, John Merryday, Rich: Kemball, Richard Pearson, John Early, Willm. Deane, John Hall.

Dorchester Co. Judgment Records
1728-1729

p.19. John Eccleston and Susanah, his wife and Henry Trippe, executrix and executor of the estate of Henry Trippe, deceased bring suit against Thomas Brannock, Nehemiah Beckwith, and John Brannock to pay 3750 lbs. of tobacco to the estate of the deceased Henry Trippe. The court ruled in the favor of the Trippe estate and added the amount of 588 lbs. for damages.

p.43. John Hughes swore that Thomas Shehaune assaulted him. Thomas receives a subpoena.

Sarah Walters, also known as Elizabeth, indicted for fornication swore that John Bramble, Junr. is the begetter of her bastard child. Sarah is to appear in November court to give evidence agst. the said John.

Rebecca Busik(?) swore Samuel Adam was begetter of her bastard child.

p.44. Torrince Gillaspie pleas with the court that his man servant named William Cullen ran away for 29 days, and he has expended sums of money to retake him. The court rules that after the date of expiration of William Cullen's servitude, he shall serve his master 6 days for every day he was missing.

Stephen Orooms(?) petitions the court that he has an old Negro woman named Grace who is not able to do anything toward her maintenance and he would like her to be set levy free. It was ordered that Grooms(?) no longer has to pay tax for her.

p. 45. William Warner, Sr. brought into court a young boy called Edward Fromer (?) to have his age adjudged which the court adjudged to be 11 years.

Ordered by the court that the orphans of John Elliott who are very much abused by him should be taken from him and given to Matthew Travers.

p.46. William Parker petitions the Court hat he is old and past his laboring years and asks for something to maintain him. The said William is allowed 500 lbs. of tobacco by the year.

John Roberson petitions the Court that for several years he has been afflicted with severe sickness and other misfortunes that hath made him unable of doing anything for a living, he humbley asks the court for something to maintain him. The Court ordered that he be allowed 300 lbs. of tobacco.

p.48. Robert Clarkson, James Cannon and Richard Andrew are holders firmly bound unto Mary Cannon and Joshua Cannon, children and orphans of Matthew Cannon for the sum of £67.6.9 and 2 farthings current money of Maryland. There is a balance due the orphans of £33.13.4 pence and 3 farthings which shall be granted the children when they are of age.

p.49. Thomas Tharpe petitioned the Court that he came into this county as a servant to David Movall(?) and has honorably served his time, but his master keeps back all of his freedom. The court ruled that if Movall is found in this bailywick that he should appear in Court. But he was not found

p. 50. Sarah Walters, also known as Elizabeth Walters, begot a bastard child, and should appear in Court if she is found in this bailywick. She was brought into Court in the custody of James Woolford and admited that she is guilty of fornication. She is fined 30 shillings current money of Maryland. 1500 lbs. of tobacco to John Krumley.

p.51. Rebena Busik(?) committed fornication with an unknown party and begot a bastard child. William Phillips, planter, undertakes for Rebena the penalty of 2000 lbs. of tobacco and six hundred lbs. of tobacco unto the Court.

p. 53. Thomas Shehanne admitted in court that he did assault and wound John Hughes. Shehanne is fined 50 lbs. of tobacco.

October Court 1728

p.55. William Stevens bringeth into Court a certain Negro girl named Jean, his servant, to adjudge her age. She was adjudged to be the age of 12 years.

p. 58. Nicholas Horld the servant of William Warner petitioned the Court that his master is not doing his part to the servant by providing him with sufficient maintenance--as for victuals, only corn--no salt or fat, and as for clothing--only what you see. The Court fined Warner 100 lbs. of tobacco.

The Court sends Mary Stanly(?) bastard child to George Ponuce (?), he paying 600 lbs. of tobacco for her.

p.59 Abraham Walker bonds his son John Walker to John Vicars(?) until the age of 21 years. His son is to receive one year of schooling before the expiration of his servitude.

p. 60. James Woolford is fined by the Court 200 lbs. of tobacco for assaulting Jon Ryder.

p. 61. John Vicars petitions the Court to allow him additional maintenance for his brother Isaac who is becoming worse and worse. The Court increases the amount to 1000 lbs. of tobacco.

p.62. Anthony Chiluitt petitions the Court that he is now above the age of fifty od(d) years and because of losses and crosses of the world he has little profit and hopes to be relieved of his future levy. So be it.

p. 72. Susannah Sanders did not deny that she committed fornication and have a bastard child. The Court fines her 1000 lbs. of tobacco and court fees.

p.73. Susannah Sanders swears that William Stanford is the begettor.

p. 74. In Court William Stanford does not deny that he is guilty of adultery and is fined £3.

p. 78, Samuel Allen did appear in Court and acknowledge that he begot the bastard child of Rebena [Rebeca?] Busik(?). He is fined 30 shillings.

p. 83. Phillip Lecompte did severely beat and wound Charles Deane. He is fined 50 lbs. of tobacco.

p. 84 Mary Stanley, spinster, the servant of George Benne(?) did commit fornication with a certain Negro person and begot a bastard Mulatto child. The Court ruled that after the expiration of her time of servitude with her said master, she shall become a servant for and during the period of 7 years according to the forms of the Act of Assembly in such cases.

p.109. The Court ruled that Darby Bryan who had runaway from his master William Stevens for a period of time, be made to spend an additional time of 5 months as servant to Stevens after the expiration of his servitude.

Elizabeth Hines (?) is indicted for begetting a bastard child and swears that Samuel Long is the begetter.

p. 109a. William Clarkson appeared in Court with Elizabeth Scrivony(?), the daughter of Elizabeth Scrivony, deceased, and prayeth that the justices bind her to him as a servant.. The Court ruled that during the time of her servitude with him, she should learn to read, spin, sow, and all other housewifery works and should at the expiration of her time of servitude she should be paid one new suite of stuff, a cap and shift of fine linene, a pair of stockings and shoes. If he does not comply, he would pay 2000 lbs. of tobacco. Her servitude would end at the age of 18 years(she now being of the age of 6).

Edward Evans petitions the Court that he is near 80 years of age and very ailing and not able to work, and crippled in the foot, and humbly prayeth that the Court will discharge him from paying taxes. The Court orders that Evans is discharged from paying taxes for the future.

p.111. William Miller brought into Court Sarah Rider, daughter of Hanna Rider. and prayeth that the Court bind her to him. The Court ruled that during the time of her servitude, Sarah should learn to read, knit, spin, sow and all other housewifery works and should at the expiration of her servitude have a new suite of stuff . Miller agrees that if he does not comply, he will be fined 5000 lbs. of tobacco. She shall serve until the age of 18.

Mary Shorter being indicted for the begetting of a bastard child swore that John Robson is the begetter.

p. 112 Mary James being indicted for the begatting of a bastard child swore that William Cullen is the begetter and it is ordered that the said Mary appear at Court to give evidence against William.

p.113. Upon the motion of Thomas Nevett, Francis Allen is appointed guardian to a certain Edward Pinder, being a minor.

The Court ordered that Anthony Lecompte be fined 5 shillings for the assault and beating of John Stewart. Locompte shall remain in he custody of the sheriff until the fine is paid.

p. 141. Mary James is indicted for having a bastard child and is fined 30 shillings.

Mary Church admitted that she begot a bastard child and is fined 1000 lbs. of tobacco. She is to be whipped at the public whipping post with 11 lashes on her bare back. Mary Hambrooke undertook the penalty of 1000 lbs. of tobacco.

p.142. John Johnson is indicted by the Court for evilly beating Ann Simpson and caused great damage to the said Ann. He is fined 10 shillings. Thomas Woolford undertook the penalty of 1500 lbs. of tobacco.

p. 143. John Johnson is indicted by the Court for assaulting Barnaby Fallon. Same terms.

p.144. John Jones was assaulted and injured by James Cannon and Joseph Mills. James Cannon is fined ten shillings and Joseph Mills is fined five shillings.

p. 145, Grace Wallis is indicted for having a bastard child. She is sentenced to a public whipping on her bare back of 21 lashes. James Carter undertook her penalty of 1500 lbs. tobacco.

p. 146. Mary Shorter is charged with having a bastard child which she does not deny. She is fined 30 shillings Patrick Collins takes her under the penalty of 1500 lbs. of tobacco.

p. 148. Elizabeth Hines did have a bastard child and is in the custody of Samuel Long for 1500 lbs. of tobacco. She is fined 30 shillings.

p. 149. Elizabeth Brickle--public whipping of 21 lashes.

p. 150. Elizabeth Murray--5 lashes penalty for having bastard child.

p. 154 Thomas Stewart has assaulted Nehemiah Lecompte and is fined £10.

p. 155. Sarah Walter appeared in Court to give evidence that she commited fornication with John Bramble and was fined 10 pounds.

p. 176. Thomas Grey appeared in Court and chose of Mr. Peter Taylor as his guardian.

p. 214. Thomas Brannock, Junr. is to be brought into Court to answer to Thomas Nevett of a plea that he vendor unto him the full amount of 6820 lbs. of tobacco which to him is oweth and unjustly detaineth. The Court orders that the debt be paid and damages also by Brannock.

p. 233. Walter Stevens late of Great Choptank parish did committ fornication with Elizabeth Handley and did begat a bastard child and is fined 30 shillings.

p. 235. Elizabeth Salsbury did begat a bastard child and is ordered to have a public whipping. John Salsbury pays 1500 lbs. of tobacco. Elizabeth swears that the begotter is Michael Ward.

p. 241. Elizabeth Handley did begat a bastard child and is fined 15 shillings. Thomas Cannor (Connor?) pays the fine 1500 lbs.. Elizabeth swears that Walter Stevens is the begeter.

Samuel Long swears that he committed fornication with Elizabeth Hinds and begot a bastard child. He is fined 30 shillings

p. 243. Mary Gray, spinster did beat severely and assault Rose Read and is fined 5 shillings.

p. 244 John Robson did commit fornication with Mary Shorter and begot a bastard child and is fined 30 shillings.

p. 245 John Willy, Junr. severely beat and assaulted Elizabeth Cannon and is fined 50 lbs. of tobacco.

Phillip Lecompte did beat and assault Samuel Long and is fined 200 lbs. of tobacco.

p. 249. Matthew Fields petitions the Court that he has a grievous rupture and many other pains, and has been living with his son-in-law but is becoming an increasing burden, so he asks for maintenance. He is allowed 400 lbs. per year.

John Macgraw petitions the court that he has had problems for two or three years and is a poor man and asks the Court to be dismissed from paying taxes. So granted.

p. 250. William Kennerly brings into court a young Negro girl named Dinah for adjudgment of her age which is determined to be 13 years.

p. 250. John Lamee brings into Court a Negro boy name Francis to have his age adjudged. He is considered by the Court that he is 12 years old.

Peter Rich brings into Court his servant William Read who had run away and was recaptured. It was ordered that after the expiration of his servitude, he should serve 6 months more to account for his runaway time.

p. 251. John Marshall appears in Court to ask for maintenance because he has a long weak condition. Granted 1000 lbs. of tobacco a year.

Thomas Moors brings into Court to be bound to him Thomas Layton and Mary Layton. During his servitude Thomas is to learn to be a weaver and to read and write and at the end of his servitude is to receive a new suite of cloaths and one pair of gears(?). Mary is to learn housewifery works at the end of her servitude would get a new suite of stuff cloaths. He would get fifty pounds and Mary would get 25. Thomas is to be bound until he is 21, he is now 13 last Feb. Mary is to be bound until she is 16, being eleven next March.

p. 252. Edward Southol brings into court Edward Southal to be bound to him until the age of 21 and he will learn the trade of carpenter. He will learn to read and write and upon the expiration of the servitude Edward the minor will receive one new suite of apparel, a new ---, broad ax, hand saw, two augers, one drawing knife, and fifty pounds. He is to be bound until the age of 21, he now being 13 years the ninth day of last April.

William Dorrington comes into Court and chooses John Brannock as his guardian.

Thomas Nevett brings into Court William Hognatos(?) and a Negro boy named Jack and prayeth that the Court adjudge their ages. The Justices considered that William is 7 and Jack is 5.

p. 253. William Williamson petitioned the Court that the Aumack(?) [possibly Accomac] County Court in the Colony of Virginia did choose Shaddrack Feddman (?) as his guardian without labour or service. Whereas Shaddrack left those parts and persuaded the petitioner to come into this county and then bound him for the period of three years to Thomas Goldsborough to be instructed in such business as Thomas should follow. The petitioner would like to return to the place of his residence among his relations and prayeth that the Court and Shaddrack release him. Freedom granted.

August Court 1729

p. 264. Patrick Brauhance was fined £10 for assaulting and injuring Thomas Thompson

p.267. We Alce Phillips, Peter Rokos and James Trego, planters, firmly bound unto Thomas Phillips and James Phillips children and orphans of Phillip Phillips in the sum of 58 pounds and 12 shillings current money of Maryland to be paid until these children. The children and orphans are to be paid the remainder due them.

p. 290. Margaret Bruff did committ fornication and have a bastard child. John Woolford came to Court and payd £10 on condition that the said Margaret should not personally appear in Court. Margaret was fined 30 shillings.

p. 283. Mary Cook appears in Court and is charged with stealing from Ephraim Wilson 5 gallons of cyder brandy the value of 20 shillings, from Elinor Ervine a pair of bodws (?) the value of 20 shillings and also from others. She is sentaenced to a public whipping of 12 lashes on her bare back well laid until the blood appear and that she stand in the pillory half an hour.

p.285. John Stanford petitions the court that he is of the age of 14 and his parents are dead, and chooses Richard Pritchard as his guardian. Agreed.

p. 287. Susannah Bryan did committ fornication and bore a bastard child. She is sentenced to a publick whipping of 29 lashes on her bare back.

p. 290. Francis Barnoto brings into Court Francis Jenkins and Samuel Jenkins to be bound to him unil the age of 21. They are to learn to be carpenters, and to learn to read and write. Francis is 15 and Thomas is 13.

p. 291. The residents of Taylors and James Island petition for a ferry. Thomas Travers, Richard Keene, Henry Keen, William Travers, Issac Partidge, William Prichard, John Pritchard, William Cullen, John Barnes, Henry Travers, Senr., Zebulon Keene, Edward Keenne, John Pollard, John Sumors, Jacob Pattison, Senr., Thomas Pattison, senr., Oliver Hain(?) John Granger, Benjamin Granger, Senr., John Granger, Junr., George Blades, Thomas (?), Oliver Woolen, Benjamin Nolon,, Matthew Travers, William Travers, Senr, John Sanders, Roger Hooper, James Hooper, Henry Travers, William Johns, William Robson, Benjamin Grangor, John Woolford, John Stevens, Junr., Thomas Hooper, John Rumley, John Abbott, Junr., Thomas Burnes, Ambrose Aron, Charles Barners, Tobias Piner(?), John Robson, William Murphy, John Barnes, William Murphy, Junr., John Pri????, Richard Chapman, James Daniel, John Aron, Mordicay Carr, Matthew Travers, Junr, Robert Hark(?), William Adam, Thomas Atkinson, George ????, Matthew Driver, Dunken Markfar Grantham, Josias ????, Edward Elliott, Alexander Farguson, Lewis Griffen, Senr., Ezekel Keene, James Insley, Thomas Nevett, Thomas Smith, Jacob Locerman, Jacob Loocerman, Thomas Stewart, Noah Pearson, Richard Pearson, Richard Manning, Solomon Robson, David Robson,

Peter Stokes, J Wheel, John Brannock, Junr., Nathaniel Maury, Henry Hooper, James Woolford, Bazel Neal, Thomas Luxs(?), Benjamin Keene, Curtis Evans, John Cullen, James Hayes, John Ennalls, William Evans, Thomas Thomson, Edward Newton, William Stanford, John Kirke, Philip(?) Lecompte, Thomas Ennalls, Will Gun(?), Samuel ????, John Hughes, Henry Trippe.

p. 293. Margaret Bruff appeared in Court to answer that John Woolford is the father of her bastard child.

Dorchester County Judgment Records
1733-34
Acc No. 8921 - MSA No. C704-3 (not on microfilm)

At a Court of the Right Honourable Charles absolute Lord and Propty of the Province of Maryland and Avalon Lord Baron of Baltimore .... November the ... following before ... Coll. Henry Ennalls, Mr. Charles Nutter, Mr. Tobias Polard, Mr. Walter Campble, Mr. Thomas Woolford, Mr. John Hodson, Mr. Thomas Nevett??, Mr. John White.

p. 9. Petition of Elizabeth Cockayne of this co. that whereas your petitioner having been left disolute by the death of her husband and through sicknesss and trouble your petitioner put two of her children namely Betty and Mary Cockayne unto a certain Jacob Pyatt that will not lett your petitioner have them but abuses them very much and unex... ... great grief and trouble of your petitioner which your petitioner humbly prayeth your worships would take ... to deliver your petitioner's children unto her ...

p. 20. John Eccleston, marriner, complains against George Griffith and Elizabeth his wife otherwise lately called Elizabeth Taylor, Gentlewoman.

p. 30. Sheriff should take Elizabeth Woolford, widow, Thomas Woolford, Gent., and Thomas Woolford, Gent., execs. of the will of Roger Woolford, DO Co. to answer Stephen Conley(?)

p. 48. Petition of Rose Casdey?? that Petitioner was bound to Govert Loockerman she to arrive to the age of 18 years your petitioner further sheweth that she arrived to the age of 18 years but is yet contrary to all law and right detained as servant by Jacob Loockerman

Petition of Richard Batcherly. That petitioner is held as servant by John Stevens, Jr. contrary to law.

p. 49. Petition of John Mandider? that he became a servant to Mr. Philemon Lecompt for the term of two years and one month but is still detained beyond that time.

August 18 1733

p. 53. Petition of Vachel Denton that petitioner is leased in the .. of and in a tract of land called *Hackedstay* of which the boundaries are uncertain.

p. 54. Petition of Thomas Shehanne to grant a commission to examine evidences ... re bounds of a tract called *Taverton*.

p. 56. To Mr. Charles Goldsborough of DO Co. Whereas Joseph Ennalls, exec. of the last will of William Ennals ... that a certain Charles Smith of sd. co. is runaway or removed in a secret manner and that he is judged unto the estate of the sd. Mr. Ennalls the sum of 2382 lbs. of tobacco and he prays attachment of the same.

p. 56. Petition of Henry Dyas being a very poor lame deraged(?) and sickly poor creature and no ways capable of getting my living by reason of my ... requests an allowance.

p. 58. Frances Beckwith to answer Catherine Bruff. That Frances Beckwith, widow, extx of last will of Nehemiah Beckwith ... debt. [Itemized list of purchases.]

p. 71. Ordered that an information be exhibited agnst. Benjamin James Bennsden for assault and battery on Jacob Mills.

Presented that John Hodson quartered late of St. Marys White Chappell Parish in the co. afsd. 10 July 1732 with Sarah Haddaway did beget a bastard child. to which he confessed.

p. 72. Presented that George Langrell, Jr. of St. Marys White Chappell Parish on 10 July 1732 committed fornication with Mary Hurly and begat a bastard child. Fined 30 shillings.

p. 74. Presented that Isaac Patridge late of St. Marys White Chappel Parish on 10 July 1732 did commit fornication with Rachel Price and begat a bastard child. Fined 30 shillings.

p. 75. Presented that Elizabeth Riggen of St. Marys White Chappel Parish, spinster, on 1 March 1732 did commit fornication and begat a bastard child. To be whipped with 16 lashes.

p. 76. Presented that Mary Higman late of Great Choptank Parish, spinster, on 30 June 1732 did commit fornication with a certain person and begat a bastard child. To be whipped with 6 lashes. Mary Higman swears that Charles Beckworth is the begetter of the bastard child.

That Daniel Sulivant beat wounded and evilly treat so that of the life of John Newton with... and arms from the custody of the said Daniel did taken and refuse and that the afsd. John Newton himself from the custody Daniel and Daniel did require David McCollister of afsd. Parish, Isaac Brown of same Parish and Richard Clarkson of same Parish, Richard Tull of same Parish and Thomas Sumers of same parish to assist and they did refuse.

p. 81. Thomas Stewart agrees to put good substantial windoe shutters to the court house to hang them upon iron hooks and hinges with iron bolts and forelocks.

p. 82. Informed that Jacob Pattison, of Dorchester Parish, DO Co. on 20 Nov 1732 assaulted Jane Pollard, wife of Tobias Pollard.

p. 86. Mary Henry acknowledged owing Proprietary £5 - that she should make her personal appearance before the court second Tues in Aug next to give evidence against William Barnett for committing fornication with the said Mary and begetting a bstard child.

p. 88. Presented that Tobias Pollard late of Dorchester Parish; Jane Pollard of same parish, wife of afsd. Tobias Pollard; Negro Tom, labourer, the Negro slave of afsd. Tobias Pollard; Negro Trish, labourer, the Negro slave of the same Tobias Pollard - on 26 Nov 1732 with force and arms to wit with clubs swords whip and staves wrongly and unlawfully in disturbance of the peace of the Lord Proprietary at the Parish afsd. and on the high road of the parish assembled and gathered together and as being assembled, then and there made upon a certain Jacob Pattison of the same Parish an assault. Tobias and Jane each to pay 5 shillings.

p. 90. Appearing to the court that Henry Hooper guardian of John Elliott, an orphan has misused the said John (one Negro woman being dead) the residue of his estate is put and placed in the hands of Mathew Travers of this co., Gent., who the said Elliott chooses for his guardian and the said Hooper from his guardianship is discharged.

p. 91. Presented that Peter Taylor, Junr. of Great Choptank Parish,Gent., on 16 April 1733 assaulted Sarah Coarson, wife of John Courson. Fined 5 shillings.

p. 92. Presented that John Sullivant of Great Choptank Parish assaulted Thomas Corson on 10 April 1733. Fined 5 shillings.

p. 94. Informed that Thomas Sumers of Great Choptank Parish on 10 April 1733 assaulted Thomas Corson. Fined 5 shillings.

Robert Medford and Mary Medford each proved 6 days attendance for his Lordship agt Peter Taylor, John Sullivant and Thos. Sumers.

Moses Poole swears 5 days attendance for his Lordship agnst Peter Taylor, John Sullivant and Thos. Sumers. Isabell Sumers, John Courson and Sarah? Courson each proved 5 days attendance. Thomas Corson swears 5 days attendance agt Peter Taylor, John Sullivant and Thos. Sumers.

p. 88/96. Ordered that warrant issued agnst Isaac Patridge returnable immediately to answer the damage for begetting a bastard child on Rachell Collins servant to James Jarrard where upon it was commanded unto the sheriff of the count afsd that he should take the afsd. Isaac if he should be found in his bailwick.

p. 88/96. John Brannock, to pay unto John Eccleston, Susanna his wife and Henry Trippe £10.4.6 and 1200 lbs. of tobacco.

New page 100. The Road that formerly lyed from Hunting Creek Church to William Kirks is ordered to be carried to the upper bridge of the Northwest Fork and John Young is appointed overseer.

p. 100. Informed that John Dean, St. Marys White Chappell Parish on 10 July 1732 did commit adultery with Susannah Reid and begat a bastard child. Fined 1200 lbs. of tobacco.

p. 106. Presented that Henry Davis feloniously killed and bore away a hog of Harmon Johnson.

Second Tuesday Nov 1733

p. 118. Hugh Spedden brings into court William Clarke an orphan and prays that he may be bound unto him - William Clarke, 10 years old is bound to afsd. Hugh as an apprentice until he arrives at the age of 21.

Ordered no more subpoenas issue against Anna Daughity as exec of George Daughity for the balance of estate till next June.

Ordered that his Lordship's presenter exhibit an information agst Samuel Greenly for fornication with Agnes Lawson.

p. 112/122. That Samuell Greenly, Great Choptank Parish, planter, on 10 Nov 1733 did commit fornication with Agnes Lawson and begat a bastard child. Fined 30 shillings.

p. 113. John Rex/Rey?? is appointed overseer of the road in the room of Richard Norman.

Ordered that his Lordships atty. exhibit an information against Frances Beckwith for burning the mare of Willm. Beckingham and that John Robson entered into recognizance to give evidence agst her.

Acquittal on an indictment for assault on Shadrack Feddeman and the cost of the jurors in cost to the plaintiff.

Presented that William Kitt of Great Choptank Parish, labourer, on 20 May 1733 with force and arms ... one broad hoe of the value of 20 lbs. of tobacco belonging to William Downes did steal. Not guilty.

p. 119. Presented that Elizabeth Long of Great Choptank Parish, widow, on 2 Aug 1733 did commit fornication begat a bastard child. Fined 30 shillings. Joseph Ennalls security. She made oath that the begetter of the child was John Baxter.

p. 121. Petition of Tench Francis stating that being seized of a tract called *Paradice* he prays for a commission to prove the boundaries of the tract.

Petition of Thomas Stuart, stating that he has a Negro woman who is taken as a taxable this year but for as much as the sd. Negro is now at this present very ailing and sick beyond all hopes of recovery most humbly prays that he be acquitted from paying tax for sd. Negro.

Petition of Wm. Goldsborough. That he has applied himself to the study of the law and that he now desires to be admitted to the Practice thereof. His is admitted.

p. 122. Petition of William German who has issue a child who is a natural fool who is now four years old. He being a poor man who has a wife and several small children who finds abundance of difficulty and had labour to maintain the same he prays to allow him what your worships may think sufficient for the maintenance of the child.

Petition of Alexander Argoe stating that now grown antient and almost past my labour; prays that the court acquit him of paying tax.

In a complaint it is stated that Michael Kelly was indebted to James Woolford for £1.3.9 and that Michael Kelly is runaway out of this Province for 3-4 years past.

p. 124. Petition of Elizabeth Minner stating that she is very antient and decriped and fallen to poverty and has nothing to live on and requests a small allowance.

Petition of Rosannah Reed having cured a certain Walker Crager an object of the county's charity which in some kind of her sickness after ...? and dyed which your petitioner buried in a Christian like manner and prays allowance for the same. She was allowed 100 lbs. of tobacco.

Petition of Isaac Middleton being a very poor child who hath been and is a very great grue? and trouble to my poor mother who is a very poor woman .. prays for an allowance. Peter Taylor given 1000 lbs.of tobacco to maintain him.

p. 125. Walker Campbell states that Benjamin Brunsden is absented himself and runaway.

On 25 Aug 1733 Samuel Greenless, taylor, acknowledges being indebted to his Lordships. Charged by Agness Lawson single woman that he had carnal knowledge of her body at several times and that she is now with child by him.

p. 130. Petition of Henry Ennalls, Jr. who hath a servant John Watson who has lost his right hand; prays to discharge him of tax.

Petition of Elizabeth Travers stating that the road going through her plantation is of great prejudice to her and prays that she may have liberty to turn this road round her plantation. Approved.

Petition of George Drew that he is poor antient man almost 70 years of age and very feeble and wishes to be acquitted of paying tax. Approved.

p. 201. Thomas Richardson agt the Vestry of St. Marys White Chappel.

Thomas Dell, principall vestryman of St. Marys White Chappel Parish, Peter Taylor, James Brown, Joseph Allford, Edward Hargeton and Moses Nicolls of the same parish and county Gentlemen Vestrymen of same Parish.

p. 221. Petition of Joshua Kennerly: Elizabeth Orrell, an orphan child, dau. of John Orrell of the co. dec'd. was bound to Marget Kirke alias Simpson to her and no other person and her mistress now being dead and your petitioner marrying with her sister Martha and the said Elizabeth being a minor and not of age to choose her guardian, prays that your worships grant petitioner, Joshua Kennerly, guardianship.

Petition of Thomas Heather that petitioner is left as orphan of this county and my father leaving a tract of land lying near the mouth of Hunting Creek and my mother after the death of my father married with one Wm. (or Mr.?) Watson who liveth in Queen Anne's Co. who keepeth the right and possession of the land from my mother being now dead also and I being informed that since the death of my mother that my said father in law hath no right and I being but a minor as yet most humbly pray that to grant liberty of choosing William Green Jr. my guardian . Admitted.

p. 224. Vienna Hodson bringeth into Court Sarah Norton who is judged to be 7 years old. Sarah is now bound to Vienna.

p. 224. That Jane Thomas, als Vincent of Great Choptank Parish, spinster, on the last day of June 1732 did commit fornication with a certain person and begat a bastard child. Fined 30 shillings. Jane Thomas swears that John McCormack is the father of the bastard child whereof he is indicted.

p. 226 Ordered that Mary Cook find sureties for her attendance at this court.

p. 227. Presented that Margarett Ryon of Dorchester Parish, spinster, on 1 Nov 1733 did commit fornication and begat a bastard child. Ordered to be whipped with 14 lashes. Margaret Ryon swears that Michel McCormack is the father.

p. 228. Thomas Smith prays that the court adjudge the age of John Thomas. The Court adjudged his age as 16 years the 6th of July next. He was bound to Thomas Smith until age 21.

p. 229. Presented that Mary Glaster of Great Choptank Parish, spinster, on 10 June 1733 did commit fornication with person unknown to Jurors. Ordered whipped with 10 lashes. Mary Glaster swears John Poole is the father.

p. 230. That Agnes Lawson of Great Choptank Parish on 5 Nov 1733 did commit fornication and begat a bastard child. 10 lashes.

p. 231 That Mary Jane of Great Choptank Parish, spinster, on 1 July 1732 did commit fornication and begat a bastard child. To be whipped with 25 lashes.

p. 232. That Mary Wheeler spinster of White Chappell Parish on 1 April 1733 did commit fornication and begat a bastard child. 10 lashes. Mary Wheeler swears that John Cremeen is the father.

p. 234. Petition of Thomas Shison sheweth that whereas one Edward Southell of this co. keeps and detains a son of your petitioner's brother, one Samuel Shison late of this co., dec'd., after a most shamefull manner and your petitioner being uncle to the said child he having no friend to speak in the behalf of the said child the said Southel having no manner of indenture for to hold the said child prays to bind the child to him.

p. 235. Ordered that an information be exhibited against John Anderson for assault and battery on Thomas Walkers/Walkins?

The court agrees with Susannah Brown to keep Samuel Seager's child for one year and to receive 1000 lbs. of tobacco.

p. 247. Presented that John Baxter late of Great Choptank Parish, mariner, on 10 Feb 1733 did assault Benjamin Ball.

p. 265. Petition of Martha Willoby that she accidentally and unfortunately with his gun shot his hand and arm in such manner that one of his hands is almost lost and become useless. Requests he be freed from paying a levy. approved.

p. 265. Petition of William Standford showeth that your petitioner having a cousin of whom he has kept this five years, one Wm. Standford, son of John Standfod dewayod(?) and he having a tract of land befallen him by the death of an elder brother prays that your worship grant the liberty of looking after the said plantation in behalf of the said child, he being a minor. William Stanford approved as guardian to the minor.

p. 266. Petition of James Cannon and John Pritchett showeth that on 25 March last they entered into bonds for Anne Holton admin on the estate of William Holton of DO Co., dec'd., and she which appraisement she made inventory thereof returned and since she hath taken no farther care to comply with the creditors but is taken up with one Dennis Buns a strainger man and wasting and destroying the estate and hath conveyed several of the household goods over the Bay so that the creditors and orphan will be defrauded.

Petition Thomas Armsby that I have served my master John Anderton of this co. but he denies to pay my food and dews [dues].

John Cremeen fined £3.

June 1734
p. 389. Presented that Mary Grayley on 10 June 1733 did commit fornication and begat a bastard child. 10 lashes. She swore that the father was Joseph Pearson.

Rachel Young, William Williams of Northwest Fork and James Bond are bound to Mathew(?) Young, child and orphan of Mathew Young, dec'd, in sum of £40.16.8 . Also to Levi Young child and orphan of Mathew Young for same amount.

p. 402. Richard Pearson, Isaac Meekins and Noah Pearson are bound to Milcah Pearson child and orphan of Richard Pearson, late of said co. in the sume of £35.16.3

p. 412. Elizabeth Orrell is bound to Matha Kennerly until she arrives to 16 years of age. Thomas Brannock and William Kennerly, secureties.

Anthony Pendergrass is bound to Willm. Lecompte son of Moses Lecompte until he arrives to 21.

Dorchester County Judgement Records
1742-1743
MSA CR49,053

25 April 1743
Indenture between Joshua Kennerly of DO Co., printer, and his wife Martha on the one part and Howes Goldsborough of the same co. of the other part.

p. 3. Whereas John Machon [Mahaun, Mohon] late of afsd. co. dec'd. did by his last will nominate and appoint James Brown, Francis Hayward and James Cannon to apportion and divide his land equally between his four daus. namely Anne, Margaret, Esther and Priscilla. [Portions described.] {See Maryland Wills 20:856}

Aug 1743
p. 5. John McKeele for £140 hath sold in open markett unto Thos. and Daniel Sulivane a Negro man called Tom, and a Negro boy called Ned.

Nov 1743
p. 12. Richard Keene gives to his son Pollard Keene, a tract of land on Taylor's Island: *Tobias Lott*, 100 a.; *Provintial Contatr.*, 51 a.; *Susanna's Chance*, 50 a.; *Keenes Closer*, 50 a.; *Maidens Lott*, 54 a.

p. 15. Petition of Elenor wife of Thomas Sprigs(?) praying for the assistance of a doctor. Allowed £4.

p. 17. Wm. Twyford, Sr., petitions to be exempt from paying levys because of age. Wounded in the shoulder by a fray with an Indian.

p. 17. James Becket petitions to be relieved of paying tax because of infirmness.

p. 18. Henry Davis petitions that whereas he had been a resident of the county for 60 years - unable to make a living, destitute. Allowed £4.

Petition of John Willey Sr. that he and his wife above 60 years of age and not able to labour and hath neither servant nor children to help them. Requests to be free from paying taxes. Approved.

To the Justices of DO Co. a petition of the inhabitants of the freeshes(?) of afd. co. showeth whereas there was formerly a road cleared from the Northwest Fork of Nanticoke to Cabin Creek but for some years past it has been neglected and not cleared from Thomas Williams to Cabin Creek. Your Petitioners humbly pray that the same road may be cleared from the said Thomas Williams to Cabin Creek or until it intersects the road from Hunting Creek to Cabin Creek -Isaac Nicolls, Thomas Nutter, Charles Brown, David Pollett, Thomas Layton, Richd. Dawson, Mathew Smith, Henry Smith, James Addams, Absolom Adams, Christopher Nutter, Richd. Harison, Richard Addams, Joseph Pollett, James Brown, John Marrett, Roger Addams, William Marine, Thos. Brown, Henry Williams, Jos. Outerbridge, Joseph Brown, Charles Mar..., Robert Harison?, Jonathan Marine, James Brown, Junr., Isaac Brown, William Williams, John Brown, Jr., Thomas Andrew, Thomas Joyns?, James Hales, Richd. Layton, Henry Cannon, Chas. ..., John James, Jonathan Williams, Jacob Palmer, Meredith Williams, George Chillett?, James Rawley, James Dent, Jonathan Clifton, Jonathan Flower, Daniel Andrews, William Shores?, It was granted.

15 July 1742

p. 18. There was found by Cooper's Negroes in his tobacco ground a white child (girl) and brought into my house Levin? Abbot by Elinor Nealle being left by some body not seen by any body, by a jug of water left in the field thought to be no more than 3 or 4 days old. The court agrees to allow the said Richard Cooper from this time until Nov next at rate of 12 shillings by the month.

p. 19. John Stafford, Jr. bringeth into court a Negro boy called Broaden and a Negro girl called Nan and prayeth the court to adjudge the ages of the said Negroes whereupon the court judged the boy of the age of 14 and the girl of the age of 13.

p. 19. Ordered that his Lordship's prosecutor exhibit an information against Elinor Wall for committing fornication and having a bastard child.

William Stevens bringeth into court a Negro called Sabina and prayed the court to adjudge her age. Adjudged 9 years.

Francis Sayward presented for committing an assault on Barterton Fletcher.

John Polk son of William Polk presented for committing fornication with Elinor Wall and begetting a bastard.

Walter Stevens brings a boy called Solomon Nights and requests the court to bind him to him. The Court binds him to the age of 21, he being of the age of 13 on 10 April last.

Walter Stevens brings an orphan girl called Anne Knights and prays to bind her to him. Bound to age of 16, she being of the age 10 years on 10 Oct last.

p. 20. The court determines that George Lang the servant of Coll. Joseph Ennalls is incapable of labour. The said Ennalls is exempt from paying of levy for afsd. George Lang.

Henry Beckwith brings into court a Negro boy called Grassfoot to adjudge his age. Adjudged age of 9.

John Magraw brought in orphan boy called John Cotter. He was bound to age of 21, he being adjudged of the age of son 14 April next.

Ordered that the prosecutor exhibit information against Winefred Laver for fornication with a Negro slave and having a bastard mulatto child.

The court sells the bastard mulatto child of Winefred Laver to Mary Willis for £1.11.0 she being the highest bidder.

The court fines Harrison Johnson 500 lbs. of tobacco for not attending the last June court as an orphan juror.

Margaret, wife of Solomon Bryan brings into court a piece of linen and swears that the flax of which the same is made grew in this county. Adjudged the 4th best.
Frances, wife of William Trippe, ...ditto. 5th best.
Anne, wife of John Trippe...
Elizabeth wife of Daniel Fraizer...
Rosannah wife of John Hodson, (forrest) ...
Elizabeth Fooks ...

Presented that Owen Owens late of St. Mary's White Chapel on 10 May 1742 assaulted Edward Nuby, shoemaker. Fined 5 shillings.

Presented that on 10 Aug 1742 in town of Cambridge John Hayward, Jr., of Great Choptank Parish assaulted John Hayward, son of Henry. Fined 5 shillings.

Presented that on 10 Aug 1742 that Francis Baynard of St. Mary's White Chapel on 10 July 1742 assaulted Batterton Fletcher.

Elinor Wall fined 30 shillings. William Wall promises to pay. She answers that John Polk, son of William Polk is the father of her bastard child.

p. 25. Presented that Winefred Laver late of Grean Choptank Parish, servant to Mary Willis, on 10 June 1742 committed fornication with a Negro slave and begat a bastard mulatto child. Given an additional seven years of servitude.

p. 52. James Peterkin presented for assaulting on 23 Aug 1742 [name unreadable]. Fined 10 shillings.

p. 53. Presented that Ezekiel Keene of Dorchester Parish assaulted on 7 Aug 1742 Charles Stanford. Fined £5.

Presented that William Cannon of Dorchester Parish assaulted James

Peterkin. Not guilty.

p. 54. Christopher Nutter, son of William Nutter, chooses William Nutter his guardian. And sd. William Nutter, William Owens and Robert Clarkson, his sureties, acknowledged themselves to owe the afsd. Christopher Nutter £166.

Presented that Mary Sudden of Great Choptank Parish, spinster, on 1 Feb 1741 allowed an unknown person to have carnal knowledge of her and begat a bastard child. Fined 30 shillings. John Barney promises to pay all fees.

p. 55. The court agrees to allow John Thompson 12 shillings per month to keep an orphan called William Johnson until next June Court.

Presented that Mary Holland of Great Choptank Parish on 10 April 1742 did commit fornication and begat a bastard child. 10 lashes ordered at the whiping post.

Edward Cato brings into court an orphan called William Johnson and prays that the court bind him to him Edward Cato. Bound to age 21, he being now of the age of 5.

Presented that John Polk son of William Polk of St. Mary's White Chapel Parish on 10 June 1742 committed fornication with Elinor Wall and begat a bastard child. Fined 30 shillings.

p. 56. Presented that Poolley Jones, planter, of St. Mary's White Chapel Parish on 10 May 1742 assaulted Thomas Cockley, planter. Fined 5 shillings.

p. 57. Presented that Eleanor Reardon of Dorchester Parish, spinster, on 10 Oct 1742committed fornication with a person unknown and begat a bastard child. 10 lashes. John Jones promised security to endemnify the co. from maintaining the child for 7 years.

p. 59. Presented that Mary Magdalen Warner of Great Choptank Parish, spinster, committed fornication and begat a bastard child. Fined 30 shillings. David Peterkin her surety. Child is called Stephen Warner.

Edward Newton brought into court Francis Green, an orphan and prayed to have the orphan bound to him. He was bound until the age of 21, he being adjudged by the court to be 10 years old.

p. 60. Presented that Sarah Smith of St. Mary's White Chapel Parish, servant to Mathew Hardikin, on 10 July 1742 committed fornication and begat a bastard child. 10 lashes.

p. 63. Priscilla Mahaun chooses as her guardian Isaac Brown.

Thomas Brawhaun brought into court an orphan called Solomon Beck and prayed to have the orphan bound to him. Bound to the age of 21, his age adjudged by the Court to be 12 years.

Presented that Abraham Jones of St. Mary's White Chapel Parish, planter, on 10 Aug 1742 assaulted Richard Andrew, Jr. Fined 5 shillings.

p. 64. Presented that Moses Poole of Great Choptank Parish on 10 Oct 1742 assaulted Michael Scackdom of DO Co., blacksmith. Acquitted.

p. 82. William Littleton submitted a petition to show that he hath an orphan boy, son of Charles Littleton that has lost the use of his limbs so that he is not capable of doing any labour. Requests allowance for the maintenance of said orphan. Granted.

Richard Harte submits a petition that he is 62 years next May and have by a fall from a horse about 2 years ago lost the use of one of my arms; also have lost one finger from each hand and am not capable of getting my living and have a parcel of small children to maintain and no estate valuable in the world. He prays to be set clear of paying tax. On 1 Nov 1742 the following persons confirmed that the statement was true: Timo. Macnamar, Joh. Macnamar, Wm. Evans, John Rumbley, Sr., David Rogers, Phillip Wingate, Anglow Wingate, Andrew Insley, William Boon, John Muse, Anthony Shorter, Ambros Wrotten, Sol.? Chaplin?, Richard Woodlan, Henry ---?, George Slacom, Job Slacum, Phillip Wingate, Wm. Harper, Richard Kendal Foxwell, Andrew Gowtee, Jacob Gowtee, George Boaz, John Nuner, John Wingate, William Dean, Richard Lane, Abraham Foxwell, Francis Willey, William Dean, Ezekiel Keene, Zed: Pritchett, Jr., Lewis Griffith, Jr., Isaac Partridge? Approved.

p. 83. Presented that Ennalls Hooper of Great Choptank Parish on 10 Oct 1742 assaulted Michael Stockdown, blacksmith. Acquitted.

Presented that Thomas Ross of Dorchester Parish, planter on 10 Oct 1742 assaulted Allen Thomas, planter. Fined 5 shillings.

p. 84. Constables appointed:
Moses Nicolls, Bridge Town Hundred
John Nicolls, Jr., Great Choptank Hundred
John Woodgate, Fork Hundred
John Trippe, Jr., Little Choptank Hundred
Thomas Loockerman, Fishing Creek Hundred
James Edmondson, Armitage Hundred
Edward Pritchett, Jr., Streights Hundred
James Hodson, Nanticoke Hundred
John Twigg, the elder, Transquakin Hundred

p. 85. Thos. Cook petitions that he is now 65 years of age and incapable of hard labour and paying a very great rent, having no land. Freed from paying any levy in the future.

Petition of John Dean, stating that at my house is an object of your worships' charity, one Alexander Mecotter who hath lost the use of his lower parts so that he cannot either stand or go or do any kind of thing towards his maintenance and his mother is dead and his father hath absented himself. £5 to be levied to Major Henry Trippe for the use of Alexander Mecotter.

Petition of Thomas Thomas, having a wife and child left by one Henry Hill who is absconded and left his wife and child in a most deplorable condition and she is incapable of maintaining herself or child and she is daily addicted to fitts and hath also since her being brought to bed thro the occasion of her fitts fell into the fire and burnt herself to a great degree and if her mother had not been nigh at hand in pulling them out for she had her child in her arms, it would have endangered both their lives. Allowed £3 for the use of afsd. woman and child.

p. 86. Petition of Lewis Griffith. has a old Negro woman named Cate who is above 60 years of age and is past labour and unfit for any service. Freed from paying future taxes on her.

Petition of Daniel Sare who maintained Mathew Skillett, one of your (the court's) pensioners from July to Nov Court and before he received satisfaction the said Skillett was taken sick in Nov and remained sometime sick and died in March. Allowed 50 shillings

Petition of Joseph Pollock requests bounds of *Little Goshen*.

Thomas Foster states that a road was lately layd out from James Vinsons's Causway to Melvills mill so nigh to your petitioner's plantations that your Petnr. is greatly damaged thereby as a road may go layd out equally convenient to the inhabitants of the county. Prays that the road be altered.

Presented that Abraham Johnson of Great Choptank Parish, on 10 May 1742 committed fornication with Eliner English and begat a bastard child. 10 lashes.

November Court 1742

p. 93. The court agrees to allow Winefred Aron at the rate of 20 shillings per month for accommodating Ann London?, an object of charity.

Solomon West brings into court a boy called Ezekiel Cavanaugh and prays the court to bind the boy to him. to trade of shoemaker. bound to age of 21, he being of the age of 3 years on this 19 Nov.

The court agrees with John Barnes to keep a ferry over Slaughter Creek from Western Point to the Loer? side of Majr. Tobias Pollards Pasture fence near his Landing

p. 94. The court agrees with Mr. Thomas Ennalls of Choptank to keep a ferry from Mrs. Mary Enall's to Chancellor's Point and to keep a boat sufficient to carry five horses and men for £30 by the year.

The court agrees with Mr. Charles Dickinson to allow him to keep a ferry from Barker's Landing to Hogg Island at £35 per year

Thomas Stewart prays to keep an ordinary in the town of Cambridge.

Licensed for one year.

Joseph Bailey prays to keep ordinary at the town of Vienna. Licensed.

p. 95. Elizabeth Jones petitioned that she was a servant to Solomon Bryan and has served her time. Nevertheless the sd. Solomon refuses to pay her freedom dues. Awarded 192 lbs. of tobacco.

p. 96. William Holloway requests that his pension continue. Approved.

Sarah a mulattoe woman requests exemption from future tax. Approved.

March Court 1743

p. 176. Presented that John Fallon of Dorchester Parish on 10 June 1743 committed fornication with Susannah Chaplin and begat a bastard child. Fined 30 shillings.

p. 178. Presented that Daniel Sulivane of Great Choptank Parish on 10 Feb 1743 assaulted Thomas Pain. Fined 5 shillings.

p. 179. Presented that John Woolford Great Choptank Parish, Innholder, on 10 Feb 1743 assaulted Margaret Noble. Fined 5 shillings.

Presented that Thomas Clark of St. Mary's White Chapel on 10 June 1743 committed fornication with Jane Slone and begat a bastard child. Fined 30 shillings.

p. 180. Presented that Hannah Smith of St. Mary's White Chapel spinster on 10 Aug 1743 committed fornication and begat a bastard child. Fined 30 shillings. John Smith, her surety.

p. 181. Presented that Rosannah Mitchell of Great Choptank Parish, spinster, on 10 Sep 1743 assaulted David Peterkin. Fined 2 shillings, 6 pence.

p. 182. Presented that Ann Bryan on 10 Feb 1743 committed fornication and begat a bastard child. 10 lashes.

Presented that James Tregoe of Dorchester Parish, on 10 Nov 1743 assaulted Elisha Stevens. Fined 5 shillings.

p. 185. Nehemiah Staiton chooses James Staiton as his guardian. Robert Polke, surety.

Henry Stafford, John Stafford and Daniel Sulavane of DO Co. stand justly indebted to Proprietary. Sd. Henry to build a new bridge where the old upper bridge stood over the North West Fork, 10 feet wide

p. 186. Presented that Henry Bradley of Choptank Parish, planter, on 10 Feb 1743 assaulted Jane Thomas. Fined 5 shillings.

The court agrees with Thomas Ruley? to keep the orphan of John Lister? from 22 Dec last til next Nov Court at the rate of 12 shillings per month and to find the orphan clothes.

187

Presented that William Ellis of St. Mary's White Chapel Parish, planter, on 10 Jan 1743 assaulted Isaac Mead. Fined 5 shillings. Fined 5 shillings.

p. 188. Presented that John Orrell of Great Choptank Parish on 10 Feb 1743 assaulted Henry Hooper. Fined 10 shillings.

Presented that Thomas Clifton of St. Mary's White Chapel Parish on 10 Aug 1743 assaulted James Hickman? Fined 5 shillings.

p. 189. Presented that Sarah Hickman, wife of James Hickman, of St. Mary's White Chapel Parish on 10 Oct 1743 assaulted John Woodgate, Constable of North East Fork Hundred, in the execution of his office. Fined 20 shillings.

p. 190. Presented that John Walter of Great Choptank Parish on 10 Feb 1743 assaulted Robert Glover. Fined 5 shillings.

p. 192. Presented that John Lee of Great Choptank Parish servant of Jacob Nunar on 5 Feb 1743 stole one shift of Joseph Cox Gray and that Sarah Kinley spinster knowing the felony that the afsd. John Lee had done did comfort, feed and assist him. John Lee after his expiration of his servitude to pay Joseph Cox Gray 400 lbs. of tobacco, 4 times the value of the shift.

p. 193. Thomas Chamberlain states he is held a servant by John Smith contrary to law. Petition dismissed and that the afsd. John recover against the afsd. Thomas 315 lbs. of tobacco his costs and charges by him about his defense.

p. 195. Presented that Hannah Carr of Great Choptank Parish stole two turkeys. Not guilty.

Presented that Thomas William Cockcraft of Great Choptank Parish on 1- Feb 1743 stole a hog and a sheep. 17 lashes.

p. 198. The court agrees with Thomas Graham to keep Mary Ann Richardson orphan of Joseph Richardson til next June Court at the rate of 10 shillings per month. Dr. Joseph Ennalls to do what he can to cure Mary Ann Richardson, an object of charity and to bring his accounts at Nov Court next.

p. 205. Thomas Sharpless petitions that he was detained by David Peterkin as servant without any legal powers to do. Complaint dismissed.

John Trippe petitions that a commission be appointed to determine the bounds of the tract called *Sandy Neck* on North West Fork of Nanticoke.

p. 206. Petition of John Dehorty statomg that he hath a very old Negroe man called Cufey, that has had one of his legs lately broke so that he is come incapable of doing any bodily labour. Requests exemption from paying any levy on him. Approved.

Edward Evans petition - being very ancient and past his labour. Year before last your worships were pleased to allow him 40 shillings to hire work to make bread for himself and family. Court approves continuing the charity.

Lenard Jones' petition states that he is 77 years old - requests exemption from paying taxes. Approved.

p. 207. Petition of William Grantham for a commission to determine bounds of tract *Mulgrave.*

Petition of Athow Pattison to determine bounds of tract called *East Billing* and *Addition to Crows Lodge.* which bounds depend on the bounds of *Weston* belonging to John Eccleston.

Petition of Charles Robson for a commission to determine the bounds of *Robson Range* on w. side of N.W. side of Blackwater River and on e. side of Gum Swamp.

Petition of Thomas Pattison tract of land called *Armstrongs Hog Pen* on Jameses Island.

p. 208. Presented that Ann Fleharty of St. Mary's White Chapple Parish on 10 June 1740 committed fornication and begat a bastard child

August Court 1743

p. 231. Presented that Sarah Willis of St. Mary's White Chapple Parish, spinster, on 10 May 1743 committed fornication and begat a bastard child. Fined 30 shillings. Andrew Willis her surety to to endemnify the inhabitants of the county for 7 years from keeping and maintaining her bastard child.

Jane Slone of St. Mary's White Chapple Parish spinster on 10 May 1743 committed fornication and begat a bastard child. 5 lashes. Joseph Willson to pay court costs. Jane Slone swears that Thomas Clark of TA Co. is the father.

Prosecutor to exhibit an information agnst Mary Rogers and Susannah Chaplin for committing fornication.

p. 233. Presented that Susannah Chaplin of Dorchester Parish on 10 May 1743 committed fornication and begat a bastard child. Fined 30 shillings. She swears that John Fallen is the father of the child. Fees paid by Solomon Chaplin.

p. 234. Presented that Elizabeth Hughs of St. Mary's White Chapple Parish, spinster, on 10 May 1743 committed fornication and begat a bastard child. 5 lashes. Moses Nicolls pays court costs. Elizabeth swears that George Scott of TA Co. is the father of her bastard child. Moses Nicolls provides indemnification. Child is called Prudence Hughs.

p. 236. Rachel Paul of Dorchester Parish on 10 May 1743 committed fornication and begat a bastard child. Fined 30 shillings. Rachel swears that William Pope is the father. Child is called Mary Pall. Rachel Pall, together with Job Slacomb, her surety, stand to indemnify the county from maintaining the child.

p. 237. Presented that Bethulia Ramsey of St. Mary's White Chapel

Parish, spinster, on 10 March 1742 committed fornication and begat a bastard child. Fined 30 shillings. Bethulia swears the father is Joshuah Ward. Fees paid by Henry Trippe. to indemnify the county from maintaining the child called Elizabeth Ramsey for 7 years. Bethulia Ramsey and William Granger her surety for £40.

p. 239. Presented that Mary Rogers of St. Mary's White Chapel Parish committed fornication on 10 March 1742. 5 lashes.

p. 240. Presented that John Finch, Jr., of Great Choptank Parish on 1 Aug 1743 committed fornication upon Mary Lowe of the same co., dau. of John Lowe to ravish and carnally know and did beat and evilly treat. Fined £5.

p. 242. Presented that Moses Poole of Great Choptank Parish on 10 July 1743 assaulted Levin Hodson of same co., planter. Fined 5 shillings.

p. 243. Presented that Mulatto Judy of Great Choptank Parish on 10 June 1743 committed fornication with Negro slave and begat a bastard child. She is ordered to become a servant for 7 years after she has served her time of servitude now due with Joseph Ennalls, her present master.

Presented that Mulatto Agnis of Great Choptank Parish on 10 Feb 1743 committed fornication with a Negro slave and begat a bastard child. She is ordered to become a servant for 7 years after she has served her time of servitude now due with Joseph Ennalls her present master.

p. 246. Thomas Roe, planter, and Francis Lee, Gent., of DO Co. are bound to Benjamin Roe, child and orphan of William Roe of sd. co., dec'd., in the sum of £36, on 11 Aug 1743.

p. 247. Thomas Roe, planter, and Francis Lee, Gent. of DO Co. are bound to Thomas Roe, Jr., grandson of William Roe, dec'd., in the sum of £18.

Nathaniel Manning and Daniel Bruffet of DO Co. are bound to Thomas Cook, child and orphan of Mary Cook, dec'd., of said co. in the sum of £2.
Also to Ann Cooke, child and orphan of Mary Cook of DO Co. for the same amount.

p. 249. Obbediah Dawson recognizance in £2.0.0 to give evidence agnst Owen Connerly for cutting the ear of John Connerly.

p. 251. Petition of Nathan Manship unable to do bodily labour and prays discharge from payng levy. Approved.

Petition of Atthow Pattison who possesses tracts, *Addition to Crows Lodge* and *East Billin* and wishes to have a commission determine the bounds.

p. 252. Inhabitants of N.W. fork of Nanticoke and between the sd. forks. pray for road from Upper Bridge of afsd. Fork to the lower Bridge be cleared, above said the under the direction of John Richards as overseer: Isaac Nicolls, John Richards, Jonathan Marine, Floyd Williams, James Dent, William Williams, Sr., Edward Williams, William Bradley, William Bradley, Jr., Absolam Addams, Peter

Carter, Richard Andrew, Henry Smith, William Cannon, Jr., James Addams, Henry Williams, Thomas Smith, Henry Smith, Stephen Smith, Jr., James Vaulx, Thomas Dawson, Morris Carvin?, Edward Smith, Timothy Kensey, Thomas Andrew, Sr., Richard Dawson, Dan Sulivane, John Rumbley, James Brown, Jr., William Owens, William Nutter, C. Manarthy, Thos. Nutter, Timothy Causey, David Mills, Andrew Gray, James Newner, Daniel Andrew, Richard Shockley, Henry Stafford, Edward Ludman, Marnaduke Story?, Thomas Williams.

Dorchester County Judgment Records
1743-1745
Microfilm CR49052

November Court 1743

p. 67. Petition of Rosannah Loockerman that Negro man called Pallypus because of his great age is unable of labouring. Requests exemption from paying levy.

Petition of Joseph Argoe incapable of helping himself or family, prays exemption from paying levy.

Petition of Ann Morris. Unable to get her living; prays she that she might be exempt from paying any taxes.

p. 68. Petition of Comfort Phillips, who has an old Negro called Gaxsledg age 67 years and past all labour. Prays to be exempt from paying anymore taxes.

Petition of Richard Covey who is seized of a tract called *Wairfields Trouble* and wishes to settle the boundaries.

p. 69. Petition of Tobias Pollard who has a Negro woman Bess who is past her labour. Prays that he be exempt from paying levy. Approved.

Petition of Ishmael Rideu. is in a very low and sickly condition afflicted with a anguishing and wasting distemper so that for this five months he has been unable to help himself. Prays that he and his wife be allowed at the rate of £5 each.

Petition of Roger Addams. He hath a tract called *Beckless* and prays to have his bounders settled.

p. 70. Petition of Joseph Cox Gray. who possesses a tract called *Taylors Promise* and prays to have the bounders settled.

Petition of James Edmondson prays that the road that goes through his plantation and through his orchard be redirected about 30 yards lower. Approved

Petition of William Williams that his plantation lying in the road from the n.w. fork bridge up ... which Capt. Charles Nutter did ... and the said road runs through the petitioners plantation so that it is ...

p. 71. Petition of Henry Trippe to practice law in the court.

Presented that Charles Littleton of Great Choptank Parish on 10 Oct 1742 committed fornication with Mary Williams and begat a bastard child. Find 30 shillings. William Littleton his surety to indemnify the county from keeping and maintaining the child.

p. 73. Presented that Mary Williams committed fornication and begat a bastard child. Fined 30 shillings.

p. 74. Presented that Elizabeth Thompson of St. Mary's White Chapel Parish committed fornication and begat a bastard child. Fined 30 shillings. Edward Trippe to pay court fees.

p. 75. Presented that William Gray of St. Mary's White Chapel Parish on 10 Oct 1742 committed fornication with Elizabeth Thompson and begat a bastard child. Fined 30 shillings. Abraham Gauther to pay court fees.

p. 76. Presented that Sarah Neall of Great Choptank Parish spinster, on 10 June 1742 committed fornication and begat a bastard child. Fined 30 shillings. John Trippe to pay court fees.

p. 77. Presented that Henry Hayward, Jr., of Great Choptank Parish committed fornication with Sarah Neel and begat a bastard child. Fined 30 shillings. John Stewart his surety to endemnify the county from maintaining the child for 7 years.

p. 79. Presented that Hannah Dawson of St. Mary's White Chapel Parish, spinster, on 10 Feb 1742 committed fornication and begat a bastard child. Fined 30 shillings. She swears that Dennis Kelley is the father.

Presented that Dennis Kelly committed fornication and begat a bastard child. Fined £3. Thomas Foster and William Addams his sureties.

p. 91. Presented that Sarah Stanford of Great Choptank Parish on 10 June 1742 committed fornication and begat a bastard child. 10 lashes.

p. 92. Presented that John Wright of St. Mary's White Chapel Parish, planter, on 10 Dec 1742 stole 2 linen and cotton shats of the value of 150 lbs. of tobacco and one linnen shift of the value of 100 lbs. of tobacco and one holland handkerchief valued at 10 lbs. of tobacco one course towell of the value of five lbs. of tobacco, one holland pillow case of vale of 10 lbs. of tobacco one ... table cloath valued at 20 lb.s of tobacco of the goods and chattles of Zabdial Potter. To stand in the public pillory for one hour and whipt 15 lashes and to pay the said Zabdial Potter four times the value of the property. David Wright his surety.

p. 147. Presented that Samuel Bradley of Great Choptank Parish, planter on 10 April 1742 committed fornication with Mary Whitely and begat a bastard child. Fined 30 shillings. George Morris his surety in maintenance of child for 7 years.

p. 149. The Court agrees with Summer Addams to keep the foundling child, kept by him last year, until November Court at rate of 10 shillings per month.

Elizabeth Tolly chooses as her guardian Major James Billings.

p. 150. Presented that Elizabeth Sutton of St. Mary's White Chapel Parish, spinster, on 10 Sep 1742 committed fornication and begat a bastard child. Fined 30 shillings. Richard Webster to pay the fees.

p. 228. Petition of Mathew Travers states he has got an old Negro man named Sam who is past his labour and has been lame in one of his knees for several years. Discharged from paying taxes on him.

Petition of Alexander McCotter who being a cripple, has lost use of his lower parts and not capable of labour. Discharged from paying taxes.

Petition of John Cook. Sickly and incapable of labour. Discharged from paying tax.

p. 229. Petition of Thomas Howell he hath a Negro man that has been for the 6 years past has had fits and several times burnt. Incapable of getting a living. Discharged from paying levy on said Negro.

Petition of John Sherwood who is seized of a tract called *Richardsons Folly* and wishes to settle the bounds.

Petition of Samuel Lawson, stating that he together with three other families or inhabitants of Lawsons Island have no publick roads on the said island nor any ferry for the said inhabitants. Ordered that a road be cleared and kept in good repair from the Widow Comfort Hopkins to Holland Straights and that Samuel Lawson be appointed overseer.

p. 230. Petition of Thomas Mackeel. on 5 June 1743, states hat the county road leads through the middle of his plantation, prays that the road be straightened. Approved.

Petition of William Harper, states that March court of last year appointed him overseer of the road from Vinsons Causway to Harpers Landing on Great Choptank River and because of his age is unable to discharge this duty. Nicholas Parish is appointed in his stead.

p. 231. Petition of Charles Goldsborough who is seized of a tract called *Littleworth*, seeks to settle the bounds.

Petition of Phillip Wingate to settle bounds of a tract on Fox Creek adj. a tract called *Maidens Lott*.

Petition of Lot Pritchett to settle the bounds of a tract called *Edenburough* which bounds depend on a tract called *Northampton*.

p. 232. Petition of Thomas Hickman, old and unable to get his living. Allowed £5 next Nov court.

Petition of Henry Smith in North West Fork Hundred on 8 March 1742. He says he had been infirm for many years. Upward of 60 years of age Discharged from future levies.

p. 233. Petition of William Harundy aged near 60, crippled for 15 years by the stroke of an adz that cut the main sinue of his leg in two and now grows much worse. He has a wife and four small children. And by misfortune has lost almost all his living being very weak and void of help. Discharged from paying future levies.

Inhabitants on the w. side of the n.w. fork of Nanticoke Riere show that your petitioners are in want of a road from the upper bridge of the said fork to the lower bridge for the conveniency in carting or travelling from one bridge to the other once cleared but now is stopt up. John Sullovon, Bruffitt Vinson, Henry Webster, Richard Layden, John Hubert, Joseph Causy, Jr., Solomn. Hubbert, Cha: Mackeal, James May, John Richards, Hen: Causy, Hen Smith, Isa: Obeair, Wm. Stafford, John Safford, Senr, James Stafford, Thos. Dell, Richard Webster, William Perry Wyass, John Stafford, Edward Pool, Roger Rotten, Daniell Map...?, Wm. Moubrey, Wm. Taylor. Ordered that Peter Taylor lay out the said road and be overseer.

Petition of Tho. Griffith near the n.w. fork, aged 59 years and laboured several years under infirmities. Discharged from future levies.

Wm. Meekins, surety for his wife Elizabeth Meekins, who is to appear at June Court to give evidence against Moses Lecompte, Jr. for assault against Edith Winstanly.

Surety for Magret Puckington wife of Abraham Puckington at June Court.

p. 242. Presented that Andrew Taylor of Great Choptank Parish on 10 June 1743 assaulted Jon Rich. Fined 5 shillings.

p. 243. Presented that Wm. Robson, Jr., of Dorchester Parish on 10 May 1743 assaulted Mansfeild Street, planter. Fined 10 shillings.

p. 244. Presented that Ann Owens of Great Choptank Parish, servant of John Stevens, on 10 March 1742 committed fornication and begat a bastard child. 10 lashes.

p. 246. Presented that Sarah Addams of Great Choptank Parish, spinster, on 10 June 1742 committed fornication and begat a bastard child. Fined 30 shillings. Court fees paid by John Rix. Surety to keep the county from maintenance of the child: John Richards.

p. 248. Presented that Mary Sudden of Great Choptank Parish, spinster, on 10 June 1742 committed fornication and begat a bastard child. Fined 30 shillings. John Barundy to pay court fees and act as surety to keep the county free from maintaining the child for 7 years.

p. 250. Ann Cook an object of charity hath heretofore been allowed £9 by the year. to now be allowed £18 per year and two shift cloaths to be bought of Capt. Thomas Nevett.

Alexander Strawhaun to keep orphan of Garrett Corbutt called Thomas Corbutt until November Court next at the rate of 10 shillings per month.

The court adjudged the age of Negro boy called Tom belonging to John Reed to be 11 years of age.

p. 251. The court agrees with Joseph Allford to keep the orphan of Thomas Webster at the rate of 12 shillings per month, to be allowed from 5 Feb last to next November Court.

James Phillips bringeth into court John Corbutt, child and orphan of Garrett Corbutt, and prays to bind the orphan to him. to learn the trade of shoemaker. Bound to the age of 21, he being the age of 8 years last March.

June Term 1744

p. 40. Presented that Neil McCallum of Dorchester Parish, minister of Dorchester Parish, on 10 Sep 1742 joined together in marriage John Anderson and Ann McHill?;/McKell, the said Ann being the said John Anderson his wife's mother's sister and the said John being the said John being the said Ann her sister's daughters husband, the said Neil knowing the affinity afsd. Not guilty.

p. 42. Presented that Larany Spicer of Great Choptank Parish, spinster, on 10 Feb 1743 committed fornication and begat a bastard child. 7 lashes. Fees of the court paid by Capt. Henry Traverse.

p. 43. Presented that Mary Spicer of Great Choptank Parish, spinster, on 10 Feb 1743 committed fornication and begat a bastard child. 10 lashes. Benjamin Granger paid the fees. [The name of the child is later given as Richard Spicer.]

p. 44. Presented that Moncy Lee of Great Choptank Parish on 10 Jan 1743 committed fornication with a Negro person and begat a bastard child. To become a servant for 7 years after the expiration of her present time of servitude with her said master John Trippe.

p. 45. Presented that Mary Willey of Dorchester Parish, wife of William Willey, on 10 Feb 1743 committed fornication and begat a bastard child. Fined £1.10. Fees paid by John Willey.

p. 46. Presented that Susannah Reed of St. Mary's White Chapel Parish committed fornication and begat a bastard child. 10 lashes. John Nicols, Jr. paid court fees.

p. 47. Presented that Rosanna Ensley of Dorchester Parish on 10 Feb 1743 committed fornication and begat a bastard child. Fined £1.10. Court fees paid by John Willey.

p. 48. Presented that Noah Peirson of Dorchester Parish on 13 June 1744 assaulted Hugh Hudson. Fined 10 shillings.

William Travers surety to indemnify the county from maintenance of the bastard child of Larany Spicer.

p. 50. The Court agrees with Edward Cannon to keep the orphan child of James Ramsey called John Ramsey until next November Court at the rate of 10 shillings per month.

The court agrees to allow James Rawley at the rate of 10 shillings by the month for keeping Penelopy Hill, and 10 shillings per month for keeping the child of said Hill till November Court next.

p. 52. Ordered that Mr. Thomas Nevett supply Anne Loaden, an object of charity, with oznabrigs for the making of two shifts, a petticoat and jacket.

Ordered that William Hurst take into his possession the orphan of James Hurst and the same orphan bring to August Court next.

Orphans bond. Joseph Griffith, Richard Tubman and Lewis Griffith of DO Co. are bound unto John Ennalls child and orphan of William Ennalls of said county, dec'd., in the full sum of £124.14.4 to be paid on 16 June 1744. He to receive £62.7.2 when of age. Also the same unto Sarah Ennalls, child and orphan of William Ennalls ... [same amount].

p. 53. Also the same unto Thomas Ennalls ... [same amount].

Edward Pritchett, Jr., Marcus Andrews and John Brawhawn of DO Co. were bound to William Pritchett child and orphan of Zebulon Pritchett of said co. in sum of £51.12.10. Also Jeremiah Pritchett child and orphan of Zebulon [same amount].

p. 54. Also Ezekiel Pritchett, child and orphan of Zebulon [same amount].

On 12 June 1744 Oliver Hackett, Thomas Hackett and James Nunar of DO Co were bound to Rosamond Kemmy, child and orphan of John Kemmy for £6.18.6. to pay her £3.9.3 when of age.

p. 55. Also Job Kemmy, child and orphan of John Kemmy [same amount]. Also John Kimmey, child and orphan of John Kemmy [same amount]. Also Betty Kemmey, child and orphan of John Kemmy [same amount].

p. 56. Also Margary Kimmey, child and orphan of John Kemmy [same amount]. Also Abraham Kimmey, child and orphan of John Kemmy [same amount].

p. 57. Petition of Thomas Pattison to settle the bounds of tract on James Island called *Armstrongs Folly* to settle bounds.

Whereas last March court it was ordered that a road be made from Mr.

Richard Keene's to the road that leads from Oyster Creek to Brans's Ferry which will be a great hardship to your petitioners, it being three miles and most of the way deep swamps and when done can be of no service to two or three families at most so that we hope Your Worships shall put a stop to the afsd. road.: Luke Summers, Matthew Traverse, Charles Barnes, Richd. Chapman, Snr., John Barns Senr, Richd. Roberts, William Keene, James Cannon, Benjamin Granger, John Lewis, Jr., John Pagon, John Aron, Jr., Thos. Fargason, Richard Gadd, Jacob Pattison, John Barnes, Oyster Creek, John Rosen, John Woollen, Senr., James Hays, Bartholomew Hays, John Aaron, Senr., Richard Chapman, William Traverse, John Willen, Junr, James Barnes, William Woollen, Edward Woollen, James Murphy, John Stevens, Wm. Pagon, James Pagon, Lewis Aaron, Thomas Chapman. Approved.

p. 58. Petition of Margaret Brannock, having a servant Negro man called Jack who is now become of very little service by reason he has one of his leggs cut off. Discharged from paying any tax or levy for her said Negro man called Jack.

Petition of Thomas Hancock having been an inhabitant for the past 20 years and having lost sight of one of his eyes30 years past through an accident and sight in the other eye has grown so dim of late as to require spectakles. He was born in 82. Exempted from paying taxes or levy.

Petition of William Harris. afflicted with very sore legs for a long time and unable to perform labour. Exempted from paying taxes or levy.

Petition of Moses Lecompte. Has a Negro woman named Rose who for three years past has been afflicted with pains in her limbs and broke out into running sores in several parts of her body and petitioner has been at great expense with several doctors but all to no purpose she being now in worse condition than ever. Exempted from tax or levy on her.

p. 59. Petition of Joseph Ennalls, exec. of William Ennalls, now possessed of a Negro man called Ben belonging to the children of afsd. William Ennalls, that is by age and other infirmities, almost incapable of doing any service. Exempted from tax or levy.

Petition of Charles Goldsborough that John Edmondson of TA Co., dec'd., being possessed of land in this co. called *Richardson's Folly* did make a deed of gift of part thereof to his son William Edmondson and the residue of the said tract the said John devised to his son Thomas Edmondson in tail which is now become the right of your petitioner. Petitioner prays for a commission to perpetrate the bounders.

Petition of John Sexton who has a tract in the head of Dorchester Co. called *Bunhill Field* and the bound thereof is decayed and prays for a commission to perpetuate the memory of the bounds.

p. 60. Petition of Abraham Oneal who hath a tract called *Mount Silley* and prays for a commission to settle the bounds.

Francis Sanders in her petition states she has maintained two orphan children belonging to William Smith for 22 months and humbly desires that he be given an allowance; the one he has had for 18 mos. and the other for 4 months. To be allowed for keeping the children to this time, £4.

Petition of Joseph Argo hath a wife and several small children and is very poor and has lost the use of his of his limbs so that he cannot walk nor stand without being held up. Prays for an allowance. Allow £5 until next November Court.

Time of servitude of John Coffin is extended to his master Isaac Mercier - 6 months for 26 days runaway time and 4 months for the money and tobacco expended in taking him up.

Time for Joseph Cups, servant of John Barney, is extended to his master of 3 mos. for 19 days runaway time and 3 mos. for £2.18.6 in expenditures.

August Term 1744

p. 101. Presented that John Cole of Dorchester Parish on 10 Jan 1743 committed fornication with Ann Bryan and begat a bastard child. Fined £1.10.

p. 102. Presented that William Bonner of St. Mary's White Chapel Parish, carpenter, on 2 June 1744 assaulted John Cushney of the same co., planter.

Presented that Mary Harvey of Great Choptank Parish, spinster, on 10 May 1744 committed fornication and begat a bastard child. Fined £1.10.

p. 103. Presented that Elinor Fitzgerald of St. Mary's White Chapel Parish on 10 May 1744 committed fornication with a Negro slave and begat a bastard mulatto child. To become a servant for 7 years.

p. 104. Presented that Thomas Loockerman of Dorchester Parish, Gent., on 10 June 1744 assaulted William Trego of the same co., planter. Fined 5 shillings.

p. 105. Presented that Anne Trego of Dorchester Parish, wife of William Trego, on 10 June 1744 assaulted Ann Mills, wife of Govert Mills. Fined £2.6.

p. 106. Presented that Ann Mills, wife of Govert Mills, of Dorchester Parish on 10 Aug 1744, assaulted Anne Trego, wife of William Trego.

p. 107. Presented that Lewis Bramble of Dorchester Parish, planter, on 10 June 1744, assaulted Adam Foxwell, planter. Fined 5 shillings.

Ordered that Michel Caffey be allowed £4.7.6 for keeping Rachel Caffey, object of charity for 5 months, and burying her.

Mary Harvey, surety Jonathan Bestpitch, indemnifying the county from maintaining her bastard child for 7 years.

p. 108. The court sells the bastard mulatto child of Elinor Fitzgerald for

£3.2.6.

William Hurst acknowledges himself to owe James Hurst £20 and Edward Wright and Patrick McCollister £10 - with the condition that William Hurst shall teach James Hurst the trade of brickmaker and bricklayer.

Ordered that Lewis Griffith, son of John, be discharged from being overseer of the roads, it appearing that he has not done his duty as overseer and it is ordered that Zebulon Keene be overseer of the said roads.

p. 109.

Linnen adjudged of yard wide:	Linnen of 7/8 wide
1st John Hudson the fourth	1st Joseph Thomas
2nd William Trippe	2nd Rachel Shocknessheeth
3rd Mary Fooks	3rd John Hodson Forrest
4th Samuel Hubbert	4th John Magraw
5th John Hodson (servant)	5th Henry Windoes

p. 113. Solomon West, William Bonner and John Lowe of DO Co. are bound unto Isaac Cavenaugh, child and orphan of Bryan Cavanaugh, dec'd., in the full sum of £8.17.5. To be paid £4.8.8 when of age. Also Daniel Cavanaugh, child and orphan of Bryan Cavanaugh, dec'd. - same amount. Also Bryan Cavanaugh, child and orphan of Bryan Cavanaugh, dec'd. - same amount.

15 Aug 1744

p. 114. John Combs, Edward Pritchett and John Gowtee of DO Co. are bound unto Mary Dean, child and orphan of John Dean in the full sum of 98.1.6. to pay her when she arrives to full age £49.0.9 Also Elizabeth Dean, child and orphan of John Dean in the same amount. Also Dorothy Dean, child and orphan of John Dean in the same amount.

Petition of John Trippe who hath a Negro man named Jack who is incapable of doing his master's service. Exempt from paying tax or levy.

Petition of James Edmondson that whereas the road that leads from Barneses Ferry at Slaughter Creek runs through the middle of his plantation to his great damage. Ordered a new road be made.

p. 115. Petition from the inhabitants that work upon the road from Thomas Maces bridge to Mannings gate. Sheweth that they there are too few working on the road and that they are informed by Wm. Stoakes that a new road must be cleared and Caswayed from Arthur Whiteley's plantation to Mr. Stephonses plantation which we think for to be impossible for your petitioners to perform and mind their own in many places of the deep swamps and pray that they be acquitted from working upon the said new road: Thos. Vickers, Arthur Whitley, Benjamin Woodward, John Vickers Sr., John Miller, John Vicers, Jr., Peter Stoakes, Thos. Stoakes, Henry Brannock, James Stoakes, Nicholas Mace, Edward Dossey, James

Jarrard, Wright Mills.

Petition of Peter Button who sheweth that he is very poor and that he hath a child that is now going of 12 years old and is a cripple that it can neither stand or walk and that he hath severall other small children. Prays for a small allowance. Allowed £2.10 at next November Court.

Petition of Ann Wing who has a tract of land called *Sharps Point* adj. a tract called *Addition* to the same. Prays that a commission be appointed to perpetuate the memory of the bounds.

Petition of John Morgan who owns a tract in the freshes of Nanticoke on N.W. Fork known as *Shear Ditch* and prays to have a commission appointed to perpetuate the memory of the bounds.

p. 116. Petition of Thomas Whiteley who owns a tract called *Whiteleys Choice* adj. *Moasleys Angle, Andrews Choise, Stapleforts Lot, Measleys Outlet* and sundry others and prays to have a commission be appointed to perpetuate the memory of the bounds.

Petition of Edward Trippe who owns a tract called *Paradice* affected by an older survey of *Habnab at a Venter* and prays to have a commission appointed to perpetuate the memory of the bounds.

p. 117. George Griffeth has discovered 4 tracts on the Hungar River which have become escheat to his Lordship, viz., *Measleys Angle, Andrews Chance, Staplefords Lot* and *Measleys Outlet* and has filed a petition to patent the land. Wishes to settle the bounds.

p. 121. Presented that John Anderson, Dorchester Parish, Gent., on 10 Sep 1742 married Ann Mackeel, spinster, she being the said John his wife's mother's sister. Ann Mackeel similarly indicted.

p. 123. The court adjudges a boy called Francis Barney belonging to Philemon Cubbidge of the age of 15.

Presented that John Jones of Dorchester Parish, Gent., on 10 Oct 1743 assaulted William Mather (Mathews?) Fined £2.6.

p. 124. Presented that James Marshall, taylor, of St. Mary's White Chapel Parish on 4 July 1743 assaulted Charles Manarthy of the same co., Doctor of Physick. Fined 5 shillings. Court fees paid by William Adams, son of Roger.

Presented that Ann Griffith of Great Choptank Parish on 10 Oct 1743 committed fornication and begat a bastard child. Fined 30 shillings. William Greenwood to pay the court fees.

p. 125. The court agrees that Sarah Nunar keep an object of charity called Ann Leadin at the rate of £12 by the year and 20 shillings to be allowed for bed cloathes for the said Leadin under the care of Mr. Thomas Nevett to be levied at next November Court.

That James Hickman enter into recognizance to give evidence against Thomas Clifton and Sarah his wife.

p. 126. John Jones, one of the Magistrates of the co., made a motion that William Madkin did call him the said Jones a dam'd. rogue and a rascal for issuing an execution against him the said Madkin on a judgment rendered against him the said Madkin for killing a deer contrary to the Act of Assembly. Fined 500 lbs. of tobacco.

The Court sells John Finch, Jr. to William Madkin for £17.10.0.for the space of five years he being the highest bidder.

Presented that Joseph Thompson of Great Choptank Parish on 10 Aug 1743 assaulted Zachariah Nicolls, planter. Fined 30 shillings.

p. 127. Presented that Owen Connerly, planter, of St. Mary's White Chapel Parish assaulted John Connerly, planter, on 10 June 1743. Fined £10.

The court to allow Allexr. Strahawn for keeping an orphan called Thomas Corbutt at the rate of 12 shillings per month to be levyed next November court.

Thomas Cook, son of John Cook, chooses as his guardian John Stevens who accepts.

Presented that Robert Medford of St. Mary's White Chapel Parish on 10 Sep 1743 assaulted Rachel Medford. Fined 20 shillings.

p. 128. John Fountain, son of Massey Fountain, chose Joseph Andrew his guardian. Joseph Andrew and Henry Cannon and Edward Newton his sureties stand bound to afsd. John Fountain in the sum of £40.

David Meddux, Thomas Ross and Nehemiah Hubbert of DO Co. acknowledge themselves to stand bound to Daniel Bradley in the sum of £40 to learn the boy the trade of bricklayer, bound to the said David until age of 21, he being 15 ½ years old.

p. 129. John Hodson the third and John Pollard appointed Pressmasters for the county.

Ordered that Hannah Hayes, an object of charity be allowed £5 to be levied this year.

Ordered that the ferries be continued as last year except the one at Chancellors Point kept by the widow Mary Ennalls.

p. 133. John Nicolls, Jr., John Harris, and Edward Leadenham of Do Co. stand bound unto Isaac Summers, child and orphan of John Summers, dec'd., in the sum of £11.0.2. to pay him when of age £5.10.1. Also William Summers, child and orphan of John Summers, dec'd. - same amount. Also Mary Ann Summers, child and orphan of John Summers, dec'd. - same amount. Also John Summers, child and orphan of John Summers, dec'd. - same amount.

p. 134. Also Joseph Summers, child and orphan of John Summers, dec'd. - same amount.

William Stokes, Matthew Driver and Phillip Tall of DO Co. are bound to Elizabeth Robson, child and orphan of David Robson in the sum of £3.8.10. to pay her when of age £1.14.5. Also William Robson, child and orphan of David Robson in the same amount. Also David Robson, child and orphan of David Robson in the same amount.

p. 135. Richard Andrew, Jr., Owen Connerly, Jr., William Nutter are bound to Mary Nicolls, child and orphan of John Nicolls in the sum of £44.19.0 to pay her when of age £22.9.6.

Matthew Driver bringeth into court the following account against Ann Narsh his servant, vizt., Ann Narsh on 13 Nov 1743 to the trouble of my house and paying the midwife for you having four base born children.

p. 136. Richard Cooper prays for an allowance for keeping a foundling infant child from last November Court. Approved.

Inhabitants having lands and plantations in Hambroosk Neck and no road to care or bring away any of the produce of their plantations without going through Mrs. Rosannah Loockerman's plantation pray that a road should be cleared round her fence: Rosannah Loockerman, John Stewart, James Wallace, Thos. Stewart.

Petition of Thomas Brannock, Jr., in possession of tract called *Winfeilds Trouble* lying on Island Bay, prays for a commission to settle the bounds.

Petition of Elizabeth Marvel, having lived in the county all her youthful days and having lost her eye sight, is incapable to maintain herself. Allowed £6 to be levied this court.

Petition of Thomas Mackeel that at his own cost he hath cleared and straightened the road adjacent to his plantation without the assistance of overseer and prays to allow him to move his fence to the said new road. Granted.

p. 137. Petition of John Dean hath kept a certain Alexander McCotter, an object of charity, and is not capable of helping of himself. Prays for a larger allowance. Increased from £5 to £9.

Petition of Ann Wing who owns a tract called *Sharps Point* prays for a commission to settler the bounds.

Petition of James Billings on behalf of Richard Gildart, Esq. he having a Negro fellow for some time unfit for any service by loss of the use of his limbs. Discharged from paying tax or levy for the said Negro.

Ann Griffith swears that John Baxter is the father and begetter of the bastard child of which she is convicted.

November Court 1744

p. 175. John Stevens exhibited expenses against his servant, Mary Holland. To the trouble and scandall of the house for having a base born child. To ten shillings paid to Col. Hooper 0.10.0.
To tobacco ppd. Howes Goldsborough 145
To tobacco paid Edward Trippe 195
To serve John Stevens an additional 6 months.

Petition of Thomas Mackeell who has three tracts of land called *Fishing Creek Point*, *Cedar Point* and *Charles's Desire* and desires to settle the bounders.

p. 176. Petition of Joseph Ennalls, Seized with two tracts on Little Choptank River and prays to have the bounders settled.

Petition of John Munday, a cripple and near 70 years of age, who was sometime ago set levy free but is now reduced to very low estate by his wife's indisposition for past 4-5 years. Allowed 40 shillings.

Petition of Edward Able has tract called *Nuthead Choice*.

Petition of Howes Goldsborough who possesses two tract one on Fishing Creek in DO Co. the one called *Markhams Desire*, the other called *Scotts Hall* and prays to have commission settle the bounds.

p. 177. Petition of David Fowler, having lived in the county and paid his tax for about 45 years past and he now being in the 68th year of his age and afflicted with sickness as well as he loss of his right leg and thigh. Allowed 40 shillings.

18 Nov 1744

p. 178. Know that wee Mary Alford, extx. of Edward Alford, Joseph Alford and Alexander Frazier are bound to William Allford, Edward Alford, John Alford and Thomas Alford, children and orphans of Edward Alford in the sum of £42.5.2 to pay these children when they reach the age of 21.

p. 179. John Salsbury, Thomas Phillips, Blackwater and James Brightall of DO Co. stand bound to pay John Granger, child and orphan of John Granger late of the said co., dec'd.,in the sum of £18.12.5 to pay him the sum of £9.6.2.4 farthings. Also Abner Granger, child and orphan of John Granger in the same amount. Also Sarah Granger, child and orphan of John Granger in the same amount.

Benjamin Wheland, Ennalls Hooper, Daniel Sulivane stand bound unto Sarah Kennerly, child and orphan of Thomas Kennerly in the sum of £253.10.8 ½ to pay £126.15.4 when of age. Also Mary Kennerly, child and orphan of Thomas Kennerly in the same amount.

Alse Pullett, John Pullett and John Ainge of DO Co. stand bound unto Margaret, Richard, Magdalen, Sarah and Mary Pullett, children and orphans of William Pullett. in the sum of £227.1 ½. To be payed £22.14.1 each.

p. 180. The court appoints Thomas Foster to meet one of the Justices of QA Co. in order to agree with the workman to repair Great Choptank Bridge and to make a report at March court.

William Haskins chooses Jacob Hindman his guardian who accepts the guardianship.

Presented that James Fookes of Dorchester Parish on 10 June 1744 assaulted William Readford. Fined £2.6.

p. 182. Presented that William Holdbrook of Great Choptank Parish, labourer, on 20 Aug 1744 stole one silk handkerchief the value of 100 lbs. of tobacco belonging to John Baxter. 10 lashes and pay to John Baxter 4 times the value.

p. 183. Presented that Thomas Lewis of Dorchester Parish on 10 June assaulted Summer Adams. Fined £2.6.

p. 185. Ordered that Ann Kirren? keep John Ramsey, an orphan till June Court next at 10 shillings pr month.

Constables appointed:
James Voss, Jr., BridgeTown Hundred
Richard Dawson, Fork Hundred
John Nicolls, Great Choptank Hundred
Thomas Loockerman, Transquakin Hundred
John Smith, Nanticoke Hundred
Thomas Mackeel, Little Choptank Hundred
John Tootle, Fishing Creek Hundred
James Edmondson, Armitage Hundred
William Dawson of Wm., Streights Hundred

Ordered that Mary Cratcher be allowed 400 lbs. of tobacco as an additional allowance for keeping Ferry - to be levyed the next November Court.

Ordered that Col. Joseph Ennals be allowed sum of £10 for the repair of Transquakn Bridge.

The court appoints William Byus and Joseph Allford, Pres Masters.

p. 186. Elizabeth Williams, wife of Hugh Williams stand charged with assault.

March Court 1744

p. 248. Petition of sundry inhabitants of the county. Sheweth that many people dwelling on and near unto Hoopers Island are often obliged to pass and repass to and from the said island about their lawful occasions notwithstanding the great difficulty they are sure to meet with in getting a passage and swimming their horses across Fishing Creek which in the Winter Season is almost impossible. Your Petitioners therefor pray your worships to erect a ferry over the said creek: Thos.

Traverse, Matthew Traverse, John Traverse, James Traverse, William Traverse, Matthew Traverse, Benjamin Traverse, John Williams, George Williams, William Shenton, Henry Keene, Tho. Phillips, Zebulon Keene, James Hooper, William Phillips, James Edmondson, John Trippe, John Goote, Alexander Farguson, Godfry McGraw, John Barns, Thomas Mackeel, H. Goldsborough, Henry Ennalls, Jr., Richd. Keene, John Woolford, Levin Hicks, Edward Keene, Tho. Ennalls, Enn. Hooper, Roger Hooper, Roger Hodson, Jacob Pattison, John Traverse, Senr, John Hodson, 3d, Wm. Traverse, John Hayward, John Hodson, 2d, Edward Pritchett, Peter Stoaks, Joseph Ennalls, Ignatius Shenton, Dan Silivane, B. Ennalls, Benja. Wheland, John Stevens, John Taylor, Wm. Lcompte, J Muir, For? Noblet, Wm. Kennerly, John Stewart, Junr, Tho. Howell, Wm. Byas, John Brown, Thos. Vickers, Jos Griffith, George Griffith, William Standford, John Tootle. Whereupon the Court agrees to allow any person who agrees to undertake to keep the said ferry at the rate of £10 by the year.

Petition of Catron Thomas that she is uncapable of getting her living and desires that the court will consider her infirmities, that is, she has lost the use of her limbs and is 70 years of age. Allowed £3 per year.

p. 249. Petition of Richard Bruff that he possesses a tract called *Eason* and prays to have a commission settle the bounds.

Petition of Walter Macdaniel states that he is very old and incapable of doing any bodily labour. Discharged from paying tax or levy.

James Vaulx appointed constable for Bridgetown Hundred.

Edward Hardekin brings charges against his servant Edward Hyde. To serve an additional 12 months for runaway time and for charges in getting him back.

Petition of William Lewis very aged and decriped and not fit for any manner of labour discharged from any further taxes.

Petition of Charles Goldsborough who possesses a tract called *Claw Haman* and prays to have a commission appointed to settle the bounds.

Petition of Jacob Mills who possesses a tract called *Snake Point* and prays to have a commission appointed to settle the bounds.

p. 250. Petition of Benjamin Wheland who hath a Negro slave whose name is Judey and formerly did belong to Joseph Cannely which slave thru age is so impotent that she is not able to perform any manner of service nor hath for two years past. Discharged from paying taxes or levy for the said Negro.

Petition of John Anderson who possesses part of two tracts on Fishing Creek, one called *Addition to Spring Garden* and the other called *Taylors Regulation* and prays to have a commission appointed to settle the bounds.

Petition of James Insly who possessed a tract called *Andrews Fortune* and prays to have a commission appointed to settle the bounds.

Petition of John Sherwood of TA Co. who possesses a tract in DO Co. called *Skillingtons Right* and prays to have a commission appointed to settle the bounds.

Petition of William Fishburn who possesses a tract on the Freshes of the said county called *Bryney? Ridge* and prays to have a commission appointed to settle the bounds.

p. 251. Your Petitioners have laboured on the roads many years and hath but little benefit of them we living down the neck where there is no road nor way to go to publick worship but through thick swamps for four or five miles we therefor rely on your worships for ordering of a road from Jacob Goutees till it intersects the road that leads from Marcus Andrews to the chappel and your Petitioners in duty bound shall pray: James Safford. John Goutee. John Cole, George Boze, George Boze, Jr;., Phillip Wingate, Andrew Gootee, John Cawowan?, Jacob Gootee, Joseph Gootee, Timothy Macknamar, John Macknamar, Jacob Gootee, Jr., William Edgar. Granted.

Petition of James Cavender, Sr., sheweth that whereas he hath been in these part upwards of 40 years and hath been a taxable in the said county but is now the age and other infirmities of the body have rendered him incapable of performing any manner of service and hath no other support but the labour of his children who are all almost their own men and so that he thinks it very hard that they should not only be obliged to support him but also to pay his taxes. Discharged from paying any tax or publick levy for the future.

Matthew Hargaton, Edward Hargeton and Abraham Gambell of DO Co. are bound unto Elizabeth Bullock, child and orphan of John Bullock, of his co. dec'd., in the sum of £72.2.1/2 to pay £30.1.and a farthing when she is of age. Also Priscilla Bullock, child and orphan of John Bullock, of his co. dec'd., in the same amount.

p. 252. James Carter, John Trice and John Brown bound unto Jeremiah Carter, child and orphan of John Carter in the sum of £7.15.9.

James Carter, John Trice, and John Brown, pedlar of DO Co. are bound unto Mary Carter, child and orphan of John Carter in the sum of £7.15.9. to pay her £3.17.10 ½ when of age.

A road from John Pritchetts at the Streights and runs to the head of Foxes Creek to the further side of a bridge that leads over a branch of said creek Funback Pritchet overseer..... about 3 pages of overseers.

p. 255. Petition of Henry Hicks who possesses a tract called *Luck by Chance*

p. 262. Presented that Thomas Veach of St. Mary's White Chapel Parish, planter, on 10 Oct 1744 assaulted Francis Dean of same co., planter. Fined 5 shillings.

Presented that Jane Griffin of Great Choptank Parish spinster on 10 Feb 1743 committed fornication and begat a bastard child. Fined 30 shillings. William Noble promises to pay court fees.

p. 263. Presented that Julen Perry of Dorchester Parish on 10 March 1743 committed fornication and begat a bastard child. Fined 30 shillings. She swears that Thomas Hancock is the father.

p. 264. Presented that James Morgan of St. Mary's White Chapel Parish, planter on 10 Feb 1744 assaulted Sarah Davis, spinster. Fined £5.

p. 265. Presented that Eleanor English of Great Choptank Parish on 10 Feb 1744 committed fornication and begat a bastard child. Five lashes.

Presented that William Robinson of Great Choptank Parish, labourer, on 20 Aug 1744 stole a silk handkerchief of John Baxter valued at 100 lbs. of tobacco. Not guilty.

p. 266. Presented that Peter Rich of St. Mary's White Chapel Parish, planter, on 10 Feb 1744 assaulted Richard Cooper. Fined 5 shillings.

p. 267. Presented that Mary Nites of Great Choptank Parish, spinster, on 10 Sep 1744 committed fornication and begat a bastard child. Fined 30 shillings. Walter Stevens promises to pay court fees.

p. 268. The court sells Ann Nash to Howes Goldsborough for the space of 7 years for the sume of 3500 lbs. of tobacco.

Presented that John Anderson of Dorchester Parish, Gent., on 10 June 1744 assaulted John Mackeel of same co., Gent. Fined 10 shillings.

Presented that William Kendey of Great Choptank Parish on 10 Feb 1744 committed fornication with Eleanor English and begat a bastard child. Fined 30 shillings. Jacob Lowe, blacksmith, gives security to indemnify the county from maintaining the child for 7 years.

p. 270. Presented that Susannah Martin of Dorchester Parish, spinster, on 10 [blank] 1743 committed fornication and begat a bastard child. Fined £32.6.0

June Court 1745

p. 278. Dorothy Loockerman, widow, to answer unto Rosannah Loockerman, extx. of the will of Jacob Loockerman.

p. 328. Petition of Walter Edgell sheweth that your petitioner is unjustly held as a servant by William Adams. Adams is summoned.

Petition of Solomon Wheelar and Charles Graham sheweth that in Nov 1743 they became bound for a certain Rachel Granger upon her administering on the estate of Richard Granger her dec'd. husband and the said Rachel having married John Cox of this co. having given cause to fear that the said Cox hath and doth intend to make away with the estate whereby not only the children of the above Grainger are like to suffer but your petitioners are in fear of trouble. Cox is summoned.

p. 328. Petition of Andrew Russel sheweth that Grace Mills his servant has had a mulatto bastard child in your petitioner's house. Ordered that she serve an additional 8 months.

Petition of Neil Maccallum sheweth that the road to Dorchester Parish Church from where it formerly was is turned to a very ill convenient and miry place as several parishioners are hear to testify. Ordered that the road be altered.

Petition of Ann Trippe who hath a servant man named Shepherd and a Negro woman that are both so lame that they are unfit for service and prays to set them levy free. Approved.

Petition of Richard Woodland. has a tract called *Northampton* and prays to have a commission appointed to settle the bounds.

Petition of Ann Trippe has right by descent to tract called *The Endeavour*.

Petition of Margaret Brannock is seized of a tract called *Margarets Fancy* and prays to have a commission appointed to settle the bounds.

p. 329. Petition of John Eccleston who hath a Negro woman that is an idiot and likewise troubled with fitts. Discharged from paying any levies on the Negro woman.

Petition of George Stapleford who hath a Negro man named Pall who is very old and almost past his labour. Discharged from paying levy or tax.

Petition of Thomas Howel hath a very old Negro man Robin, past his labour. Discharged from paying tax or levy.

Petition of William Twyford that whereas the main road which now leads from Cabbin Creek to the North West Fork bridge and runs through your petitioner's corn field proves a great prejudice to your petitioner and may be prevented by turning the said road about 40 or 50 yards the other way. Wm. Twyford, Richard Dawson, John Magin, Thomas Flowers. Approved.

Petition of Henry Hooper sheweth that he hath three slaves to wit, Henry, Cuffey and Lucy that are grown aged and past their labour. Discharged from paying levy or taxes.

p. 330. Petition of John Kendrick sheweth that whereas he hath been a labourer n the county these 30 years but now hat pleased God to inflict him a very sore leg that he is very incapable of labouring whereby to get his living and having one child and having neither land nor other estate to live upon prays for some allowance. Discharged from paying taxes or levy.

Petition of Matthew Driver who sheweth that the road which leads to

Dover Town, Kent Co. on Delaware goes through the middle of his plantation and is very prejudicial to him and is not laid out so straight and well as your petitioner conceives it might be. To be turned according to the directions of Mr. Thomas Foster.

Petition of William Alford, son of Edward Alford late of this county, dec'd. sheweth that he is seized of a tract called *Skipton* and prays to have a commission appointed to settle the bounds..

Petition of William Stanford states he has a Negroe boy incapable of labour. Discharged from payment of tax or levy for the future.

Petition of inhabitants of Transquakin pray that a new road be created from Kennerlys Mill down Transquakin along by Henry Haywards and so over Haywards Dam into Transquakin road by where Mathus Skillet formerly lived: Francis Hayward, John Traverse, John Hayward, Henry Hayward, James Soense?, Samuel Kenton, John Noel, John Sard, John Hayward, Ezekiel Keene, Joseph Recards, Enn. Hooper, Thos. Stewart, Charles Stanford, James Cullen, Charles Powell, Lewis Griffith, Jr., James Hooper, Eben White, Benjamin Wheyland, Moses Pool, Thomas Williams, Solomon Wheelor. Granted.

Petition of Howes Goldsborough who has two tracts on Fishing Creek one called *Scotts Hall* and the other *Markhams Deisre* and prays to have a commission appointed to settle the bounds.

p. 331. Petition of Sarah Thomas who possesses a tract called *Britts Hope* on Hunting Creek and prays to have a commission appointed to settle the bounds.

Petition of John Pollard who possesses a Negroe fellow named Jobe that is lame and so old that he is not able to earn his own victuals. Discharged from paying taxes or levy.

Petition of John Harris who owns a tract called *Wakefield* on Hunting Creek and prays to have a commission appointed to settle the bounds.

Sarah Owens, Roger Addams, and David Owens are bound to Mary Owens, child and orphan of William Owens, dec'd., in the sum of £62.18.1 ½ to pay her £31.9. and 3 farthings. Also Ann Owens, child and orphan of William Owens, dec'd., in the same amount. Also William Owens, child and orphan of William Owens dec'd., in the same amount.

p. 332. Also Robert Owens, child and orphan of William Owens, dec'd., in the same amount.

p. 335. Presented that Rosannah Pickering of Dorchester Parish on 10 Feb 1744 committed fornication and begat a bastard child. 10 lashes.

Bartly Owens chooseth Richard Cantwell for his guardian who accepts.

p. 336. Presented that Mary Mitchel of Great Choptank Parish, spinster, on 10 March 1744 committed fornication and begat a bastard child. Fined 30 shillings. Francis Carr, her surety, to indemnify the county from maintenance of her bastard child called Levin Mitchel for 7 years.

p. 337. Francis Bickham, John Pritchet Fisher and Robert Hobbs are bound to the apprenticeship of Billy Williams to Francis Bickham in the trade of shoemaker.

Presented that Thomas Wheelar of Dorchester Parish on 10 May 1745 assaulted Betty Mingo. Fined 5 shillings.

Ordered that Grace Stockdale be allowed 3.12 for keeping the orphan child of James Stewart from November Court last till this Court to be levyed next November Court.

p. 338. Presented that Grace Mills of St. Mary's White Chapel Parish, spinster, on 10 Dec 1744 committed fornication with a certain Negro and begat a mulatto bastard child. To become a servant for the use of the county for 7 years. The court sells the bastard mulatto child to Andrew Russel for 350 lbs. of tobacco.

p. 339. Presented that James Fargason of Dorchester Parish, labourer, on 10 Feb 1744 assaulted Noah Pearson, labourer. Fined 5 shillings.

Thomas Swigget chooses George Williams his guardian who accepts, John Williams his security.

p. 340. Presented that Julia Perry of Great Choptank Parish spinster on 10 Feb 1744 committed fornication and begat a bastard child. 8 lashes. She swears that Edward Trippe, son of Edward Trippe is the father.

p. 341. Presented that Mary Hinds of Dorchester Parish on 10 Jan 1744 committed fornication and begat a bastard child. 8 lashes. She swears that Daniel Forbus is the father.

Presented that Money Lee of Great Choptank Parish, servant of Ann Trippe, on 10 March 1744 committed fornication with a Negro slave belonging to Ann Trippe named Will and begat bastard child. Her servitude to be extended another 7 years. The court sells the bastard mulatto child of Mooney Lee to John Eccleston for 500 lbs. of tobacco.

Presented that William Walker alias Taylor of Great Choptank Parish, labourer, on 10 Feb 1744 assaulted Thomas Wing, planter. Fined 2 shillings, 6 pence.

p. 343. Presented that Ann Bryan of Great Choptank Parish, servant of Joseph Bowes, on 10 May 1745 committed fornication and begat a bastard child. 8 lashes. She swears that David Poole is the father.

p. 344. William Grantham together with William Standford, his surety, acknowledge themselves to stand indebted unto Mary Reardon in the sum of £20, an apprentice to learn to read, spin, sew and knit and at the expiration to give her a new suit of cloaths, two shifts, a cap, handkerchief and a pair of shoes and stockings until she arrives to the age of 16 she being now by the judgment of the court 3 years old come next Oct.

Robert Vass chooses Capt. John Eccleston his guardian who accepts.

The court agrees to allow Capt. Bartholomew Ennalls the sum of 29 shillings per month for keeping Mary Kews [Hews?] and her 3 children.

Presented that Bartholomew Gibbs of Dorchester Parish, planter, on 1 May 1745 assaulted Daniel Follin, planter. Fined 5 shillings.

p. 346. Presented that Edward Nuner of Dorchester Parish labourer on 10 Feb 1744 assaulted William Standford, Jr., labourer. Fined 5 shillings.

Elizabeth Jarrard together with Thomas Howell her surety acknowledge themselves indebted unto Elizabeth Locksly in the sume of £20, as an apprentice until age 16, she being of the age of 4 years come next October in the judgment of the court.

p. 347. Presented that Sidney Cornish of Great Choptank Parish spinster on 10 Feb 1744 committed fornication with a Negro slave and begat a mulatto bastard child. Not guilty.

p. 348. Presented that James Tregoe of Dorchester Parish, planter, on 10 May 1745 assaulted Phillip Tall, Jr. Fined 5 shillings.

John Mace together with Noah Pearson, his surety, acknowledge themselves to stand indebted to Robert Job in the sum of £20 to learn Robert Job the trade of a weaver until age of 21. [age not given].

Presented that Margaret Pratis of Great Choptank Parish, spinster, on 10 Feb 1744, committed fornication and begat a bastard child. 10 lashes.

Presented that Thomas Brannock of Great Choptank Parish, planter, on 10 May 1745 assaulted Elizabeth Soward. Fined £3.

Presented that Mary Keene of Great Choptank Parish, spinster, on 10 June 1743 committed fornication and begat a bastard child. Fined 32 shillings, 6 pence.

October Court 1745

p. 404. Petition of Joseph Webb of TA Co. possesses a tract called *Rochester* and prays to have a commission appointed to settle the bounds.

Petition of Levin Denwood who possesses a tract called *Hogyard* whose bounds depend upon the bounds of tract called *Pinney Ridge*; he prays to have a commission appointed to settle the bounds.

Petition of Samuel Griffith prays for an allowance for maintaining a poor old decrepit lame woman named Elizabeth Spores who has not been able to help herself this three years. Allowed 600 lbs. of tobacco.

Petition of Elizabeth, widow of Patrick Carawin who is aged, sick, and lame in both legs and arms very often and not able to support herself with her labour. Ordered that Elizabeth be allowed at the rate of £3 to be levied at next November Court.

p. 408. The court agrees to allow any Doctor of Physick that will undertake to cure Richard Dollen the sum of 1000 lbs. of tobacco.

Presented that Mary Hughs of Great Choptank Parish, spinster, on 10 June 1745 committed fornication with a Negro slave and begat two bastard mulatto children. Ordered to become a servant for the use of the county for the next 7 years. The Court sells Mary Hews and her two bastard mulatto children to Mr. Henry Hooper, Junr for 3100 lbs. of tobacco he being the highest bidder.

p. 410. Ordered that a warrant issue to the sheriff returnable immediately to bring Samuel, Thomas, and Moses Griffith, orphans of John Griffith, that the said orphans may be bound to trades they having no estates.

Ordered that an attachment issue against William Hopkins and Samuel Lawson, son of Hance Lawson, witnesses to attend this court for Thomas Woolford against Comfort Hopkins for their not attending this court.

Presented that Sarah Hart of Dorchester Parish, spinster, on 10 May 1745 committed fornication and begat a bastard child. 10 lashes.

p. 413. Presented that Thomas Brannock of Great Choptank Parish, shipwright, on 10 May 1745 assaulted Welcome Soward, child of Francis Soward, an infant about one year old. Fined £4. [Elizabeth Soward proved 7 days attendance at Court giving evidence against Thomas Brannock.]

p. 415. Presented that Jane Smith of St. Mary's White Chapel Parish, spinster, on 10 Feb 1744 committed fornication and begat a bastard child. 10 lashes.

Presented that Esther Rotten of Dorchester Parish, spinster, on 10 May 1743 committed fornication and begat a bastard child. 10 lashes. Thomas Wrotten the third, planter, promised to pay the court fees.

p. 416. The court adjudged a boy called Martin Crossgreen belonging to Thomas Little of the age of 15 years.

Presented that Stephen Ross of Dorchester Parish, planter, on 10 May 1745, assaulted John Mackeel. Fined 5 shillings.

p. 417. Presented that David Poole of Great Choptank Parish committed fornication with Anne Bryan and begat a bastard child. Fined 30 shillings.

Presented that Thomas Stoaks of Dorchester Parish, planter, on 10 Aug 1745 assaulted George Williams. Fined 5 shillings.

Presented that Sarah Ross of St. Mary's White Chapel Parish on 10 May 1745 committed fornication and begat a bastard child. Fined 30 shillings.

p. 419. Presented that Elizabeth Davis of Great Choptank Parish committed fornication and begat a bastard child. 5 lashes. Elizabeth Davis swears that Joseph Warrington is the father.

Presented that Diane Boze [or Boaz] of Dorchester Parish, now the wife of John Coal on 10 May 1744 committed fornication and begat a bastard child. Fined 30 shillings. John Cole to pay court fees. Dianah Boaze swears that John Gowtee is the father of the child.

Presented that Sarah Jones of Great Choptank Parish, spinster, on 10 Jan 1744 committed fornication. Fined 30 shillings.

Presented that Job Slacomb of Dorchester Parish, planter, on 10 Aug 1745 assaulted Jacob Gowtee, planter. Fined 10 shillings.

Presented that Thomas Bently of Dorchester Parish, planter, on 10 May 1745 assaulted Elizabeth Winstanly. Fined 5 shillings.

Presented that John Gowtee of Dorcheser Parish committed fornication with Diannah Boaze and begat a bastard child. Fined 30 shillings.

Presented that Daniel Fallen of Dorchester Parish on 10 Aug 1745 assaulted Barnaby Fallin. Fined 5 shillings.

Joseph Bond together with Obadiah Dawson, his surety, stand indebted in the sum of £20 to learn [apprentice] Samuel Shorson? the trade of house carpenter.

Samuel Griffith, Jr together with John Rix his surety stand bound unto Moses Griffith to learn this the trade of house carpenter.

p. 425. The court sells Winifred Claver to Col. Joseph Ennalls for £13.10. for 7 years servitude.

November Court 1745

p. 429. Presented that Richard Woodland of Dorchester Parish, planter, on 2 April 1745 stole 276 fence rods of the value of 300 lbs. of tobacco, the goods and chattels of Lot Pritchard. Acquitted.

p. 460. Petition of William Magraw ... that he is detained as a servant by Robert Wensitt contrary to law. Petition is dismissed.

p. 461. Petition of Edward Trippe the elder, seized of tract called *Paradice* which is affected by a survey called *Hapnab at a Venture;* prays to have a commission appointed to settle the bounds.

Petition of Francis Lee, in possession of a tract called *Rhehoboth*, prays to have a commission appointed to settle the bounds.

Petition of Wm. Grantham, in possession of a tract named *End of Controversy*, 70 a., prays to have a commission appointed to settle the bounds.

Petition of William Hurst having purchased a tract of one John Beard called *Hog Quarter* on northwest fork of Nanticoke River on e. side, 300 a. and prays to have a commission appointed to settle the bounds.

p. 462. The court allows Elizabeth Gore the sum of £3 on behalf of an orphan that is a cripple.

Petition of Elizabeth Mears in behalf of her dau. who it appears to this court is a natural fool. The said Elizabeth Mears is allowed the sum of £5 toward her maintenance.

Petition of Elizabeth Carwin on behalf of herself and dau. who appear to this court to be objects of charity; the said Elizabeth Carwin is allowed the sum of 1000 lbs. of tobacco.

Petition of inhabitants to clear a road from Choptank Bridge nigh mouth east course up and by the said river to the uppermost inhabitants of the county that pays levy therein and appoints an overseer therefore. Jos. Sherwood, Richd. Cooper, Flower Fisher, Thomas Sewell, Richard Harrington, Peter Harwood, Martin Willowby, William Edge, James Cooke, Alexander Mackme, John Oldfield, John Cook, William Oldfield, William Broadaway. Ordered by the court that the road be cleared according to the petition afsd. that Mr. Thomas Foster appoint the labourers and layout the said road and that Joseph Sherwood be overseer thereof.

Petition of Thos. Smith, sheweth he hath a Negro wench named Deddy who for some years past hath been deprived of her usual senses occasioned by frequently having fitts which render her incapable of any service. Discharged of paying levy or tax until such time as she shall be capable of doing service.

p. 464. John Hodson, John Baxter and Arthur Whiteley of DO Co. are held bound unto Levin Ward, child and orphan of Owen Ward, dec'd., in the sum of £18.1.6 ½; when of age to pay him £9.0.9 farthings. Also Ann Ward, child and orphan of Owen Ward, dec'd., in the same amount.

p. 465. Also John Ward, child and orphan of Owen Ward, dec'd., in the same amount. Also Sarah Ward, child and orphan of Owen Ward, dec'd., in the same amount. Also Sumers Ward, child and orphan of Owen Ward, dec'd., in the same amount.

p. 466. Sarah Hayward, John Stevens and Thos. Stewart are bound unto William Hayward, child and orphan of John Hayward, dec'd. in the sume of £28.17.5; when of age to pay orphan £14.8.8 ½. Also Rosannah Hayward, child and orphan of John Hayward, dec'd. in the same amount. Also Thomas Hayward, child and orphan of John Hayward, dec'd. in the same amount. Also Priscilla Hayward, child and orphan of John Hayward, dec'd. in the same amount.

p. 467. Thomas Long, John Long and John King are firmly bound unto Mary Courson, child and orphan of Thomas Courson, dec'd. in the sum of £57.3.0;

to pay the orphan when of age £28.11.1/2 Also Elizabeth Courson, child and orphan of Thomas Courson, dec'd. in the same amount.

p. 470. Peter Rich together with John White and Daniel Silivane are bound in his carrying on an ordinary at his own house in Dorchester Co.

Ann Coburn together with Henry Turner and John Nicolls, Jr., her sureties, to carry on an ordinary at her house in DO Co.

p. 471. James Stafford, bricklayer, together with Lot Pritchet his surety are bound unto Thomas Griffith, an orphan, in the sum of £20 who will serve an apprenticeship to the trade of a bricklayer and plaisterer til the age of 21 he now being by the judgment of the court 13 years of age.

Presented that Mary Smith of Great Choptank Parish, spinster, on 10 May 1745 committed fornication and begat a bastad child. Fined 30 shillings. John Spedden promised to pay the court fees.

Presented that Edward Price of Great Choptank Parish, planter, on 10 Oct 1745 assaulted Abraham Jones.

p. 473. Presented that Gideon Gambel of St. Mary's White Chapel Parish, planter, on 10 Oct 1745 assaulted Zachariah Nicolls.

p. 474. Presented that Johann McDaniel of St. Mary's White Chapel Parish, spinster, on 10 May 1745 committed fornication with a Negro person and begat a mulatto bastard child. To become a servant for 7 years. The court sells Johannah MacDaniel and her mulatto child to Joseph Sherwood for 3050 lbs. of tobacco, he being the highest bidder.

p. 475. Presented that Jane Price of Great Choptank Parish on 10 Oct 1745 committed fornication with a Negro and begat a bastard child. To become a servant for 7 years.

Presented that Solomon Bry of Great Choptank Parish, planter, on 10 Oct 1745 assaulted Isaac Merry, planter. Fined 5 shillings.

p. 476. Constables appointed:
William Dawson of Bridgetown Hundred
William Edmondson, son of Solomon of Great Choptank Hundred
Richard Dawson of North East Fork Hundred
Moses Pool of Transquakin Hundred
Thomas Loockerman of Nanticoke Hundred
Thomas Wing of Fishing Creek Hundred
Thomas Chapman of Armitage Hundred
John Macnamar of the Streights Hundred
John Stewart, Jr. of Little Choptank Hundred

John Harris and John Anderson appointed Presmasters.

Howes Goldsborough together with Thomas Nevett, his surety, are bound to Thomas Corbut, to learn him the trade of shoemaker, in apprenticeship until age of 21, he being in the judgment of the court 3 years of age.

The court agrees with Doctr. Joseph Ennalls to his endeavour to cure William Moffet and to board and find said Moffit sufficient clothes for one year for the sum of £20.

p. 477. Presented that Elizabeth Stapels of Dorchester Parish, spinster on 10 May 1745 committed fornication and begat a bastard child. 30 shillings.

Part of March Court 1742 from Liber PA No. R folio 151.

Presented that Jane Johnson of Great Choptank Parish, spinster, on 10 Oct 1742 committed fornication. 10 lashes.

p. 484. Ordered that Sarah, wife of Zabdiel Potter give security for her appearance to give evidence against Elizabeth Morgan.

Presented that William Soward of Dorchester Parish, planter, on 10 Sep 1742 assaulted William Herrin (Kerrin?), shoemaker. Fined 30 shillings.

p. 486. Presented that Mary Claridge of Great Choptank Parish, spinster, on 10 Oct 1742 assaulted Elinor Killman, spinster. Fined 5 shillings. John Claridge, planter promiseth to pay court fees.

David Wright, the father of John Wright, by the consent of the said John Wright cometh her into court and bindeth said John Wright to Mr. John Adderton of this co. for 7 years, David declaring the said John Wright to be of the age of 14 years.

p. 489. Presented that Brigett Mackrow of Great Choptank Parish, spinster, on 10 Oct 1742 committed fornication and begat a bastard child. Fined 32 shillings.

QUEEN ANNE'S COUNTY JUDGMENT RECORDS
1709-1716
Liber ETB

November Court 1709

p. 3. Susanna Butler, servant to Robert Jones, complained of hard usage.

Richard Hammond petitioned that Bryan Brother d. and was bur. at the charge of the petitioner and left an orphan boy who is at present with the petitioner.

Thomas Yewell brought an orphan boy named William Jones to be bound to the age of 21, to learn the trade of shoemaker.

Edward Tomlins petitioned to commit to his care the Wading Place Ferry being the former ferryman.

p. 4. George Phillips being last court committed to the sheriff's custody until he should find security regarding his fathering a bastard child to be born of Jane Cockrun.

Capt. William Hackett brought his servant Arthur Arling who confessed he had deserted from his master's service 23 days.

Thomas Hynson was bound to Richard Thursby [Hursly?] to learn the trade of weaver.

p. 7. It was presented that Cath. Hawkins of St. Paul's Parish in QA Co., servant to John Hawkins on 10 July 1708 committed fornication and begot a bastard child. John Hawkins is to have the service of the said mulatto child (now being 2 years old) until it attains the age of 31 years he paying the county 500 lbs. of tobacco. Cath. Hawkins to have her time of servitude extended.

p. 9. The Grand Jury presented the following Sarah Lee for fornication; Catharine Hawkins for having a mulatto; Honor Glardy for fornication; Elizabeth Chaffine(?) for fornication.

Charles Marshall presented an inventory of his estate, 600 acres of land on the east branch of Tuckahoe called *Marshalls Outlett* and lumber worth £2.2.6 and was thereupon discharged according to the Act of Assembly for the Relief of Poor Debtors.

Catherine Walls petitioned to choose her guardian which was granted and she chose John Coursey.

Charles Hollinsworth produced an inventory worth £5.6 which £5 is allowed and 4 shillings to the clerk of this court.

p. 17. Allowances made in the county, 26 Nov 1709:
Humphrey Walls for 6 crows heads
Charles Lowther for 17 crows heads

Mathew Griffin for 7 crows heads
Nathl. Wright for 1 wolf's head Indian killing
Nathll. Tucker, Junr. for 1 wolf's head his own killing
To the same for 9 crows heads
John Johnson for 1 wolf's head Indian killing
Capt. William Hackett for 1 wolf's head his own killing
Henry Willcocks for 1 wolf's head his own killing
Thomas Ruth for 1 wolf's head his own killing
Ja: Kersey up the river for 1 do and 2 crows heads
William Boone for 1 wolf's head Indian killing
John Hackett for 2 wolves' heads killed by himself
Henry Pratt for 7 wolves' heads his killing
Mr. Charles Blake for 1 wolf's head
John Doyle for 3 days labour att laying out Mortt Town
John Keld for 1 wolf's head his own killing
Colo. Richd. Tilghman for 1 wolf's head Ind. killing
Mr. Solo. Wright for laying out and the platt of the town at Tuckahoe
Mr. Arthur Emory for 1 wolf's head & 5 crows heads
Edmond Prior for 4 crows heads
Walter Nevill for 3 crows heads
Major William Turle for 7 crows heads
To the Sheriff 29 days labouring Men's wagers, carrying and fetching the
burgesses att 20 pr diem
To ditto for summoning the men
To ditto for executing two writts of election
To do allowed per order of court for the court house August last over & above
the first allowance
To the Secretary for ... not allowed last year
To ditto this year
Geo. Matter Shaw (?) for 3 1/2 days work att Marlberrough
Dr. Chethames widdo. on acct the care of Robt. Stansell
Colo. Edward Loyd for fees of the Great Seale
Sherf. for sum. 7 men & attending att Tuckaho Towne
The widdo. of Wm. Sparks for keeping Cath. ----? 1708 & 1709.
Edward Hamblton for Mary Royston
Do for the grand jury in March 1708/9
Do for the grand jury in August 1709
Edward Jones for keeping & cloathing Anne Mordick(?)
Joseph Clifts for 3 days att laying out Tuckaho Town
Thomas Smith for Mary Underwood
Henry Everett for keeping & cleansing the court house
Bryan Connelly a poor man

Barnard Powell and old poor man
Majr. Hawkins for Thomas Howe order'd formerly
Richard Moore for Edwd. Wenlock a poor man
Thomas Howe a poor lame man
Robert Jones coroner for 4 inquisitions.
Issabella Broom a poor woman
James Kersey for keeping Mary Underwood.
Doctor Edward Chatham for 22 days allowance as Justice
Majr. William Turle for 17 days ditto
Mr. John Selter for 20 days ditto.
Mr. John Wells for 21 days ditto.
Mr. Thomas Fisher for 7 days ditto.
Mr. Arthur Emory for 4 days do.
Mr. Solomon Wright for 2 ditto.
Mr. John Whittington for 9 days do.
Mr. William Sweatnam for 1 do.
Majr. Jno. Hawkins for allowance of 4 tax last year
Stephen Camperson for burying &c. of Richd. Hill.
John Oldson for keeping the ferry last year.
Jacob Covington for keeping Eliz. Gibson till June.
Samuel Hunter for 2 grand jurys in June and August last.
Evan Thomas for severall services.
Coll. Richd. Tilghman for insolvent tax. and amercements as per August
delivered.
To the same toward building a prison house.
To the sheriff for salary
Nicholas Lowe, clk. of the indictmts.
Docto. Maclanan for Mary Carter a poor lame girle.
Majr. Hawkins for 4 tax alld. this year

March Court 1709

p. 18. William Willis alleged he should be free from his master John Jones who detains him as a servant. To the court it appears that he must serve until 21 Nov 1711.

Richard Cotton petitioned that a summons be issued agst. William Sweatnam to show cause why he detains a certain horse of the petitioner. Granted.

It was ordered that Major John Hawkins be overseer of the highways from the town to Chester Church.

It was ordered that Mr. Thomas Fisher be overseer of the highways from Elizabeth Town to Tuckahoe Bridge.

p. 19. Margarett Skinner complained agst. Robert Noble for the hard usage of Jno. Newnam her son & not performing his part of an indenture.

p. 19. John Nicholson petitioned to have a road from his house to George Powell's land through Thomas Wyaetts land to go to church and mill.

John Worldley petitioned for liberty to clear a road beginning att Edward Satterfoots plantation with the road of Mr. Grundy to church, Queens Town, and Mill, which was granted.

William Ridgway a poor man prayed to allow him a cow to give him milk. Approved.

It was ordered that Richard Holding for being drunk and abusing the court be put in stocks one hour.

March Court 1710

p. 27. It was presented that John Salter of Town Hundred in QA Co. on 20 Jan 1708 killed and carried a cow of Jeremiah Miles, late of the county, merchant, dec'd.., then in the possession of Anthony Ivy, Gent., admin. de bonis Non, worth 500 lbs. of tob. Acquitted.

p. 28. Joseph Attwell dwelling upon Parson's Point on Kent Island, his neighbors have fenced in an ancient road; he prays that it be restored. The court so ordered whilst being considered by the court.

It was presented that Susannah Whaley, wife of Daniel Whaley, on 28 Nov in Town Hundred stole a gown and pettycoat, apron, a dowlas shirt, a dowlas shift and 2 balls of yarn, the goods of Andrew Cornelinson. Not guilty.

p. 32. Edward Tomlin appointed crier in place of the late cryer who died.

Margaret Downes and brought one Frances Seachiverell(?) an illegitimate girle and prayed to have her bound to her until age 18, being 7 years old on 5 Nov last. Richard Hynson and Charles Downes, securities.

p. 33. It was ordered that David Pagett be overseer for the road from this town to the wading place of Kent Island & from thence to Mr. Bennett's plantation & from thence back again.

Mary Deroachburn prayed for an allowance for accommodating and dressing the sores of a poor distemper'd woman named Elizabeth Malogon [Malague] and for salves afsd. about her and likewise an allowance for the keeping a man living with the petitioner and often mad and out of his senses.

Sarah Stansell complained agst. William Hopper for the hard usages of her son.

It was presented that Daniel Whaley of Queen Anne's Co., planter, on 28 Nov 1709 in St. Paul's Parish stole one gown and pettycoat, one apron, one dowlas shirt, one dowlas shift and two bolts of woolen yarn, property of Andrew Corneliuson. Benj. Wicks, foreman. Found guilty. Ordered to receive 20 lashes and put in the pillory for 1 hour.

p. 34. It was ordered that William Hollingsworth be committed to the sheriff's custody until he find security for his good behaviour, and fined for his abusing and contempt of the court and also to be put in stocks for an hour.

It was presented that Elizabeth Cheshire of Worrell Hundred, spinster, on 4 June 1709 committed fornication and got with child. She states that James Flood is the begetter of her bastard child. Fined 30 shillings.

It was presented that Mary Jones of the Upper Hundred, servant to James Evans on 25 Oct 1709 committed fornication and suffered herself to be gott with child. She states that Edward Welsh is the father of the child. To receive 15 lashes.

p. 35. It was presented that Elizabeth Graves of Queen Anne's co., spinster, on 20 March 1709, committed fornication and begot a child. She states that Thomas Hill is the father. Fined 30 shillings.

p. 39. Mary Sergeant was required to answer a plea of trespass by William Martin and his wife Phebe, regarding the possession of some jewelry and silver.

p. 46. Thomas Jackson charged Anthony Ivy with unpaid bills while Jackson kept an ordinary in Queens Town during the period, 6 May 1707 through 20 May 1708. The court ruled otherwise.

p. 49. Richard Poore (Power?) of QA Co. was required to answer unto John Rickard of said county, carpenter of a plea - that Richard did break and enter into Rickard's house and Susannah, dau. and servant of him the said John, did unlawfully and carnally know and have company with and for a long time unlawfully frequent her and did beget a child. As a consequence Rickard the family has fallen into poverty. The court ruled that Rickard did not prove his case and that he pay for court costs of Power.

p. 68. Mary Chethame, widow and extx. of the last will of Edward Chetham demanded payment of James Gold admin. of Mathew Smith, for administering physick, visits and chirurgery performed by her late husband to and for Mathew Smith. Nothing awarded.

June Court 1710

p. 72. William Tarbotan (Tarbutton), taylor brought to court Michael Ely and prayed he might be bound to him until he arrives to the age of 21 years which is granted requiring him to find security and to learn him to read, write and the trade of taylor, being 9 years old since March last. Securities: Thomas Ruth and John Fowler.

Thomas Ruth prayed that Anne Ely, an orphan girle may be bound to him to the age of 18 years being five years old last march which is granted; he is to learn her to read, all manner of houswifey work and provide her with a suit of cloaths with the expiration of her time. Richard Power and Jno. Fowler, securities.

Trustram Thomas brought John Badsey, an orphan, praying he might be bound to him until he arrives to the age of 21 being 14 years old last February. Granted. Will be taught the trade as shoemaker. John Jones & James Gould, securities.

It was argued that Doctor Andrew Imbert had undertaken to make a sound and perfect cure of a certain lame distempered woman named Elizabeth Malldge(?) and requested payment.

John Gibbs set forth that John Gibbs, father of the petitioner gave him a cow calfe of a different mark from his own and told a certain Thomas Lewis requesting him to get the same recorded which being neglected the widow of John Gibbs. The court orders that Christopher Pinder who married the widdow of the said John Gibbs deliver unto Thomas Lewis for the use of the petitioner, one good cow & calfe forthwith.

p. 73. Peter Peterson became bound to our Sovereign Lady the Queen in the sum of £20 to make an appearance next November Court. Renatus Smith and Anthony Joy, securities. John Johnson bound himself to give evidence against said Peter Peterson.

It was ordered that the road be cleared from the town to Coll. William Coursey's plantation to Major William Turle's house.

Richard Smith son of George Smith prayed he might have liberty to close his guardian which was granted and he chose Richard Powell. William Sweatnam, security.

Richard Power brought Elizabeth Ely praying that she be bound to him until she arrives to the age of 18 years being a 12 month old the 20th of August last. Granted. Thomas Ruth and John Hawkins, Junr., securities. She is to be taught to read and housewifery work. She is to be given a suit of cloathes at the expiration of her time. It is ordered that Richard Power be allowed the sum of 1000 lbs. of tobacco at the laying the next levy.

John Holt was fined for swearing 3 oaths within the hearing of the constable.

It was ordered that the road be cleared from the town to Coll. William Coursey's plantation to Major William Turle's house.

John Atchison prayed for his freedom from his master William Hopper; the time of his servitude he alleges is expired. Denied.

Joseph Sparks chose John Nabb to be his guardian. Solomon Clayton and Nathaniel Tucker, Junr., securities.

p. 74. It was presented that Edward Tobin, of St. Paul's Parish, Queen

Anne's Co., taylor, on 1 Sept. committed fornication with Margaret Costigin and begot a child.

It was presented that Thomas Hill, planter, on 20 March 1709 and divers other days and times as well committed fornication with Elizabeth Graves. He confessed and was fined 600 lbs. of tobacco.

p. 75. Anne Mathews petitioned to be discharged from her master Mr. William Sweatnam. Denied.

Charles Lowther set forth that the petitioner having a kinswoman att Doctor Thomas Goodmans which is now att age and still detained; praying that she be released. Ordered that she continue to serve until age 21, now being 17 years old.

It was presented that Mary Sanders of Worrell Hundred on 30 Aug 1709 committed fornication and begot a child. She states that John Roberts is the father. Mathew Mason to pay her fine of 600 lbs. of tobacco; she is to serve said Mathew Mason 6 months for keeping her child after the expiration of her present time of servitude.

August Court 1710

p. 82. The petition of John Worley Smith, servant to John Worley was heard, praying relief agst. his master in that he neglects to comply with what he is obliged to perform by virtue of an indenture signed by the petitioner's father and the sd. John Worley. Denied. John Worley made oath to 60 days runaway time agst. the said John Worley Smith; additional time of servitude is added.

Edward Tomlins the ferryman of Kent Ferry surrenders up the same when the year is expired; thereupon John Oldson late ferryman by his petition prays readmittance which is granted.

John Atchison, servant to William Hopper prayed to be relieved agst. his master for detaining him in his service his time being expired. [Approved.]

Richard Smith prayed for another guardian instead of the former Richd. Powell for some reasons in his father's will & which is granted; he chooses Richard Bishop. Sureties Majr. John Hawkins & John Meredith.

Abraham Johnson & Mary his wife prayed that John Lane be compelled to pay the petitioner what is due to his wife by a contract formerly between them [she as a servant].

p. 83. Upon a motion of Evan Thomas, clk. of the court, having urgent business to go to England for some small time, prayed that Philip Feddeman may be admitted deputy in his absence. Granted.

It was presented that William Cooper of Tuckaho Hundred, planter, otherwise called William Cooper of Tuckaho Hundred, cooper, on 29 April

1710 took a certain quantity of bacon belonging to John Pitt of Talbot Co., Gent., of the value of 900 lbs. of tobacco. Ordered to stand in the pillory 1/2 hour and receive 25 lashes.

John Merriday prayed to clear a road from his house to the main road.

John Prewitt, servant to John Hawkins, Junr., complained agst. his master for his negligence in getting the petitioner's legg cured which renders him incapable of his master's service and also for want of bedding to lye on.

p. 84. It was presented that Frances Roe, spinster, of Wye Hundred, on 1 March 1709 and at divers other days committed fornication and begot a child; she named Edward Tobin as the father. Fined 600 lbs. of tobacco which was paid by her father Thomas Roe.

p. 86. Mary Sargeant set forth that Patrick Cavener being a servant of the petitioner hath and still doth absent himself from the petitioner's service whereas it is shown that Patrick Cavener is the servant of Samuell Hunter.

Theodorus Bonner was readmitted to practice before the court.

November Court 1710
p. 113. George Mathers, master of Thomas Osburn, became bound with Charles Conner and Francis Barnes in the sum of £18.6.0 due to the said orphan as of his father William Osburn's estate.

Elizabeth Sanders to summoned Johannes Deliney to show cause why two of the petitioner's children being bound to the said Deliney and by him abused, may not be sett att liberty from him and it appears to the court that he had much abused George Sanders one of the children by beating and is therefore fined 200 lbs. of tobacco.

William Jackson with John Jones and Daniel Walker his security became bound for the sum of £190.4.8 3/4 the remainder of the estate of Robt. Robinson.

John Sutton, together with Thomas Marsh and William Kerby his security, became bound unto the orphans of Roger Baxter in the sum of £31.5.0 to pay unto the said orphans the sum of £15.12.8 1/2 their portion and part of their father's estate.

Samuel Hunter became bound with Francis Barns and Bryan Shield, his securities, unto Lewis, William, John, Hanse, Mary and Elizabeth Meredith in the sum of £74.14.10 ... to pay unto the afsd. children the sum of £37.7.5 proportionably as of their father Lewis Meredith's estate.

Robert Jones prayed liberty to remove the main road through his plantation round his corn field. Granted..

p. 114. Mr. Robert Grundy brought his servant John Connor, praying judgment for 7 days runaway time that the said servant absented from his service to which the servant confessed.

Patrick Creagh was ordered to testify before the Grand Jury.

It was ordered that Elizabeth Gibson continue with Mr. Jacob Covington a year for the sum of 1000 lbs. of tobacco to be paid him in the next year's levy and att the same rate per annum for a longer time, and the said Jacob Covington being to salivate her is to be paid therefore if cured 1500 lbs. of tobacco, otherwise nothing for the salivation. [Is the Doctor being paid to spit on her as a possible cure?

Daniel Harris set forth that he had served his time but his master James Evans would have longer time, also would not pay his cloathing.

p. 115. It was presented that Mathew Collins of Queen Anne's Co., on 25 July 1709 att St. Paul's Parish did traffick, barter and deal with Henry Smith then being a servant to William Clayton, Junr, of Talbot Co. Acquitted.

Charles Neale was appointed constable of Wye Hundred for the ensuing year.

Mathew Collins and his wife Ursula were summoned to answer a plea of indebtedness to William Clayton. That Ursula when she was single, known as Ursula Griffin, on 15 July 1709 entertained Henry Smith (for 8 nights) then servant to William Clayton of TA Co. being then unlawfully absented form his master's service. The law stated she had a financial responsibility to Henry's master as a consequence. The verdict was quashed and held for nought.

James Smith, an orphan chose as his guardian his mother Margarett Smith. John Salter and John Whittington, her security.

p. 117. It was presented that William Carman of QA Co., planter, on 2 Nov 1710 att St. Paul's Parish, assaulted Mary Creagh the wife of Patrick Creagh, merchant, in the house of her husband. [Charge dropped.]

It was presented Elenor Knowland for had a base born child about 23 Oct 1710. She named William Willson as the father. She is fined 600 lbs. of tobacco.

It was presented that Edward Tobin of QA Co., taylor, on 5 March 1709 and divers other times committed fornication with Frances Roe, spinster. Fined 600 lbs. of tobacco.

p. 118. It was presented that William Carman assaulted Jean Halfe(?) spinster, servant of Patrick Creagh, merchant. [Charge dropped]

Allowances for the year 1710:
William Wrench for 15 crows heads
Majr. William Turle for 18 crows heads
John Merreday for a wolf's head, his own killing

John Merreday for a wolf's head his own killing
Mr. John Salter assigned by the speaker of the House, delegate for a bill past in favour of this county
To ditto by assignmt. of R. Dallam, clk. of Assembly for do.
To Mr. John Salter for William Ridge per order of court
To do. by assignment of Dorothy Offley for 8 crows heads
To do for 9 crow's heads his own killing
William Boone for 1 wolf's head his killing
John Prinrose for one ditto
John Keld for one ditto
William Kenting(?) for one ditto
John Johnson for 5 ditto Indian killing
Nath: Cl...e for 1 wolf's head his own killing
Nath: Tucker for 1 ditto his own killing
Cath: Deale the widdo. of Jno. Deale for burying Mary Gibbins
John Meraday, Senr. for 14 crows heads
George Elliott for one wolf's head his own killing
Thomas Ruth, Senr. omitted in the last levy for a wolf's head
Philip Conner for keeping Elizabeth Hoge 2 months
To ditto for his trouble abt. her and salves, &c.
Henry Wilkinson a poor man to be paid him by Mr. Whittington
Morris Clock for 1 wolf's head his own killing
Mr. John Pemberton 1 ditto Indian killing
Thomas Hony for keeping Cath: Innocence 9 months last year.
Mary Sparks for keeping ditto 3 months
Edwd. Jones for keeping Anne Morecock 8 months
Richd. Power for nursing & bringing up Eliz: Ely
Mr. John Whittington for 1 wolf's head his own killing
Nath. Conner for 6 crow's heads
Wm. Hampstead, constable of Worc... Hud. for 1 levy last year mistaken in the list
Mary Simmons for keeping Elizab: Sanders
Doctor Mackelanans widdo. for keeping Mary Carter
Mrs. Mary Chetham for 1 wolf's head
Edward Winlock a poor man on K. Island
Jacob Covington for Elizabeth Gibson's keeping a year
Jno. Hawkins, Junr. on acct. of Andr: Hamblton for the statutes
Edward Hamblton for the grand jury expenses(?)
Richard Ha....d for Bryan Brother's orphan boy allowed in Nov court 1709 & omitted in the year's levy.
Colo. Richd. Tilghman the remainder of his allowance for building the prison
John Fowler for keeping two children of John Ely's 2 months, allowed in June

court last.

Samll. Hunter for the grand jury's expenses in March last

Mary D'Roachburn for Elizabeth Malogen [Malague]

Edwd. Hamblton for the Gr: Jury's expenses in April last

Richd. Hynson for the orphan jury in June last

William Hollinsworth by assignmt. of Edward Carsh for 1 wolf's head Indian killing

Thomas Howe a cripple per order of court

Ditto for his wife's cleaning & looking after the courthouse

Robert Jones, coroner for 2 inquisitions

James Carsey for keeping Mary Underwood this last year

Edward Tomlin for keeping Kent Island Ferry

Majr. Wm. Turlo for 21 days attendance as Justice

Mr. John Salter for 22 days ditto

Mr. John Wells for 20 days ditto

Mr. Thomas Fisher for 22 days ditto

Mr. John Whittington for 9 days ditto

Mr. Solomon Wright for 20 days ditto

Mr. Thomas Marsh for 22 days ditto

Mr. Philemo. Lloyd for ferry's fees not allowed anno 1708

To the Governor for the Great Seale Anno 1709

Bryan Connelly a poor man

Tho: Hony by assignmt. from Isaac Hollinsworth for 1 wolf's head

Edward Hamblton for pt. his license halfe a year charged when not due

Colo. Richd. Tilghman for a book of laws and a skin of parchment to cover it

Mrs. Eliza. Coursey for the court house & church land

Colo. Nicho. Lowe for ... criminal fees

Evan Thomas for ... criminal's fees

To ditto for extraordinary services

Colo. Richd. Tilghman for insolvt. tax

December Court 1710

p. 126. Samuel Wright admin. of Samll. Wright, dec'd., together with Samuel Hunter & Mathew Smith his securities and became bound unto the Orphans of the sd. deceased in the sum of £176.15.8 for the paymt. of £63.7.10 the orphans' parts of the sd. estate.

It was ordered that Coll. Richard Tilghman have the use of the brick shed, while, & as long it lasted.

It was ordered that William Hamblton be paid for keeping Mary Underwood the ensuing year be allowed the sum of 1500 lbs. of tobacco.

March Court 1711

p. 127. Mary Hobbs, servant to Mr. Robert Colt complained that she is putt to more labour than was obliged to by agreement.

Richard Poore, servant to Mr. James Hindman, complained of having a sore leg, and not allowed time to dress it, neither doth his master endeavour to procure a doctor to have it cured. [The court finds no cause for complaint.]

It was ordered that Eleneror [sic] Knowland, servant to Mr. Robert Guiney [Quiney?] (she was fined here last court for bastardy) serve a whole year for charges in & trouble of his house, to commence from the expiration of her present time of servitude.

Thomas Storey prayed to be lett att liberty from his master's service having served his full time, & above since the 10th of August last. [Ordered released from service.]

The following constables were appointed Island Hundred Richard Bishop; Town Hundred William Hollingsworth; K.I. Lower Hundred Mathew Erickson; K.I. Upper Hundred John Roberts; Wye Hundred Charles Neale; Worrell Hundred Mathew Mason.

It was ordered that George Jackson be overseer of the highways from home to the wading place of Kent Island, & from thence to Mr. Bennetts.

p. 128. It was ordered that Major John Hawkins pay the sum of 500 lbs. of tobacco for Elizabeth Trundle's mulatto child, she being a servant of Major Hawkins.

Alexander Forbes of QA Co., Gent., otherwise of KE Co., was summoned to answer Griffith Jones of the City of Philadelphia, merchant, and his wife Elizabeth who was admx. of Patrick Robinson, late of Philadelphia, Gent., her late husband, that he owed her £80. The court denied the claim.

John Walles servant to Mr. James Earle, set forth that he served his master 4 years, praying he may be sett at liberty but not producing an indenture, he was ordered to serve as the law directs.

p. 129. It was presented that Patrick Creagh of Queen Anne's Co., merchant, on 29 Nov 1710 committed perjury.

p. 130. It was presented that Alexr. Forbess overseer of the Queens road in Kent Island, had not cleared the said road & minded the bridges. Fined 500 lbs. of tobacco.

It was presented that John Coursey of Worrell Hundred, Gent., on 25 March being Sunday, gott drunk. Fined 100 lbs. of tobacco.

It was presented that Charles Neale overseer of the Queen's road between Thomas Yewells & the bridge by Mrs. Alice Loyd's plantation, had not cleared the road & minded the bridges. Fined 500 lbs. of tobacco.

p. 131. William Hynson, a minor, complained that he was being held by Charles Vanderford under pretext of being exec. of John Nabb late of this county contrary to law (as the petitioner is informed) as an apprentice. [Vanderford produced the indenture by which Hynson was indentured to Nabb; however the court considered the indenture insufficient to hold the petitioner as servant any longer.

Mr. Vincent Hemsley who being bound for the said John Story's appearance at this court prayed that he might be discharged from this recognizance. Granted. John Story committed to the sheriff's custody according to law.

John Story set forth that he was by Seth Garrett of this county held a servant in manner contrary to the laws of this land and by him in diverse ways abused. [Deferred until Garrett can get a transcript of the Talbot Co. court.]

Joseph Sparks chose Thomas Frisby as his guardian. William Hollingsworth & George Sparks, his security.

William Austin complained that he was being detaining by William Pratt as a servant in an illegal manner. The court rules that in consideration that William Pratt assigns unto Judith Austin, mother of the petitioner, a certain Hannah Middlton's time of servitude & advantages thereupon, the said William Austin to remain in the service of sd. William Pratt the remaining part of his indented time.

p. 134. It was presented that Mary Lemarr, wife of Charles Lemarr, cooper, at St. Paul's Parish in QA Co., on 1 March 1710 stole a pair of stockings of Owen Sullivane. Not guilty.

June Court 1711

p. 139. It was presented that William Boone of St. Paul's Parish, Queen Anne's Co. before the last day of March 1711 profaned the Lord's day called Sunday by causing his servant to do servile labour. Fined 100 lbs. of tobacco. Also presented that he was hunting in the woods and killed a deer with a gun. Fined 100 lbs. of tobacco.

Richard Jones was charged with fathering a child by Elizabeth ---?

p. 142. John Johnson brought John Douglas an orphan child praying that he be bound to him until he attained the age of 21, being 3 years old on 15th of this June.

p. 143. Sarah Stonsell (Stousell, Stonfell, etc.?), set forth that her husband being indebted to William Hopper late dec'd. in the sum of 1450 lbs. of tobacco, in consideration thereof did bind his son Robert Stonsell(?), Junr. contrary to the mind of the petitioner until satisfaction of the debt afsd. was made & done. The indenture was made on 4 Sept 1707 when the boy was 7 years 2 months old and was bound until age 21. The extx. of William Hopper summoned. The boy was freed.

Majr. John Hawkins gave information that his servant woman named Elizabeth Trundle had lately been brought to bed and delivered of a Mulatto child.

August Court 1711

p. 144. Christopher Pindar and his wife Susannah, set forth that Doctor Imbert detained the petitioners' son agst. the consent of his parents, as a servant. The indenture is shown to the court whereby the son John Cantin [Caustin?} serves for 5 years in consideration that Doctor Imbert would cure him of distemper that he was languishing under. The term is reduced by one year to 3 years from 22 Dec 1710.

It was presented that William Senett, planter, on 20 Feb 1710 and at diverse other days and times before and since in St. Paul's Parish in Queen Anne's Co., committed fornication with Margaret Kelly, servant woman to Mary Chetham. Fined 600 lbs. of tobacco.

It was presented that Margret Kelly of the parish of St. Paul's in Queen Anne's Co., Spinster, servant to Mary Chetham, on 20 Feb 1710 committed fornication and begot a bastard child by William Sennett. Fined 600 lbs. of tobacco which was paid by Mr. Philemon Hemsley.

Mary Sanders set forth that as servant to Doctor Williams she was detained from freedom and abused. The doctor was ordered to take care of her.

p. 145. It was presented that Nicholas Massey, Peter Massey, Thomas Massey and Benja. Benham of Queen Anne's Co., planters, were malefactors and perpetrators of the peace, with swords, staves and knives on 27 of 9ber 1710 at Chester River in St. Pauls Parish broke into and entered the mansion house of Samuel French and to the terror of the people. All called to appear, except Peter Massey, and pleaded guilty. Fined 100 lbs. of tobacco each.

It was presented that Elizabeth Thomas of Wye Hundred, spinster, on 1 March 1710 committed fornication and begot a child by Thomas Louds. Fined 600 lbs. of tobacco.

p. 146. It was presented that Margaret Carrary [Carrory?], spinster, on 17 May 1711, and at diverse days and times before and since, at Worrell Hundred, committed fornication and begot a child. She states she cannot tell who the father is. Fine paid by William Merson.

It was presented that Johannes Delimsyosta (Deheniossa?) of Wye Hundred, chirurgeon, on 26 April 1711 being produced as an evidence in the court, dep. about the age of Thomas Storey then held as a servant by William Boone, and committed perjury. Bound over to the Provincial Court.

p. 147. John Creamer prayed for relief agst. Majr. John Hawkins his master. Denied.

John Gibbs asked to be bound to Thomas Lewis until age 21, according to his father's desire; to learn the trade of cooper. Thomas Lewis agrees to look after the petitioner's cattle and stock during the term.

James Gold brought John Raley an orphan boy and prayed to have him bound to him until as 21 which is granted; to learn the trade of shoe making.

Mary Hopper set forth that a boy named Robert was by the desire and request of Robert & Sarah Stansell, his parents, bound to her dec'd. husband to the age of 21, then at age 7; that the boy being small was not capable to do any service. Sarah Stansell ordered to pay 2000 lbs. of tobacco for satisfaction in keeping and maintaining the boy.

John Hackett brought James Raley an orphan boy and prayed to have him bound to him until age 21 which is granted; to learn the trade of tanning.

John Greenwood set forth that he had bound Christopher Tomkins, to learn the trade of wheelwright for 4 years but said Tomkins is runaway the court orders the indenture rescinded.

John Hackett brought into court Charles Raley and prayed to have him bound to him until age 21 which is granted; to learn the trade of shoe making.

p. 148. Dennis Kelly prayed for redress agst. Doctor Thomas Williams who detains him from his freedom dues; Doctor Thomas is given until 1 March next to satisfy the petitioner's dues.

William Boone was ordered to pay Walter Whaley's levy, being a servant when the list of taxables should have been taken.

It was ordered that William Jump and his wife Rebecca be summoned to answer Ephraim Winn of a plea that the owed him 500 lbs. of tobacco.

p. 153. Mr. Thomas Fisher assumes to pay 100 lbs. of tob. fine for Arthur Hill a convict before him for breach of the sabbath.

November Court 1711

It was ordered that John Lawrence be allowed 1500 lbs. of tobacco to build a bridge at Tuckahoe between Mr. Grundys and Mr. Pembertons and the county be at no further charge in repairing of the same.

p. 156. Edward Harris was appointed overseer of the highways from hence to Wye Mill and from thence to Coll. Coursey's and so back again to this town.

George Elliott was appointed overseer of the highways from Chester Mill to Collins' Mill

Thomas Power chose his guardian Thomas Carman.

John Griffin chose his guardian Thomas Smith.

It was ordered that Thomas Parsons be overseer of the highways from hence to Chester Mill, from thence to Coll. Tilghman's plantation & back again here.

John Dennis(?) set forth having served Bryan Shield a servitude when at the expiration of his time was to have one suit of broad cloth. Court agrees and so orders Shield.

Timothy Tracey prayed to keep an ordinary or house of entertainment at Majr. John Hawkins' house near the Wading Place. Granted.

Mr. Christopher Philipson one of the attorneys of this court was expelled from practicing in this court unless he makes an appearance here by the last day of this present court.

Thomas Lewis was appointed constable of Worrell Hundred instead of Mathew Mason.

John Oldson prayed that he continue as ferryman at the wading place. Approved.

William Jump was appointed constable of Wye Hundred instead of Charles Neale.

It was ordered that Samuel Hunter be paid for shutters to the lower windows of the back building of this court house and for repairing the front window shutters and for cleaning the house.

Charles Lowder was appointed overseer of the highways from the north side of Pearl's Branch to the head f Chester River.

p. 157. It was ordered that Bryan Sennet and his wife and Daniel Walker and his wife be summoned to answer complaint of said Margaret Thompson.

It was presented that Margaret Thompson of Queen Anne's Co., spinster, servant to James Heath, Gent., on 20 Sept 1711 in St. Paul's Parish, committed fornication. Ordered to receive 3 lashes.

Mr. Henry Chetham swore to 90 days runaway time agst. the sd. Margaret Thompson; she to serve 10 days for every one day absent.

It was presented that Elizabeth Trundle of St. Paul's Parish of Queen Anne's Co., servant to Majr. Jno. Hawkins, Gent., on 22 Dec 1710 and at divers other times, committed fornication and begot a child. Found not guilty of being [bearing?] a mulatto but guilty of fornication. Her fine of 600 lbs. of tobacco paid by Major John Hawkins. Elizabeth Trundle was ordered to served Major Hawkins until the last day of Sept next for the trouble and disgrace of his house.

p. 158. John Bowlyn was cleared by proclamation.

A cow calfe given to Elizabeth Trundle by Majr. John Hawkins was marked with a crop and 2 slits in the left ear, and a crop, a slit, etc.

p. 160. Richard Holding was summoned to answer unto Benjamin Ball, Gent., and his wife Susannah of a plea that he render unto them the sum of 3166 lbs. of tob. and cask. They were awarded 2366 lbs. of tobacco.

p. 161. It was ordered that John Lawrence be allowed the sum of 1500 lbs. of tob. for the building of a bridge at Tuckahoe between Mr. Grundys and Mr. Pemberton.

John Hawkins, Jr., was summoned to answer Mary Chetham, widow, and Henry Chetham, Gent., extx. and exec. of the last will of Edward Chetham of a plea of trespass. Nicholas Lowe, atty. for Hawkins stated that after the day of issuing the original writt, 25 June 1711, Mary took to her husband one James Heath, Gent.

p. 167. It was ordered that Robt. Jones, coroner, be paid for 3 inquisitions, vizt. Patience Semms, a Negro of Mr. Krachbulls and a bastard girle of Majr. John Hawkins.

March Court 1711

p. 169. Samuel Phillips and Grace his wife prayed for relief agst. Thomas Williams whom the said Grace served her time and was denied her freedom dues. [Williams ordered to pay said Grace her dues.]

Henry Willcocks was appointed constable for Island Hundred.

Humphrey Wells and Richard Webster were fined for not appearing as jurors are remitted.

It was ordered that a road be cleared from the landing from Nicholas Masseys to John Swifts.

James Heath prayed for an allowance for the trouble caused by Margarett Kelly begetting a bastard child.

James Gold was appointed constable of Town Hundred.

Margaret Graves a servant woman newly imported into this province is adjudged by the court to serve 5 years according to the custom of the country.

p. 170. Margaret Thompson complained of abuses as servant to Madam Chetham. Denied.

Elenor Nowell prayed that Mr. John Hawkins be ordered to pay her freedom dues. [He is ordered to pay her a pair of shoes.]

It was presented that Margaret Millburn of Christ Church Parish in Queen Anne's Co., spinster, servant to Phillip Connor of afsd. parish, planter, on 27 Dec 1711 committed fornication with Edward Wright and begot a bastard child. Ordered to receive 9 stripes (lashes). Edward Wright to pay Philip Conner 600 lbs. of tobacco for the trouble of his house and of keeping and maintaining the said child.

John Oneale prayed for relief agst. William Elbert with whom he served the latter part of his time and who refused to pay him his freedom dues. [Elbert ordered to pay him a Kersey coat, a pair of breeches, a pair of shoes and stockings, a white shirt and a hatt.

Samuel Hunter prayed that a renunciation be entered agst. Colo. Lowe & Mr. Bonner as his attorneys in all actions wherein he is plaintiff, which is granted.

Margaret Thompson was ordered to serve Charles Marshall one month for the trouble of his house about her child. [Later child is bound to sd. Marshall until he arrives at age 21.]

p. 172. Ephraim Winne, Gent. of QA Co., and his wife Mary als Mary Hartshorne of QA Co., were summoned to answer Bryon Shield of afsd. county of a plea that they render to him the sum of 319 lbs. of tob. Shield stated that Mary while sole on 18 March 1709 at Queens Town by her bill obligatory bound her self to pay the sum of 319 lbs. of tobacco.

p. 175. Upon the motion of Doctor John Button that Elizabeth Lane, servant to James Bishop, dec'd., of whom he is exec., having long since absented herself from her said master's service, and is now resident within this county and goes by the name of Sarah Howe, wife of William Howe, servant to Majr. John Hawkins, prays that the court take sd. Lane als How into his possession as exec. of sd. James Bishop. [The court so ordered.]

It was ordered that Charles Marshall be allowed at the laying off next levy 500 lbs. of tob. towards the maintenance of Margarett Thompson's child and that the child be bound to said Marshall until age 21.

p. 176. Valentine St. Lee (?) chose his guardian as Charles Lamar.

The petition of William Williston was rejected.

William Boone was summoned to answer to Charles Storey of QA Co., weaver, admin. of Hester Storey, spinster, who d. intestate who was in possession of divers property [listed] including a mare branded ES, when on 22 June 1708 she died. Boone was accused of withholding the property from the admin. Not guilty.

p. 186. Johannes Dehineyosta was fined 10 s. for swearing 2 oaths.

Edward Harris made oath that Anne Williams, his servant, absented herself 107 days. In accordance with the law she was ordered to serve 10 days for each day of absence.

p. 187. Eleanor Croney, servant to James Hindman was adjudged to be

22 years old.

Ellenor Roach, servant to Charles Vanderford was adjudged to be 20 years of age.

Robert Noble was sworn as Under Sheriff of the county.

Mr. John Wells brought James Burne(?) his servant who confessed he absented himself from his master's service 25 days.

Andrew Hamilton about the need to build a bridge over the main branch of Chester River. The court agrees to support 1/2 the costs as long as the Justices of KE Co. agree to support the other half.

Richard Kempson prayed liberty to keep an ordinary on Kent Island. Granted.

1 Dec 1711
County levy for the year 1711:
Capt. Wm. Hackett for 4 wolves' heads
John Hackett for 4 do.
John Murphey for 1 do.
Naths. Scott for 3 do.
Samll. Sheffield for 1 do.
Solomon Wright for 1 do.
James Hutchins for 15 crows heads.
Mr. John Salter for 4 do.
Henry Covington for 4 do.
William Hamilton for 2 wolves' heads
John Green for 1 ditto.
Henry Pratt for 4 ditto.
Arthur Emory for 10 crow's heads.
John Meredith for 7 do.
Francis Benton(?) for 9 do.
Peter Falcons(?) for 8 do.
Bryan Connally a poor man
Robt. Jones, coroner for 3 inquisitions, vizt. Patience Seunus(?), a Negro of Mr. Krachbulls and a bastard girle of Majr. John Hawkins.
Edwd. Scott for Wm. Ridgers debt and cost.
Wm. Hamblton for keeping Mary Underwood
Colo. Tilghman as balance last year's acct.
William Boone for 1 wolf's head & 3 crow's heads.
Benja. Falcanar for 4 wolves's heads.
John Falconar for 5 wolves' head & 5 crow's heads, whereof he assigns Mr. Bonner 200 lbs. of tobacco.
Thomas Howe a poor lame man
To his wife for cleaning the court house

Darby Cavanagh for keeping Mary Carter
Edwd. Winlock a poor man upon K. Island.
Thomas Honey for keeping Cath: Innocence.
George Powell for keeping Anne Morecock & to Mrs. John Salter for her use to buy her cloaths.
John Ouldson for keeping Kent Island Ferry this year
Majr. William Turlo for 16 days as Justice.
Mr. John Salter for 14 days ditto
Mr. John Wells for 16 days ditto
Mr. Thomas Fisher for 15 days do.
Mr. John Whittington for 11 days ditto
Mr. Solomon Wright for 11 days ditto
Mr. Thomas Marsh for 16 days ditto
Thoms. Hollinsworth for Zorababell Wells levy last year
Edward Hamblton for the grand jury's expenses in march, June & November
To Doctr. Andr: Imbert in pt. for curing Elizabeth Malogue.
Remainder of payment to remain in sheriff's hand until the cure is perfected.
Colo. Nicholas Lowe for criminall --- fees.
Mr. Amos Garrett by assignmt. of Thomas Reading for copy of the law anno 1709
Colo. Richd. Tilghman for insolvent tax ameriamt.
To ditto upon account of the president for the seal to the law October 1709
To ditto for a wolves' head Indian killing
To ditto for John Story's imprisonmt. fees servt. to William Boone
Mr. Antho: Joy for 3 tax twice charged anno 1710
To ditto for 1 tax in 1709
John Lawrance for building a bridge at Tuckaho
Mr. Benja. Wicks for himselfe & 4 men's trouble & expenses, and boat hire in fetching the county arms from Annapolis
Mr. Phil. Hemsley for bringing over the county laws
To ditto for insolt. tax. Jno. Arnoult 94, Tho: Kersey 95, Loflin Malloony 391, James Hardin 125, Thomas Rox 195, Tho: Brown 162, Weltin(?) Jones 195 and Edward Ramsey 195.
Majr. Turlo, Mr. Salter, Mr. Wells and Mr. Whittington for 1 days attendance more.
Thoms. Reading for the laws about settling the court house
To ditto for the law last Assembly
Evan Thomas for sevts. criminalls fees & other services ex office
Edward Tomlin for do.
Sheriff's salary

June Court 1712

p. 188. Joseph Earle prayed liberty to keep an ordinary within this town. Granted. Solomon Clayton and Thomas Hollinsworth, his security.

Mary Hampstead brought Elizabeth Pasckell, on orphan and prayed to have her bound to her until she is age 18. Granted. Mathew Smith & Richard Hynson, her security.

Benjamin Ball on behalf of himself and the people called Quakers, moved that the court grant them liberty to have a meeting house in this county according to the toleration given them by act of Parliament which is granted. The place of the meeting house to be at said Benjamin Ball's house upon Kent Island.

p. 189. The court was informed that Priscilla Bruin of this county, widdo. has lately been committed into the sheriff's custody upon suspicion of murdering her bastard child. The court orders that she be placed in the custody of the sheriff of AA Co. in order to appear before the Provincial Court.

John Laurence was appointed overseer of half the road from Wye Mill to Tuckahoe.

John Skinner and his wife set forth that John Newnam, Junr, about 5 years ago was bound to Robert Noble to learn the trade of cooper and carpenter, but Robert Noble keeps him to common plantation labour. Robert Noble fined 100 lbs. of tobacco.

Elizabeth Loyd set forth having lived near 40 years in this neighborhood and from her infancy hath frequently been afflicted with the Kings Evill, and now at last rendered her incapable of getting a livelyhood, prays this court to allow her a reasonable maintenance. 1000 lbs. tob. allowed at next levy.

Mr. John Wells, Mary Hobbs, Mr. John Coursey, Mary Thunderman and Anne Shelburne to testify before the Grand Jury.

p. 190. Mr. Anthony Ivy brought his servant William Humphry who confessed that he absented himself from his master's service 139 days.

It was presented that Mary Gibson of Queen Anne's Co., spinster, of St. Paul's Parish, on 28 Feb 1711 committed fornication with Thomas Wallis of county afsd. and begot a child. She is fined 600 lbs. of tobacco, paid by Bryan Shield.

It was presented that Mary Hobbs of St. Paul's Parish, Queen Anne's Co., spinster, on 28 Feb 1711 in Island Creek Hundred committed fornication and begot a child. She states the father is John Morris. She was fined 600 lbs. of tobacco, paid by Richard Moore.

p. 191. It was presented that Rebecka Parrott of St. Paul's Parish in QA Co., spinster, on 28 Feb 1711 committed fornication and begot a child. She states the father is James Silvester. She is fined 600 lbs. of tobacco, paid by

William Jump.

Following a writt of inquiry it was found that John Tillotson the defendt. had not sold, wasted or to his own use converted any of the goods or chattels which were of Patrick Halpeny at the time of his death.

August Court 1712

p. 194. Edward Hambleton brought Margarett Graves his servant who is adjudged to be 17 years of age.

p. 195. It was presented that Sarah Hopwood, spinster, servant to John Coursey of St. Paul's Parish of Queen Anne's Co., on 1 May 1712 and at divers other times, committed fornication and begot a child. She states that the father is Robert Lewis(?). She is ordered to received 10 stripes (lashes).

John Granger set forth that being bound an apprentice to John Roberts of Kent Island, turner, for the term of 6 years, which is almost expired, he promising to put the petitioner to school one whole year in the said time, whereas he has given the petitioner only 6 months schooling. [Roberts is ordered to give him 6 more months of schooling or forfeit the petitioner 5000 lbs. of tobacco.]

Anne Smith set forth that she with her estate was by the Kent County court put into the hands of her uncle Renatus Smith, who keeps her worse than a servant not affording her things necessary to sustain life. The court orders that Renatus Smith find the said Petitioner with a suit of good cloaths and other necessary cloathing.

Mary Poor, widdo. of Richard Poor, dec'd., showed that Richd. had left an orphan with real estate; the court appoints her as guardian for her dau. Sarah Poor.

Johannes Dehineyossa was presented for misusage of two children, George Sanders and John Sanders, sons of George Sanders, dec'd., by information of James Kerkum and John Leonard. Fined 500 lbs. of tobacco and upon further reasonable complaint to manumit the boys.

It was ordered that Doctor Andrew Imbert be paid 5000 lbs. of tobacco for the cure of Elizabeth Malogue (already in the sheriff's hands).

p. 196. Gilbert Tate discharged from recognizance.

It was presented that Edward Wright, planter, on 27 Dec 1711 committed fornication with Margarett Milburn of Christ Church Parish in Queen Anne's Co. Fined 600 lbs. of tobacco.

It was presented that James Silvester, planter, on 28 Feb 1711 and at divers other times, committed fornication with Rebecka Parrott and begot a child. Fined 600 lbs. of tobacco.

November Court 1712

p. 199. James Hicks was appointed constable of Wye Hundred.

Charles Neal stated that in the month of October 1692 Thomas the son of Edward Tomlins was then a sucking child and is now at the age of 20 years.

John Meredith, Junr., was appointed overseer of the highways from Chester Mill over Cattaile Bridge.

John Meredith, Senr. was appointed overseer of the highways from Thomas Punney's plantation to Chester Ferry.

Michael Moore was fined 120 lbs. of tobacco for swearing two oaths, paid by John Rawls.

p. 200. It was ordered that Patrick Sexton be allowed for the time he has kept Elizabeth Malogue, and that John Wells find her with cloaths and be allowed the same.

James Coursey was appointed constable of Worrell Hundred instead of Thomas Lewis.

It was presented that Elinor Lee, servant to Charles Connor, planter, on 1 April 1712 and at diverse other times committed fornication and begot a child. Fined 600 lbs. of tobacco (paid by Charles Connor) and to serve Charles Connor 10 additional months.

Major William Turlo brought his late servant Jane Steward who formerly had been convicted of having brought a mulatto child and having served her indented time of servitude with him. Ordered that she be sold for the term of 7 years. John King offers 2500 lbs. of tobacco for the present year.

p. 201. John Oldson was approved to continue as ferryman at Kent Island at the rate of 4000 lbs. of tobacco per year.

John Tatnam was allowed 2000 lbs. of tobacco for keeping Elizabeth Sanders the ensuing year.

Charles Lowder was appointed overseer of the highways from Pearl's Branch to the head of Chester River.

Thomas Mounsier was appointed overseer of the highways from Collins' Mill over Pearl's Branch.

George Elliott was appointed overseer of the highways from Cattaile Bridge over Collins Mill Branch.

John Early set forth that Rev. James Hindman detained him as a servant. The court ordered that John Early serve him after the rate of 1000 lbs. of tobacco per year until such debts as have been paid by Mr. Hindman to Samuel Hunter and Edward Harris.

James Heath demanded payment from Robert Betts for medicines for Sarah, wife of Robert Betts. Bill was verified by Mary Heath.

November Court 1712

County Levy
Thomas Marsh for 1 day's attendance not allowed last levy
Charles Marshall for maintaining Margarett Thompson's child
Elizabeth Lloyd per order of court in June last
Doctor Imbert for Mary Corneliuson
John Oldson for keeping Kent Island ferry
Majr. William Turlo for 13 days attendance as Justice
Mr. John Salter for 11 days ditto
Mr. John Wells for 12 days ditto
Mr. Solomon Wright for 13 days ditto
Mr. Thomas Fisher for 13 days ditto
Mr. Thomas Marsh for 13 days ditto
Mr. John Whittington for 9 days do.
Thoms. Wright for 6 wolves heads
Ditto for 6 crow's heads
John Tillotson for 6 crow's heads
Henry Covington for 4 crow's heads
Aron Edge assigned Joseph Clift 1 wolves head
William Hamblton for keeping Mary Underwood
Thoms. Atkinson for keeping Mary Morecock 3 months
Thomas Hony for keeping Cath:
Capt. William Hacket for 3 wolves' heads
Thomas Godden for keeping Mary Sparks
Henry Wilkinson a poor man
Jacob Covington for Elizabeth Gibson
Robt. Jones, coroner for inquisition on Cath: Fitzhugh
Ditto for inquisition on James Nevill
Edward Hamblton for 3 Grand Jurys
Mr. John Hackett for 3 wolves heads
William Hollinsworth for 3 wolves heads
Thomas Pratt for 1 wolf's head
Thomas Falconar for 8 wolves heads
Ditto for 8 ditto more
John Tatnam for keeping Eliza. Sanders
Bryan Connelly a poor man
Charles Connor for 10 crow's heads
Thomas Howe a poor man
Evan Thomas for criminall servts. fees

Edward Tomlin, Crier
Colo. Nics. Lowe for criminal serv. fees
Hon. President. for the seale
Thomas Yewell for 17 crows heads
Samuel Hunter for work done to the court house per agreement
John Holland for looking after & burying of John Long

March Court 1712/13

p. 203. John Meriday, Senr. was allowed for 27 crow's heads next levy.

John Falconar was allowed 800 lbs. of tobacco more for wolves' heads at the next levy.

Thomas Hollinsworth was appointed constable for Worrell Hundred instead of Thomas Lewis.

William Wyatt was appointed constable for Town Hundred instead of James Gould.

John Hawkins set forth that his servant Elizabeth Trundle hath absented herself 103 days without license. The time of 103 days is proved. Ten days additional time of servitude for each day of absence.

Richard Kemp petitioned that the widow of Richd. Bishop be summoned to show cause why the petitioner shall not have his freedom dues. Granted.

Susannah Buttler, servant to Robert Jones, prayed to be sett free, or to take some other care of her, being so distempered in her bones and so broke out that she is not able to go through her service. Robert Jones promises to doe for and towards her cure.

Rev. James Hindman brought his servant boy David Lindsey whose age was adjudged to be 10 years last November [1712].

p. 204. Came John Canlin, servant to Doctor Andrew Imbert and acknowledged to have absented from his said master's service the space of 107 days. Said Andrew Imbert states he is willing to release him on 25 Dec 1714 [despite the runaway time].

It was ordered that Mr. John Salter be requested & empowered to treat and agree with Doctor Brown(?) or any other physicians for the cure of Elizabeth Wilkinson and that the county shall be answerable for what he agrees for and for necessaries to be supplied her by the sd. Mr. Salter. And also that if her husband stays with her upon the plantation where now she live on & that the Doctor cures her there, then this court will allow a rent of 500 lbs. of tobacco.

It was ordered by this court that the sheriff receive no levys from the widow of Henry Richardson, dec'd.

p. 205. It was presented that William Whittaker of Talbot Co., cordwainer, in Wye Hundred, stole a gelding of William Willis of afsd. county, cordwainer. Not guilty.

It was presented that George Sexton of Queen Anne's Co., planter, on 28 Nov 1712 in St. Paul's Parish, stole a horse, bridle and saddle of James London, planter. Found not guilty.

p. 206. It was ordered that Darby Cavanah be allowed 1200 lbs. of tobacco for a last year's keeping Mary Cater, at the laying of the next levy.

March Court 1712/3

It was presented that Robert Lewin of Queen Anne's Co., carpenter, on 16 Feb 1711 and at divers other times committed fornication with Sarah Hopwood and begot a child. Not guilty.

p. 220. It was presented that Priscilla Bruin of Tuckahoe Hundred in St. Paul's Parish, on 26 March 1712 committed fornication and begot a child. The court ruled that the indictment be quashed.

p. 222. It was ordered that Sarah Hopwood, servant to Mrs. Mary Coursey, serve an additional year for the trouble and disgrace of her house.

p. 232. Benjamin Kerby chose as his guardian William Browne.

June Court 1713

Darby Cavanah asked for runaway time against Eliza. Freeman, his late servant. She was judged to be free.

p. 233. Thomas Wolfe set forth that being so lame he is altogether incapable of getting his living. The court asks that if Mr. Solomon Wright be pleased to see that the petitioner is well lookt after he shall be allowed at the laying of the next levy for the same.

August Court 1713

p. 234. Thomas Halfe, a poor distempered man, applied to the court for relief. The court agrees with Doctor Thomas Godman that if he makes a perfect cure of the dropsical distemper he now languishes under, to allow him 3000 lbs. of tobacco and if Halfe dies then he will accept whatever the court decided.

Richard Hammond prayed for a license for a house of entertainment in this town. Granted. Charles Neal & Mathew Smith, his security.

Samuel Hunter prayed for the same liberty as above request of Richard Hammond. Granted. Charles Neal & Mathew Smith, his security.

William Bryan prayed for an allowance being old and not able to work. To be allowed 1500 lbs. of tobacco at the next levy.

Aspatia Mihyll, servant to John Hocken, stated that she came into this province by indenture for 6 years, and was sold to David Machlefish & from him to John Hocken of Kent Island for the space of 5 years which time expired 27 May last; prays liberty to produce evidences to prove the same. Granted. The court ruled that she serve until 29 May next.

p. 243. Anthony Ivy was summed to answer to Andrew Imbart, apothecary of a plea of trespass for that Imbart complained that at various times of the year he prepared and delivered various medicines and physical preparations to Ivy who languished under a great and grievous malady and who promised to pay Imbart according to the account. Andrew has demanded 2000 lbs. of tobacco.

p. 245. Ann Smith agreed to serve Doctor Andrew Imbart until 10 March 1715 in consideration he is to give a cow and calf., a good gown and pettycoat, 2 shifts of dowlas, pair of new shoes and stockings, two new white aprons, a new black hood, 2 good handerkerchiefts, a good suit of muslin headcloaths and a good new pair of gloves and that his wife be obliged to bear her all manner of housewifery work and not be compelled to work in the ground.

November Court 1713

p. 249. Mr. John Johnson prayed liberty to practice in this court as an attorney. Granted.

Robert Walters was appointed overseer of the highway from here to Wye Mill & from thence to Colo. Courseys & thence back again here - instead of Edward Harris.

Thomas Roe was appointed constable of Wye Hundred.

Thomas Cooper prayed to have the liberty of keeping the publick ferry at the Wading Place of Kent Island which is granted to him at the usual rate of 4000 lbs. of tobacco per annum.

Mr. Francis Cook prayed the liberty to practice in the court as an atty. Granted.

p. 251. Benjamin Kerby chose as his guardian, instead of William Browne, who commits waste on his land, William Kerby, John Gwyn and John Sutton his security. Granted.

It was presented that Thomas Morrell of St. Paul's Parish, planter, Queen Anne's Co., on 2 Sep 1713 stole a sheep of Robert Grundy, merchant. Ordered to receive 10 lashes and stand in the pillory for ½ hour.

Richard Poore set forth that he had been unlawfully detained as a servant of Mrs. Hindman, the widdow of Mr. James Hindman. His is set free.

p. 252. It was ordered that Edward Atkinson a poor distempered young man be put under the cure of Doctor Thomas Godman for 5000 lbs. of tobacco.

Thomas Smith, servant to Capt. William Hackett, stated that Capt. Hackett would keep the petitioner a servant for 2 years and 2 months by an agreement made to cure the petitioner's wife whereas she died in 8 days and now Capt. Hackett will have the petitioner to be a servant. The court rules that he serve according to the indenture.

James Earle was appointed overseer of the highways from Thomas Punny's plantation to Chester Ferry instead of John Meriday, Senr.

Duncan Munroe was appointed overseer of the highway from Chester Mill to Wye Mill, and from Thomas Yewell's plantation to Wm. Clayton's Bridge.

The court agreed to allow Samuel Hunter to keep the courthouse shutters.

At November Court 1713
The following allowances are made:
Doctor Thomas Godman for pt of Tho: Halfe cure
Thomas Jackson for 23 squirrels heads and 1 crows head.
Majr. Wm. Turlo for 24 crows heads & 4 squirrel's do.
Isaac Harris for ... squirrels and 31 crows
Peter Falcom for 23 squirrels and 12 crows heads
Thomas Bright for 6 squirrels & 3 crows
James Sadler for 30 squirrels & 7 crows
James Evans for 31 squirrels & 11 crows
John Merriday, Senr., for 40 squirrels & 4 crows
Augustine Thompson for 17 squirrels heads
Do. by assignment of Jno. Primrose
To do. Primrose for remainder of 4 wolves heads.
William Legg for 4 squirrels & 1 crow
Samll. Hunter for G. Jurys expenses this court.
Edmund Thomas for 19 crows & 20 squirrels
To ditto for 27 squirrels & 6 crows
To ditto for 33 crows & 18 squirrel
Daniel Kelly for 14 squirrel & 6 crows
Darby Cavanaugh for 13 squirrels
Thoms. Hollingsworth for 31 squirrels
Humphr: Wells for 27 squirrels & 4 crows
Thomas How for 42 squirrels & 4 crows
Wm. Wrench for 17 squirrels & 6 crows
Nath: Tucker for 1 wolf's head & 12 squirrels
Thoms. Wright & James Gold for 7 wolves' heads
Mr. Solomon Wright for 1 wolves' head
Nath: Cl--- for 23 squirrels heads

Edmund Godwin for 10 crows & 1 squirrel
Henry Covington for 11 crows & 4 squirrels
Daniel ---eld for 11 crows & 15 squirrels
John Carlton for 17 squirrels & 4 crows
John Haimes(?), Senr., 33 squirrels & 5 crows
John Falkner for T. Falkner 8 wolves heads
B. Faulkner for 5 wolves heads
Nath: Connor for 58 squirrels & 1 crow
Philip Connor for 37 squirrel heads
Richd. Bennett, Esqr. assigned per Ind. John 1 wolves' head.
Richd. Moore for 15 squirrels
Fra: Barnes for 36 squirrels & 36 crows
John Willson for 44 squirrels & 2 crows
Val. Carter 146 squirrels & 16 crows
Nath: Comegys for 18 squ. & 1 crow
Wm. Maconakin for 25 sqr. heads
Mr. Salter paid Doctor Brown for Eliza. Wilkinson
Mr. Salter per acct. for provisions for do.
John Emory for 48 crows & 52 squirr.
John Merriday, Junr. for 29 squir. & 10 crows.
Jno. Johnson up Chester for 26 squirrels & 1 crow
Hen: Johnson for 9 squirrels & 4 crows
John Carter for 86 squirrels & 10 crows
Richd. Hammond for dyeting Thoms. Halfe
George Golt for 45 squirrels
Thomas Roe for 59 squirrels & 4 crows
Nath: Wright for 1 wolf's head Ind. killing
Stephen Comperson for 39 squirrels & 1 crow
Lawrence Evrett(?) for 116 squirrel heads
Math: Griffith for 10 squirrels
Charles Connor for 24 squirr. & 11 crows
Mr. John Wells for Eliza. Malogue
Mr. Thomas Fisher for 21 squirr. & 26 crows
William Jump for 44 squirrels & 5 crows
William Kenton for --- squir. & 1 crow
Edwd. Hamblton for G. Jury's expenses in Mar: last
John Leonard for 8 squirr.
John Lane senr. for 9 squir.
Thomas Jump for 23 squirl. 7 5 crows
Joseph Clift for 36 squir. & 9 crows
James Dalton for 24 squir.
Thomas Baynard for 12 squir.

Williamander Baynard for 34 squir. & -- crows
John Tatman per order of court 9ber last for keeping Elizabeth Sanders
Jno. Meriday, Senr. per order court in March for 27 crows
John Falconar per order do. court for wolves heads
Patrick Sexton for carrying Thomas Halfe to Dr. Godmans
Majr. Wm. Turlo for 14 days attend. as Justice
Mr. John Salter for 12 days ditto
Mr. John Wells for 13 days ditto
Mr. Thomas Fisher for 14 days do.
Mr. Thoms. Marsh for 14 days do.
Mr. John Whittington for 13 days do.
Mr. Solomon Wright for 9 days do.
Jacob Blangy for 275 squir. & 19 crows
Patrick Sexton for cloathing Elizab: Malogue
John Fowler for 20 squir. & 4 crows
Colo. Richd. Tilghman for insolvt. tax
Do for salary not allowed in 1710
Do by assignment of Darby Cavanagh
Do for 1 wolf's head Indian killing
Robt. Jones by assignmt. from Darby Cavanagh
Charles Erickson for 17 squir. & 1 crow
Jacob Covington for 12 squir. & 3 crows
James Hutchens for 58 squr.
John Winchester for 72 squir.
Benj. Wicks for 20 squir. Nichs. Clouds for 13 squir. & 17 crows
Marma. Goodhand for 131 squr.
Robt. Walters for 23 squir. & 4 crows
Nicho. Cummins for 32 squirr.
Alexander Toulson for 24 squirr.
Salandine Eagle for 139 squir. & 12 crows
Robert Blunt for 57 squir.
John Rawls for 20 squirr. & 1 crow
Patrick Sexton for 9 crows
William Elliot for 6 crows & 6 squirr.
John White for 34 squirr heads
Charles Stevens for 22 squirr.
John Meredith for 40 squir. & 4 crows
Mr. Heath for a levy anno 1712 (taken in pd.: for)
Thomas Honey for keeping Cath: Innocence
Do for a coffin & burying of her
William Hamblton for keeping Mary Underwood
John Atkinson for a lame man his brother & carrying him to Doctor Godmans

Humphr: Wells for Zerababell Wells levy
Henry Wilkinson a poor man
Humph: Wells for Zorab: Wells this year's levy
Patrick Sexton for Mary Malogue omitted last year
William Bryan a poor man on Kent [Island]
Robert Jones, coroner for 2 inquisitions
William Hollinsworth for 5 wolves' heads
Patrick Laughan a poor man on Kent [Island]
John Oldson for Kent ferry keeping
Bryan Connelly a poor man
Edwd. Winlock for 1710 & 1713, a poor man
Jane Howe for cleaning the court house
Majr. Turlo for 5 days attend. this court
Mr. John Wells for 5 do.
Mr. Thoms. Marsh for 5 do.
Mr. Solomon Wright for 5 do.
Mr. John Whittington for 3 days do.
Mr. Thomas Fisher for 5 days do.
The president for the great seal
Jos. Earle for the G. Jury in 9ber 1712
The president more for the great seal
Mr. Phill. Hemsley for insolvt. tax
Colo. Lowe for 13 criminals fees

March Court 1713/14

p. 255. George Jackson was appointed overseer from this town to the Wading Place from then to Mr. Bennetts plantation and from thence to this town.

Robert Hollingworth was appointed constable for Town Hundred.

Renatus Smith was appointed constable for Island Hundred.

Robert Macklyn was appointed constable for Worrell Hundred.

William Salisbury prayed that a road be cleared from the middle of Spaniards Neck to the main road below Thomas Bailys. Granted.

James Kersey was appointed overseer of the highways from Collins Mill to Cattail Bridge.

At the petition of Jno. Wetherby, Richard Smith ordered to pay him 1000 lbs. of tobacco.

It was ordered that William Typins appointed overseer of the highways from Chester to the Cattail Branch.

John Gilberd late apprentice to Mathias Boly prayed to be discharged from apprenticeship, his master being dead. Set free.

It was ordered that Humphrey Wells be overseer of the highways from Pearls Branch to the head of the Chester River.

p. 256. Thomas Murphey, sawyer, was summoned to answer Mathew Errickson and his wife Katherine late called Katherine Bowdle, one of the execs. of the last will of Mary Sergeant, widow, dec'd. and Priscilla B---, co-extx., with a demand for 500 lbs. of tobacco owed to Mary Sergeant in her life time.

Anne Williams prayed that Edward Harris may be summoned to show cause why he detains her a servant, having been free a long time. Ordered set free.

Mary Hobbs, servant to Richd. Moor prayed that she be freed. Ordered to serve 1 1/2 years more from 23 Feb last and he to find her two shifts, a pettycoat and waistcoat of country cloath, at the end of her time.

David Shulager lately hired servant to Doctor Andrew Imbert for the value of 1000 lbs. of tobacco and having demanded the same it was denied. Judgment made for 856 remaining lbs. of tobacco to be paid to him.

p. 259. Christopher Ainiger who petitioned that he was afflicted with lameness and other distempers was allowed 1000 lbs. of tobacco the next levy.

p. 260. John Chaires next friend to Sarah Poor set forth that Sarah was very much abused by Robert Walker her now father-in-law, husband to the guardian in law of the said Sarah, praying that Sarah be removed and another guardian assigned. The petition was rejected.

p. 268. Sarah Hopwood declared that Charles Young as the begetter of her bastard child. Fined 600 lbs. of tobacco. William Granger and Benjamin Wicks her security.

It was presented that Sarah Halfpeny of St. Paul's Parish of Queen Anne's Co., spinster, on 28 Dec 1712 committed fornication and begot a child. Fined 600 lbs. of tobacco. Fine paid by John Roe.

June Court 1714

p. 271. Mary Leake[?] was bound to serve John Roberts until age 18, she being 4 years old.

Francis Hayes and his wife Bridgett appears according to their recognizances.

John Obryan was bound by the court to serve Thomas Shoobrooks until age 21, he being 6 years July next.

John Burdon and his wife Rose appeared according to their recognizances.

p. 272. Thomas Baxter, orphan son of Thomas Baxter, chose as guardian Thomas Cooper.

It was ordered that Frances Lane, wife of John Lane, Jr., give security for her appearance at next court.

p. 281. Despite the petition of Christopher Denny the children of Maurice Lane remained with the father-in-law William Martin who m. Rebecca Lane, mother of the children.

George Sanders, servant of Johannis Dehenoyossa, complained of abuse by his master. The court ordered him to remain with his master.

p. 282. Thomas Greenaway, orphan boy, was bound to Thomas Hynson Wright until age 21, he being 13 years old last March.

Thomas Silvester in behalf of James Silvester, an orphan, showed that the real estate of the orphan consisting of a plant., housing, orchard, fencing, are suffered to go to destruction and are very much wasted. Thomas Silvester was appointed guardian.

William Dean, orphan boy, was bound to serve William Turbutt until age 21, he being 10 years old last May.

p. 283. Barbara Jackson prayed to prove an account due from John Seymour due to her husband Thomas Jackson.

p. 284. William Vaughan was summoned to answer Robert Baynard and his wife Sarah late called Sarah Hall, admx. of Richard Hall who d. intestate. They complained that William Vaughan owed the estate 1500 lbs. of tobacco valued at 125 shillings.

p. 288. William Wrench of QA Co., planter, son and heir of William Wrench, glasier, dec., to summoned to answer Richard Bennett, Esq. of a plea that he render to him the sum of 5202 lbs. of tobacco.

November Court 1714

p. 306. Elizabeth Williams petitioned that she was hired to Joseph Jennings and she was taken sick and lame, unable to work, and Joseph Jennings carried her to Bryan Conellys and she was unable to work since. Jennings was required to pay her 260 lbs. of tobacco.

p. 307. Thomas Head [Read?] showed that he had a son named Matthew Head [Read?] who was a very great charge to him, Matthew not having the use of his limbs. He was exempted from paying any future levies.

Barbara Jackson, wife of Thomas Jackson asked for 47 days of runaway time against a servant named Mary Sanders. Approved.

p. 313. It was presented that John Thomas, labourer, on 14 Nov 1714 stole a saddle and bridle of Edward Gray worth 40. Acquitted.

p. 320. Christopher Gould, ship carpenter, and his wife Sarah, lately called Sarah Boulton, extx. of the will of William Boulton of KE Co. to answer Micajah Perry of a debt of 449 lbs. of tobacco.

p. 329. A petition was submitted by James Butler stating that he being a servant for a term of years to Robert Jones and having two small children which would perish unless they are bound. The children were bound to Robert Jones. The son William was bound to age 21, he being 6 years old 7 Dec next. The other child, Margaret Butler, was bound to serve until age 18, she being 3 years old on 7 Nov instant.

p. 330. Frances Row, widow, submitted a petition stated that she had living with her for many years, Frances Millington, an old woman and asked for support to maintain her. An amount of 500 lbs. of tobacco was allowed.

It was ordered that John Oldson of Kent Island replace Thomas Cooper in the keeping of the ferry on Kent Island.

p. 331. It was presented that Thomas Falconer, labourer, on 15 Nov in the 12th year of the reigne of the Queen, at Wye Hundred, committed adultery with Sarah Falconer, wife of John Falconer. Witnesses Edward Hyett and Ellinor Falconer. Not guilty. His sureties were John and Benjamin Falconer.

p. 339. It was presented that Benjamin Falconer, labourer, on 30 Oct in the 12th year of the reign of the Queen stole and carried away a barrow hog, owner unknown. He was ordered to receive 25 lashes and sit in the pillory for one hour. His sureties were John and Thomas Falconer.

p. 354. The sheriff, William Sweatnam, announced election results. elected to the General Assembly John Whittington, Charles Wright, Solomon Clayton and Edward Brown.

John Salter was appointed one of his majesty's justices of the county.

p. 355. William Hackett at the request of James Kersey stood as a godfather to his son John and the said James as also Elizabeth his wife and mother of the child are both dead and the child in a manner left destitute, only under the tuition of a father-in-law. Hackett with the permission of the father-in-law took the boy home with him to be instructed and requests that the boy be bound to him. The court agreed and he was bound to him to the trade of a weaver.

p. 356. Charles Downes was appointed constable of Worrell Hundred.

John Swift was appointed constable of Town Hundred.

William Hambleton was appointed constable of Island Hundred.

Doctor Thomas Godman brought Joseph Leake and had him bound to him to the age of 21, to learn the trade of house carpenter.

p. 358. Anne Smith complained against her mistress, Elizabeth Imbert; the court summoned her to appear.

p. 359. Sarah Sweet showed that she was kept by force by Michael Moor in his service for no wages. She was freed.

William Smith stated that he had broken a rib from a fall out of a loft and has been unable to earn a livelihood. He was to be allowed 600 lbs. of tob. at the next levy.

p. 360. John Daly of Kent Island, receiving 1000 lbs. for the maintenance of old William Bryan, requests payment for the burying of Bryan's wife.

Dorothy Jones, dau. of John Jones, dec'd., chose as her guardian, Thomas Hynson Wright - John Johnson, security.

p. 361. A petition was submitted by Bryan Biggs and his wife Margaret Biggs showing that she served George Powell for 4 years by indenture from Waterford, Ireland, the said term being expired 10 years on 26 Feb last past and cannot get her freedom dues. The court ordered George Powell to deliver to Bryan Biggs, 3 barrels of corn due to the said Bryan's wife.

p. 363. John Carradyne was fined for two oaths.

p. 364. It was presented that Robert Gary, labourer, on 15 Sep 1714 at St. Paul's Parish assaulted Jane Brans(?) wife of John Brans(?).

William Kerby brought the two following writtings 24 July 1710. Be it known ... that I James Sudler of Kent Island ... acquit and discharge Elizabeth Walters of the said Island and province, widow, of and from that part or portion of Walter Kerby's estate which became due to my wife Rebecca Sudler, as her child's part or portion (viz.) the sum 10.17 as also of and from all other debts, dues and demands, from the beginning of the world to the day of the date hereof.

March Court 1714/15

p. 388. 23 March 1714/15 Then received of William Kerby the sum of . £10.11 current mony it being if full of my wife's portion or part of her father's estate this day received per George Jackson.

June Court 1715

p. 389. James Earle petitioned showing that soon after his father's decease he with the consent and advice of his guardian, Richard Tilghman, Esq., bound himself to Wornell Hunt, Esq., one of the practitioners of the law not only in the Provincial Court of this Province, but in divers of the inferiour courts within the same province, and he has completed his time and wishes to take the oath usually admitted to attorneys. He was given liberty to practice in this court.

Nathaniel Comegys was appointed overseer of the highways instead of Andrew King, from Queens Town to Chester Mill, from thence to Solo. Tilghman's plantation and from thence to the sd. town.

p. 390. George Smith chose as his guardian Richard Moor; he to learn the tract of carpenter.

Matthew Collier brought an orphan boy named Richard Bishop and prayed to have him bound to him until age 21, to the tract of smith. Approved.

William Salisbury brought an orphan boy named William Bishop and prayed to have him bound to him until age 21 to the trade of house carpenter. Approved.

p. 391. Richard Moor prayed to have Robert Smith, an orphan boy, be bound to him until age 21. Approved.

p. 392. It was presented that Anne Dazey, spinster, servant to William Hackett, on 1 April 1715 in Town Hundred committed fornication. She named Arthur Arling as the father of her child. She was ordered to receive 30 lashes.

It was presented that Jane Herring, servant to Robert Hollingworth, spinster, on 1 April 1714 committed fornication and begot a base child. She named William Nunam as the father of her child. She was ordered to receive 6 lashes.

p. 393. Effey Jones, wife of Thomas Jones made oath the she is in danger of her life or bodily injury by reason of abuses she received from her husband Thomas Jones.

In the petition of Mary Moor of Kent Island, wife of George Moor, stated that about 18 months earlier she was by threats and menaces not only from her husband but from John Hawkins of the afsd. Island of Kent to whom her husband was and still is a servant for a certain debt paid by the said Hawkins was forced to enter into a covenant with the said Hawkins for 4 years and in return Hawkins would maintain and keep one of her children. However he never was any charge or trouble in keeping the child.

p. 401. Thomas Tanner, orphan, chose as his guardian William Legg.

Francis Rochester states that having kept an orphan child of Richard Bishop about 2 years, seeks some support. Denied.

It was ordered that Thomas Cooper keep the ferry at Kent Island instead of John Oldson.

John Ryan made a complaint against his master, Philemon Lloyd, Esq.

p. 404. It was presented that John Murfey of Island Hundred on 21 March 1714 stole some Indian meal valued at 12 pence belonging to Charles Hollingsworth. Acquitted.

It was presented that Charles Young on 20 Oct 1713 at St. Paul's Parish, committed fornication with Sarah Hopwood. Acquitted.

August Court 1715

p. 423. David Clark complained of abuse by his mater Johannis Dehinoyossa.

John Ryan complained that he should be discharged from his service to Philemon Lloyd, Esq. Ordered to be freed.

p. 424. It was presented that John Johnson of Island Hundred on 1 April 1715 had given away or sold an orphan boy called John Douglas which had been bound to him and otherwise abused the John Douglas. Fined 100 lbs. of tob. John Roe was ordered to bring the boy to court.

p. 425. It was presented that John Bennett, Jr., on 20 Nov 1715 stole and bore away a hog, owner unknown.

p. 426. It was presented that Gilbert Tate of Town Hundred on 20 Nov 1714 stole and bore a way a hog, owner unknown. Acquitted.

p. 427. It was presented that William Tate stole and bore away a hog, owner unknown.

p. 428. It was presented that James Lipsey, on 11 Nov 1714 stole a bridle of Charles Lemare. Not guilty.

p. 431. Thomas Williams, chirurgion, and his wife Elizabeth als Elizabeth Thomas, widow, were summoned to answer Elizabeth Carter, widow, admx. of Richard Carter, Gent., that they render to her 2109 lbs. of tobacco.

p. 463. Thomas Jackson asked for allowance of his wife, sons and servant as evidences for Edward Heyatt defendant agst. Thomas Falconer, plaintiff. Barbara Jackson attended 3 days; Mary Sanders, servant to the said Thomas Jackson attended 3 days; Francis Jackson, son of sd. Thomas Jackson, attended 6 days, Joseph Jackson attended 5 days.

p.464. John Hawkins, Jr. requested a license to keep a public house in Queens Town and was rejected.

p. 475. John Wright, son of Solomon Wright received bounty for 33 squirrels.

p. 478. John Heath, a poor blind man upon petition was allowed 1500 lbs. of tob. toward the passage of himself and wife to England.

p. 479. Jacob Covington was allowed 500 lbs. of tob. for keeping Elizabeth Gibson, a poor object of charity some small time and burying her.

March Court 1715/16

p. 480. The election results Majr. John Hawkins, Mr. Charles Wright, Mr. William Turbutt and Mr. Edward Wright to serve as delegates of the county at the General Assembly.

p. 485. Elizabeth Salisbury prayed for runaway time against her servant

Mary Bradburn for 25 days. Accepted and ordered to serve 10 days for each day of absence.

p. 486. Elizabeth Salisbury, widow and relict of William Salisbury, brought an orphan boy named William Bishop who had been bound at June Court last as an apprentice to sd. Salisbury. Matthew Collier and William Bishop had also been appointed as guardians to two of the sons of Richard Bishop, one of them being bound to Wm. Salisbury and one bound to Matthew Collier. Elizabeth Salisbury asks that the court take him under their care and release her from her husband's obligation. William Bishop was then bound to Matthew Collier.

Barbara Jackson brought her servant, Mary Saunders and was awarded 12 days runaway time.

p. 487. James Hutchins prayed for allowance for looking after Mary Moor in her sickness and burying her, as also for maintaining a child of the said Mary Morr named George Moor.

p. 488. Valentine Carter brought an orphan girl named Mary Harris and had her bound to him until age 18, she being 9 years old last Feb.

p. 489. Perigrina Nailler stated that being formerly a servant of Thomas Silvester, when her time was nearly expired, she signed an indenture for 4 years longer, partly because of threats and partly by persuasions. Freed.

George Jackson brought an orphan boy named Edward Young and had him bound to him until age 21 to the trade of carpenter.

p. 490. William Hackett was given 45 runaway days against his servant Arthur Arnull.

John Wright brought an orphan girl Elizabeth Tryall and had her bound to him, alleging that the child's mother, Sarah Gary, left the child to his wife (in her will). She was ordered to serve John Wright until the age given in the will.

Isaac Winchester chose as his guardian Robert Jones.

p. 491. John Wood and his wife Elizabeth were ordered to testify for the court but refused and were fined 500 lbs. of tobacco each.

p. 492. Robert Ivy chose as his guardian Renatus Smith.

Augustine Thompson was appointed overseer of the road from Whittalls Bridge to Mr. John Whittington's plantation, from thence to Chester River, opposite to New Towne and from Whittalls Bridge to Thompson's dwelling plantation.

p. 493. John Thompson, illegitimate son of Anne Thompson, was bound by the court to serve Andrew Fe---.

p. 501. It was presented that Anne Thompson, spinster, on 1 Feb 1715 in St. Paul's Parish committed fornication. She named John Hammitt as the father. She was ordered to receive 6 lashes.

p. 502. It was presented that Eleanor Fitzgerrald, spinster, late servant to Arthur Emory of Worrell Hundred, had a base born child 2 March 1715. She refused to name the father. She was ordered to receive 11 lashes. Edmund Thomas asked the court for damages by reason of Eleanor having two bastard children whilst a servant. It appeared to the court that one of the children was dead. Eleanor was ordered to serve her master one additional year.

p. 515. Eliza. Watters of QA Co., widow, otherwise Elizabeth Watters of Kent Island, widow, were summoned to answer Benjamin Ball of a plea that they render him the sum of 1340 lbs. of tobacco.

TALBOT COUNTY JUDGMENT RECORDS
Liber BB2 (1662-1674)

January Court 1685

John Nowler, servant to Daniell Glover was judged to be 15 years old.

George Scarr, servant to John Boram, was judged to be 11 years old.

Robert Holland, servant to John Eason, was judged at 11 years of age.

Marey Makey, servant to Richard Sweatnam, was judged at 21 years of age.

It was presented that Mary Hackett, wife of Nicholas Hackett, accompanied scandalously with Richard Stevens. January Court 1685 ordered 39 lashes.

It was presented by Majr. Peter Sayer, high sheriff, that Thomas Jackson struck at him and gave him scurrilous language.

James Davis claimed he had served his full time of servitude by indenture to Christopher --- master of the ship Forrister who sold him to William Bishopp. The court ordered that he be given his freedom corn and paid for overplus of time.

It was ordered that the orphan George Barkhurst live with Christopher Denny until age 18.

In a petition by Peter Hadaway it was shewn that John Jordaine, son of Alexander Jordaine was left in the county by the said Alexander his father in the custody of Christopher Binder, son in law to the said Alexander who had now deserted the province. The petitioner being his uncle took charge of the said John Jordaine and requested that the boy be made over to him by law, until age 21. The court approved, stating that the last five years were to be spent by the boy in the said Peter's trade of carpenter and cooper.

It was requested by Michael Hackett that he have license to keep a ferry over the Chester River to the town of West Chester. Approved.

It was presented that Robert Macklin, planter, on 23 Dec 1685 in Spaniard Neck of TA Co. stole a hog of Thomas Jones, dec'd.

Jefferry Hardman, servant to Michaell Turbott, was set free.

TALBOT COUNTY JUDGMENT RECORDS
Liber NN6 (1686-1689)

February Court 1685

John Roach, servant to Francis Shepheard was judged to be 14 years of age.
William Lee, servant to Andrew Orem, was judged to be 13 years of age.

Henry Cross, servant to Loveless Gorsuch, was judged to be 16 years of age.

Elizabeth Rafes, servant to Frances Bishopp, was judged to be 14 years of age.

Mary Williams, servant to Morgin Thomas, was judged to be 9 years old.

Mary Godfrey, servant to Nicholas Cloudes, was judged to be 18 years old.

Hannah Raimus, servant to Nicholas Cloudes, was judged to be 18 years old.

At November Court 1685 Richard Steevens gave security for his good behaviour in not associating or coming in company with Mary, wife of Nicholas Hackett; at the next court in February 1685 he was cleared from further action.

John Hughs, in a petition, he said he was bound by his father, Thomas Hughes of Northam in the county of Devon, taylor, to serve Wm. Bishopp of TA Co., merchant, during his life or the term of 6 years, whichever occurred first. The term began with his arrival in Maryland on the ship named the *Robert and William* of Barnstable. The indenture was signed on 29 Oct 1683. Mr. Bishopp being dead the petitioner asked to be free. The court ordered that he continue his service under the executorship of Bishop's will.

Rebecca Bingham, widow of Thomas Bingham petitioned to get a bed and furniture which was promised to her when she resigned the administration of her husband's estate to Thomas Bayley.

March Court 1685/6

Charles Hall, servant to John Newman, was judged to be 18 years old.

Elizabeth Howell, servant to John Newman, was judged to be 18 years old.

Ruth Wilson, servant to Robert Hawkshaw, was judged to be 13 years old.

Anthony Penington, servant to John Kinimount, declared that he was sold to sd. John Kinemount but for 4 years as would appear in writing from under the hand of Isaac Cox, carpenters mate of London, Capt. Phinehas Hide, commander, which said Isaac Cox sold the sd. Anthony Penington to the sd. Kinemount.

It was presented that Elizabeth Loller [Chester Hundred] had borne a bastard child, she being a servant to Michaell Hackett.

Thomas Mountfort, constable of Mill Hundred, presented Mary Kenam for bearing a bastard child, being 22 Feb 1685/6.

It was presented that Mary Richardson, servant to Mr. Wollman was lately delivered of a bastard child.

It was presented that Susanah Shawe, servant to Richard Sweatnam, lately delivered of a bastard child.

A complaint was made against Thomas Jackson that he is a vagabond and vagrant. He was accused of entering the plantation of William Dixon on Miles River and entering the house without permission, took, ate and destroyed their provisions and the said Jackson assaulted sd. William Dixon's servant and child. William Allen said that Jackson threatened and terrified his wife and children. Jacob Abraham said that Jackson assaulted and beat him with the round of a ladder with a knife in his hand. The court ordered that Thomas Jackson immediately be apprehended.

John Hollingsworth sought payment for interring the body of Hugh Johnson, dec'd. which he did in Dec 1683 as ordered by William Bishopp, admin. of the estate, who d. before payment was made.

It was presented that Hugh Hunt, chyrurgeon, entered the plant. of Henrietta Maria Lloyd and took 2 hhds. of tobacco and 6 barrels of Indian corn. Ordered to pay to Henrietta Maria Lloyd 800 lbs. of tobacco and 6 barrels of Indian corn.

June Court 1686

Ann Coltman, servant to Edward Elliott was judged to be 15 years old.

Daniell Smith, servant to John Stanley, was judged to be 14 years old.

Alexander Grames, servant to Henry Greene was judged to be 14 years old.

It was ordered Mary Pearce live with William Hackett until she arrived at the age of 16 or date of marriage.

It was ordered that Sarah Pearce live with Daniel Swindell until age 16 or day of marriage.

John Norman, servant to Capt. William Combes, was judged to be 13 years old.

Mary Hall, servant to Griffith Jones, was judged to be 13 years old.

John Clement, servant to William Berry, was judged to be 15 years old.

Griffith Jones was fined 500 lbs. of tobacco for affronting Majr. Peter Sayer, High Sheriff of the county.

It was ordered that John Lewis, orphan of Thomas Lewis go along and abide with his brother-in-law Henry Everitt until the next court, then to prove that he is 14 years old.

Ann Bunsell chose as her guardian John Emerson.

William Jackson chose his brother Thomas Jackson to be his guardian.

Saffiah Furby chose John Pemberton to be her guardian.

It was ordered that Elizabeth Evirett keep Elizabeth Lloyd until she arrives at the age of 21.

Margarett Nickson, servant to Stephen Jurdaine, was judged to be 16 years old.

John Pearce was bound to John Lafield until age 18, to be taught by said Lafield and John Whittington, the trade of cooper and carpenter.

Kymton Mabbot of DO Co. petitioned for runaway time for Haniball Haskins, his servant, who ran away for 12 months.

It was presented that William Harris of TA Co., planter, late overseer to Mr. Richard Royston of the same county, abused Oney Richardson by kicking her and calling her --- whore and papist whore.

Katherine Emerson, widow, stated that her husband, in his lifetime, was ordered by the court to take under his care the estate of William Cook, dec'd., for the security of the orphans of William Jones and administer upon the same was granted to him but her husband died before the estate was settled and she wishes to be quit of the estate.

It was presented that where Mary Richardson, servant to Mr. Woolman was presented in March Court last for bearing a bastard child and when summoned, disappeared. Nor ordered to received 15 lashes.

It was presented that Susanah Shawe, servant to Richard Sweatnam, bore a bastard child. Ordered to receive 5 lashes.

August Court 1686

Ann Shongshaw, servant to Mr. Tho. Vaughan, was judged to be 13 years of age.

Thomas Mecantlis, servant, to Mr. George Mecantlis was judged to be 12 years of age.

John Burdin, servant to Mr. George Robins, was judged to be 12 years old.

It was ordered that William Jones be free from John Davies.

It was ordered that William Priske be struck out of the levies.

Katherine Catterson, widow of Francis Catterson of the town of Oxford., innholder, petitioned to receive a license in order to continue to keep an ordinary at Oxford as her husband had done for the previous two years. Approved.

James Studley, servant to Mr. William Dickinson, complained that John Sangoe, contrary to the order and approbation of said William Dickinson, whipped and beat the said James most unchristian like. John Sango was ordered to receive 21 lashes.

Elizabeth Lewis complained against the violence and injury done and threatened against her by John Goodin.

Philemon Armstrong, son of Francis Armstrong, dec'd., chose as his guardian Thomas Smithson.

Margarett Gill, late wife of Henry Gill, dec'd., stated that she was in poor disordered condition with a child to maintain out of her own labor, having received nothing from her husband's estate; Robert Smith keeping all from her including her bed.

John Hawkins and his wife Eliza. complained against John Gatterlea regarding a transaction in September 1684 when said Eliza. was unmarried.

January Court 1686

Jno. Parker, servant to Francis Harris, was judged to be 12 years old.

Tho: Browne, servant to Samuell Abbott was judged to be 13 years old.

Edmund Hurst, servant to Jno. Whittington, was judged to be 11 years old.

Tho: Chambers, servant to Samuell Farmer, was judged to be 14 years old.

George Winston, servant to Wallter Quinton, was judged to be 11 years old.

Margrett Millin, servant to Wm. Bexly, was judged to be 17 years old.

William Sillcock, servant to Wm. Bexly, was judged to be 19 years old.

George Pooly, servant to Jno. Hollingsworth, was judged to be 15 years old.

Robert Jenkinson was found guilty of hog stealing. Ordered to receive 50 lashes and ordered to stand in the pillory for one hour.

John Hollingsworth was fined 500 lbs. of tobacco for absenting himself from the jury without leave.

It was ordered that George Hurlocke either bring Eliza. Potter and --- her parents, John Coppin and Sarah his wife before the next court, or such testimony sufficient of her marriage and that he the said George Hurlocke enter into recognizance. George Hurlocke and Eliza. Potter were presented for notorious living in common fame.

It was ordered that William Jones be set free.

Daniell Harrison was found guilty of the presentment for living in common fame with Sarah Jones, wife of Edward Jones. Ordered to receive 10 lashes.

It was presented that Edwd. Pond packed --- in tobacco ---.

It was presented that Sarah Ask, servant to Richd. Goold, had a bastard child.

It was presented that Jane Willson and Eliza. Reed, servants to Robert Macklin, had bastard children. Eliza. Read named Robert Macklin as the father of her child; she was ordered to have 15 lashes. At June Court 1687 the court considered that Robert Macklin was to bear the county harmless from the maintenance of the child and to pay to Elizabeth her freedom corn and cloathes. At August Court 1688 she was ordered to receive 15 lashes.

It was presented that Thomas Bruffe by the information of John Davis, --- a mare and a horse colt.

It was presented that Thomas Bruffe of Chester entertained people and made of them drunk on the Lord's day, 29 Aug last past. By the information of John Chaier and Rebeckah Bingham.

February Court 1686

John Richardson, servant to Ralph Burges was judged to be 11 years old.

William Gabroll, servant to Wm. Dickinson, was judged to be 16 years old.

Edward Cockraine, servant to Cornelius Mulraigne, was judged to be 8 years old.

William Sanders, servant to Capt. Wm. Combs, was judged to be 12 years old.

March Court 1686
Richard Jackson, servant to Miss Mary Roe, was judged to be 18 years old.

Bennett Jump, servant to Miss Alice Rich, was judged to be 12 years old.

William Murphy, servant to the estate of Thomas Taylor of Kings Creek, was judged to be 14 years old.

George Hurlock was bound in recognizance to restore the body of Eliza. Potter to her father or mother or bring a testimonial sufficient of her marriage which he did and is clear by proclamation.

It was presented that Eliza. Fry[?] had a bastard child.

It was presented that Margarett Wright had a bastard child.

It was presented that Martha N--ld had a bastard child.

It was presented that Eliza. Price bore a bastard child.

It was presented that Mary Welch bore a bastard child.

It was presented that Issabell Cole bore a bastard child. At June Court she refused to name the father. She was ordered to receive 30 lashes and 20 additional lashes for refusing to name the father.

It was presented that Ann Moody bore a bastard child. At June Court she refused to name the father and received 30 lashes with 20 lashes more for refusing to name the father.

It was presented that Eliza. Potter had a bastard child. She was ordered to receive 30 lashes for baring the child and 20 more lashes for refusing to name the father.

It was presented that Kempton Mabbott, of Oxford, innholder, kept unlawful games in his house and keeping an ordinary without a lycence.

It was presented that John Booth, servant unlawfully absented himself from his master, John Davies.

June Court 1687
Edward Jeoffreys, servant to James Smith, was judged to be 12 years old.

George Phillips, servant to Arthur Emery, was judged to be 3 years old.

It was ordered that Mary Merirt[?] live with Robert Fortune until she was 18 years of age.

It was ordered that Charrity Jones live with John Pemberton until age 18.

It was ordered that William Tottenham live with John Pemberton until age 21, to be taught a trade as cooper.

It was ordered that Ann Barnes with the consent of her mother Ann Barns live with Michaell Russell until age 16.

It was ordered that Thomas Shanks live with Alice Rich until age 21.

It was ordered that Thomas Sutton live with Issabell Doud until age 18.

Robert Kitchin having been committed to prison for attempting to carry out of the province a woman servant belonging to Mr. Richard Smith.

A license was granted to Michael Hackett to keep an ordinary.

A license was granted to William Nevill to keep an ordinary at Chester.

It was presented that Kempton Mabbott of Oxford in his dwelling house kept a place of gaming: cards, dice and tables and other unlawful games. Found guilty. Ordered to give up his license to keep an ordinary. At August Court 1687 he was ordered to forfeit 3 shillings, 4 pence.

It was presented that Eliza. Fry bore a bastard child. Ordered to receive 30 lashes.

It was presented that Margrett White bore a bastard child. Ordered to receive 30 lashes.

It was presented that Martha Nelds bore a bastard child. Ordered to receive 12 lashes.

It was presented that Elizabeth Price having been presented for baring a bastard child, named the father as Joseph West which he confirmed.

It was presented that Mary Welch bore a bastard child; she refused to declare the father. Ordered to receive 30 lashes.

Jane Wynn, was brought into the county a servant to Humphry Davenport, late dec'd., for the term of 3 years which expired in November last and seeks to be freed but is detained by Thomas Bruffe. Ordered freed.

Thomas Vaughan stated that he had kept Garrett Fitzgarrald, son of Garratt Fitzgarrald nearly 2 years and his father has left the county; he wished to have the boy bound to him until age 21. Approved.

John Burges declared that he had taken a child of John Bowing to nurse, the child being a bastard child of John Bowing. John Burges had made an agreement with John Bowing at the house of Edward Man for to have 1000 lbs. of tobacco and all necessaries as clothing, sope and sugar to be provided by Bowing. Edwd. Man appeared and engaged before the court to take the child after the court year is expired with John Burges, the county to pay the 1000 lbs. of tobacco, and the mother to make satisfaction for the same when free.

Thomas Jackson, Jr., stated that about this time 12 month was chosen guardian to his brother William Jackson, orphan Richard Jackson, dec'd., who made Richd.

Mirax and Thomas Thompson, execs. to the estate till the said orphant be at age which estate of late has been much neglected so as the plant. and stock goes to ruin to the great loss of the orphant and the said execs. have not yet exhibited an account of the said estate according to law.

August Court 1687

James Scott stated that whereas Rebeckah Cooke, wife of William Cooke, dec'd., lay sick about 8 days and then died. James Scott seeks payment for the coffin of 8000 lbs. of tobacco. It was ordered that Eliza. Cooke, dau. of afsd. Rebeckah Cook, about 4 years of age, live with the afsd. James Scott until she arrived at the age of 16.

Henry Allexander stated he had a servant named John Lahey who absented himself 6-7 months. The court ordered that he serve an additional 2 years.

Barbarah Middleton stated she was formerly servant to Rhoda Earle, later Brooff [Bruff] and in the time of the said Rhoda's being in widowhood was servant and through ignorance served her a complete year more that the agreement. Rhoda Brooff was ordered to appear at the next court.

Rebecah Mitchell chose Michaell Turbutt as her guardian.

Mary Richardson, servant to Richd. Woolman, was ordered to serve him an additional 12 months for bearing a bastard child.

William Butler acknowledged his security to be given for his not associating or coming in company with Hannah, wife of Christopher Batson.

Eliza. Redish, being brought for bearing a bastard child, swore that sometime in March last was 12 months about midst of the day coming in from work with Robt. Bryant, her then master he desired to have carnal copulation with her pretending she was his; she answered that was none of his but at last consented and gave him liberty and he had the knowledge of her body lying with her on the cubbard bed where he usually lodged, some time after he had the like carnal copulation with her in the freemans room and where the freemans lodged, at another time he had the like were the boy lodged after several other times she cannot remember. That the first munday in Oct last the said Robt. about sun set had the knowledge of her body in one of the said Robert's tobacco houses which was the last time. She swore that Robert Bryan, cooper, was the father of her bastard child. She was ordered to receive 20 lashes. Robert Bryant was ordered to maintain the child.

It was presented that John Ponder of Chester Hundred stole rum and sugar of Tho. Harmon and Henery Robinson, merchants.

It was presented that John Price, brick maker, stole a turkey cock of Robt. Bryant, cooper.

It was presented that Robert B. Sumpter, planter, stole a blue shirt of Robt.

Bryant, cooper.

It was presented that Francis Harrison and Benony Porter, planters, committed a breach of peace on the plant. of Tho: Beondeth[?].

It was presented that Robt. Sumpter, planter, on 10 July at Tred haven Creek stole a blue shire of Edward Jones. He was ordered to receive 20 lashes.

It was presented that Francis Harrison and Benony Porter, planters, on 13 April 1687 and at divers other days and times entered the plant. of Thomas Bowdell in Island Creek called Mitcham Hall, committed a breach of the peace.

It was made known that Capt. William Lawrence of Kent gave to Mary Bexly, dau. of William Bexley, a cow calf which increase if a total of 4 head, and Mary Bexley had died, and Capt. Lawrence now has given these cattle to Rachell Bexley, sister of afsd. Mary Bexley on 13 Aug 1687.

It was presented that Alice Rutee, spinster, servant hireling to Richard Carter, merchant, stood to answer to Gr: Jones and Eliza: his wife that she assaulted said Eliza: being great with child, on 28 Feb 1686.

September Court 1687

Peter Sydes obtained a judgment against his servants Charles Wilson and William Smith of 15 days of runaway time.

It was presented that Pattrick and Charles Culliner had made their escape from the goaler of the county.

John Man and Sarah his wife, execs. of the will of Tho: Cox, were summoned to answer Robt. Merrit of a plea of debt.

October Court 1687

Payment was authorized to John Burges for keeping a bastard child of Martha Reed.

November Court 1687

It was ordered that Geo: Hays live with Edward Tomlin until age 21, to be taught the trade of a shoemaker.

John Burton having been committed to prison for being drunk and committing a breach of peace, he was fined 500 lbs. of tobacco.

It was presented that Robt. Dennum stole a saddle and furniture.

It was presented that Sarah Hanson bore a bastard child. At March Court she was ordered to receive 15 lashes.

It was presented that Mary Easgate bore a bastard child.

It was presented that Bridgett Tattenham bore a bastard child. At March Court she was ordered to receive 15 lashes.

It was presented that Moses Harris, overseer of roads, had not cleared the roads as warrants to him were directed.

It was presented that Mary Macoy bore a bastard child.

It was presented that Mary Savage bore a bastard child.

It was presented that Thomas Bruff took a mare and branded her, she not being his own.

It was presented that Elliner Hall [Hull?], servant to Wm. Hatfield, bore a bastard child. At March Court she named Wm. Warner as father. She was ordered to receive 15 lashes; the court accepted a fine.

It was presented that Toby, Negro slave to Wm. Dixon stole a hog.

It was presented that Robt. Vaus was guilty of unlawfully ranging in the woods.

It was presented that Jane Johnson bore a bastard child. At March Court she was sentenced to 21 lashes.

It was presented that Robt. Bryant, cooper, hewing cask contrary to Act of Assembly.

It was presented that Jonathan Ayrey was guilty of unlawful hunting in the woods.

It was presented that Mary Grove bore a bastard child.

It was presented that Eliza. Vincent, servant to James Downes, had born a bastard child; she named Negro Guy, servant to said James Downs as the father. He was ordered to serve an additional two years.

It was presented that Richard Stevens was guilty of unlawful ranging in the woods.

It was ordered that Barbarah Vincent, the illegitimate child of Eliza: Vincent, live with James Downes until age 21.

Jno. Bird complained that although Simon Harris and he made an agreement wherein he would teach his dau. Martha Harris to read and write, the said Symon Harris did not fulfill his part of the agreement.

January Court 1687

Edmund Godfrey, servant to William Belford, was judged to be 13 years old.

Elizabeth Butler, servant to Thomas Siffett, was judged to be 14 years old.

John Deacon, servant to Francis Neal was judged to be 14 years old.

George Everatt, servant to John Whittington, was judged to be 16 years old.

Tedy[?] Maner[?], servant to John Pope, was judged to be 17 years old.

Cornealius Dunnican, servant to William Bush, was judged to be 17 years old.

George Lane, servant to Ralph Fishbourne, was judged to be 13 years old.

Marques Harquedan, Servant to Capt. James Murphy, was judged to be 27 years old.

Anthony Gibbs, servant to Andrew Price, was judged to be 10 years old.

Marke Williams, servant to David Blany, was ordered to be freed.

It was presented that Robert Denham, planter, on 28 June 1687 at Tredhaven Hundred, stole a saddle of John Man, planter. He was ordered to restore fourfold the value of the saddle and receive 25 lashes.

It was presented that Robert Bryant, cooper, on 30 March 1687 and at other times, hew and make tobacco hogsheads contrary to the law. Fined 500 lbs. of tobacco.

James Clarke stated he had served his indenture time which was 4 years on 6 Dec 1685 to Richd. Swettnam at the expiration of which time his master set him free, serving him one year more in consideration of which his master was to pay him 1000 lbs. of tobacco which now being expired and one year more over. He was set free.

Sarah Collins requested runaway time on her servant Wm. Wiggons who has absented himself 2 years.

Dorothy Allemby, an orphant now in the possession of Tho: Anderson, to appear at next court to choose her guardian.

March Court 1687

It was presented that John Hacker was guilty of unlawful ranging in the woods.

It was presented that Edmd. Fish stole hogsheads staves belonging to James Laws.

It was presented that David Rogers was guilty of unlawful ranging in the woods.

It was presented that Nath: Wright was guilty of unlawful ranging in the woods.

It was presented that Geoffry Horney stole some hogs.

It was presented that Jno. Emerson, Jacob Gibson, Jno. Brown, James White, Frs. O--- and Wm. Proser did not properly assist Moses Harris, overseer of the highways.

It was presented that Daniell Toaes, merchant, ---- ?

It was presented that Richd. Holland stole a hog.

It was presented that Mortaugh Horney stole a hog.

It was presented that Richard Holland assaulted Wm. Wintersell and his wife.

Fra. Pecock declared that he had been sold by Wm. Dickinson to John Wade of DO Co. for 4 years and since then had been sold to Cornalius --- and his time has now expired. John Wade stated that he had bought him on his arrival in Maryland on 10 May 1684.

Mary Broadhurst stated she had been married for the 11 years to Tho. Broadhurst of the county in all of which time she had undergone great hazard to her life, and because of blows from her husband was unable to turn in her bed. Recently she had come across a letter from her husband's relations which showed he had a wife and son in Chester and that they were well in health. The court appointed Capt. James Murphey to inspect the situation and report to the next court.

Wm. Fuller was ordered to live with Wm. Webb the following year.

Mary Earley, having been presented for bearing a bastard child was ordered to receive 15 lashes.

Symon Rider was given his freedom.

Jane Collinor, a lame woman, petitioned to have an allowance for the payment of doctor bills in the cure of her sore back.

A petition was made by Thomas Osbourne and Richard Daniell in which was stated that whereas Thomas Collins, late of the county, died intestate, leaving three children and since his wife is dec'd. so that the plant. was left destitute without anyone person to dwell thereon to keep it in repair. The children were left to the care of the petitioners. It was ordered that William Scott take an account of the estate of Thomas Collins and report to the next court.

Moses Prisk declared that he had completed his time of servitude with Miss. Eliza. Hatton. She was ordered to appear at the next court.

It was presented that Richard Holland and Susannah his wife on 20 Jan 1686 at Tredhaven assaulted William Wintersell and Jane his wife and stole property belonging to them. Richard Holland was fined 400 lbs. of tobacco for breach of the peace.

It was presented that Jeoffrey Horney of TA Co., planter, on last day of June 1687 at Mill Hundred about 6 of the clock stole a barrow hog of Obedia Judkins. He was ordered to restore four fold the value to Obadia Judkins. Ordered to stand in the pillory for two hours.

It was presented that Mortraugh Horney, laborer, on 28 June 1687 at Mill Hundred stole a barrow Hog of Obediah Junkins. Ordered to restore four fold the value of the hog. Ordered to stand in the pillory for two hours.

It was presented that Daniell Toaes at Doncaster Towne on 10 June 1687 ---.

It was presented that Richard Holland, planter, on 10 Jan 1687 at Mill Hundred stole three barrow hoggs belonging to Benja: Pryde.

It was presented that Toby, Negro of William Dixon, on 10 Nov 1687 stole a hog of Micha: Turbutt. He was ordered to received 39 lashes.

June Court 1688

It was presented that Griff: Jones kept and detained Peter Dennis, son of Peter Dennis, dec'd., and did not give him an education either by a trade or teaching him.

It was presented that Henry Fox of Bay Hundred keeps a child of Robt. Colson late of the county and does not allow it a competent maintenance.

It was presented that Wm. Reede of Mill Hundred being c18 years old on 20 May last stole from Thomas Smithson a white horse.

It was presented that Wm. Thomas of Bay Hundred stole property belonging to Thomas Broadhurst.

It was presented that Micha: Turbutt, Gent. for that Rebekah Mitchell, dau. to John Mitchell, dec'd., was willing to come to this court to make her grievance known but was stopped by the said Mich: Turbutt.

It was presented that Robt. Macklin of Chester Hundred sold goods and merchandize to the value of £90 at his own house contrary to the Act of Assembly.

It was presented that Thomas Jackson, guardian to Wm. Jackson, did not comply with the Act of Assembly.

It was presented that William Berry as one of the execs. of the estate of Thomas Marsh of KE Co. did comply with the Act of Assembly for the maintenance of Mary Marsh by information of Mary Derimple.

It was presented that Thomas Symons as guardian of the wife Margritt for not allowing a competent maintenance according to the Act of the Assembly unto Margrett Walker, dau. of John Walker, dec'd.

It was presented that Capt. George Cowly did not give Eliza. Stapleford her freedom, she being at the age of 16 years and having lived with Capt. Cowley ever since her mother died which was not 10 years.

William ---, servant to Thomas Alcock, was judged to be 14 years old.

John Ryley, servant to Peter Sayer, was judged to be 10 years old.

Katherine Cattafor Stevens, servant to Margrett Peterson was judged to be 18 years old.

Marmaduke Colson, servant to Robt. Macklin, was judged to be 15 years old.

Phillipp Griffin, orphant, was ordered to live with John Burrell until age 21, to be taught the trade of carpenter.

Francis Collins, orphant, was ordered to live with Wm. Scott until she was age 16, to be taught to read and needle work.

Thomas Collins, orphant, was ordered to live with Wm. Finney until age 21, to be taught some trade.

Mary Collins, orphant, was ordered to live with Lawrence Knowles until age 16, to be taught to read and sew.

The petition of Sarah Olliver [later referred to as Sarah Olliver Millington], orphant of James Oliver, dec'd., stated that she had given her by Jno. Raynolds, one cow calf which remained in the hands of Thomas Broadhurst [her father-in-law] but the cow and its increase have been denied to the petitioner. A copy of the deed of gift shows that John Reynolds made the gift in 1678 and a statement confirming this was made on 5 Aug 1685 by John Reynolds with the consent of his wife Waddy Raynolds, Miss Wells and Alice Harris and Mary Olliver.

August Court 1688

Mary Bethorne, servant to Tho: Koggens, was judged to be 4 years old.

It was ordered that William Merier, orphant, to live with Tho: Anderson until age 21.

John Eason refused to serve on the Grand Jury and was fined 500 lbs. of tobacco.

It was presented that Andrew Imbert seduced a servant of Andrew Price.

It was presented that Sarah Conway bore a bastard child.

It was presented that Margrett Savage bore a bastard child.

It was presented that Mary Eagers bore a bastard child and privately concealed the death of the child.

It was presented that Richard Lloyd committed a felony.

It was presented that John Baker stole a hog.

It was presented that Wm. Browne and Eliza. Barker committed a felony.

It was presented that Margrett Miran committed adultery.

It was presented that Eliza. Foster[?] bore a bastard child. At September Court 1688 she was fined 500 lbs. of tobacco.

Henry Greene by consent of his mother Dorothy Greene was ordered to live with Wm. Parrott.

Eliza. Lawler, being presented for bearing a bastard child, was ordered to receive 29 lashes.

Edwd. Bell being presented by the grand jury for hogg stealing, was cleared by proclamation.

Richard Lloyd, servant to William Hemsley, was ordered to serve runaway time.

It was recorded that Nicholas Massey and Margret Morgan were married. [No date was given.] Witnesses: Wm. Wilson, Jno. ---, Jno. Don--aw, Robt. Ardis, Jno.

Richards, Tho[?] Peterson, Dorothy Mekins, John Chapman, Jane Ardis, Margritt Hoult, Woddin Raynolds [her mark].

It was presented that Margrett Miran [wife of Richd. Miran] and Andrew Imbert committed adultery on 28 July last. Richard Miran was one of her sureties. Found not guilty. She was ordered not to come in company with Andrew Imbert.

It was presented that William Browne and Eliza. Barks, spinster, on 20 Oct 1687, entered the house of Henry Bowen of Bullingbrooke Hundred and stole goods, wares and merchandise to the value of 990 lbs. of tobacco. She was ordered to restore 4 times the value and receive 11 lashes.

It was presented that John Baker on 20 July last killed and carried four hogs of Wm. Sparks. He was ordered to restore 4 times the value and stand in the pillory for 2 hours.

It was presented that John Hacker on 10 Aug 1687 and other times at Wye, Tuckaho, Chester and Mill Hundreds, unlawfully hunted and ranged the hoggs, horses and cattle of divers people. Not guilty.

It was presented that David Rogers, laborer, on 10 Aug 1687 and continually to 10 March next unlawfully hunted and ranged and chased and drove away horses, hogs and cattle of divers people. Not guilty.

It was ordered that Edwd. Man and George Robins at the widow Derumple's plant. enquire after the estate of Sarah Marsh, orphant of Thomas Marsh.

It was presented that Edmd. Fish, laborer, on 10 Feb 1687 at Treadhaven Hundred entered the plant. of James Laws and stole 100 hhds. staves. Not guilty.

It was presented that Richd. Royston, Gent. on 20 June last, killed and bore away a hog of Jasper Hall. Not guilty.

Richard Pindergrasse petitioned for his freedom clothes due from Richd. Royston[?].

William Kenton and Mary his wife stood attached to answer Thomas Anderson in a plea of debt.

September Court 1688

It was presented that John Da--s and his wife Jane of Wye River committed libel against John Hacker and Eliza. Browne.

It was presented that Richd. Pindergrass stole two sheep of Richd. Royston.

It was presented that Wm. Allyn of Mill Hundred committed breach of the sabbath.

It was presented that Bryant Kinnissy servant to Antho. Mayle stole a sheep of his master.

Eliza: Browne, wife of Jno. Browne of Wye being bound in recognizance for her good behaviour and appearance at the court appeared accordingly and ordered cleared.

Mabell Ouldman petitioned for her freedom from Ann Spooner. Ann Spooner was ordered to satisfy the said Mabell for the time she was detained.

It was presented that Susannah Bennett bore a bastard child and refused to name the father. She was ordered to receive 29 lashes but she elected the fine of 500 lbs. of tobacco.

It was presented that Wm. Alleyn of Mill Hundred sent his servant a fishing on the sabbath day. Fined 100 lbs. of tobacco.

It was presented that Bryant Kennisy, servant to Antho. Mayle, Gent., on 19 June 1688 at the plant. of said Antho. in Mill Hundred stole a sheep of his master. He was ordered to stand in the pillory one hour and receive 31 lashes.

It was presented that Wm. Allyn, planter, and his wife Joane received a stolen sheep from Bryan Kennisy, servant to Antho. Mayle, on 19 June 1688 at the plant. of said Antho. in Mill Hundred, knowing the sheep to be stolen. Wm. Allyn was ordered to restore four fold the value and stand in the pillory for one hour and Joan Allyn to stand one hour.

November Court 1688

It was presented that Wm. Browne killed and bore away a hog of Tho: Anderson.

It was presented that George Palmer and Tho. Russum, both of Bullingbrook Hundred killed some hogs contrary to act of Assembly.

It was presented that Elizabeth Smith of Bay Hundred bore a bastard child Oct last.

It was presented that Roger Sumner of Bullingbrooke Hundred had a hog in his house without ears and pretending not to know its marks.

It was presented that Jane Dames, Jno. Brown and Jno. Hacker of Island Hundred profaned the sabbath day at the at the church at the head of the Wye River by abusing each other.

It was presented that Mary Lawrence, servant to David Blany, bore a bastard child Sep last.

It was presented that Thomas Bruff of Island Hundred kept unlawful games in his house.

It was presented that Wm. Nureumb [Norcumb] of Bullingbrook Hundred scandalous lived with a woman called Grace.

It was presented that John Dames of Island Hundred clearing a highway on the sabbath Oct last.

It was presented that Allexa: De--- of Mill Hundred stole a bridle and saddle of Michl. Russell.

It was presented that Bryan Kinnissey, Wm. Allyn and Joan his wife of Mill Hundred killed and bore away a sheep of Anthony Mayle.

It was presented that Wm. Norcomb, Tho. Nurcome and Mary Norcumb stole goods and chattels of Christopher ---.

It was considered by the court that Gr: Jones be dismissed from pleading in the court.

It was ordered that Allexa. Maxwell be freed from Michael Hackett and has chosen Charles Hollinsworth for his guardian.

Coll. Henry Coursey petitioned for runaway time of 102 days from his servant Tho. Correy.

A petition of Richd. Dudly who has a servant boy named Edward Higley who has absented himself a total of 65 days and requested compensation in the form of runaway time.

Michael Earle was given a license to keep a house of entertainment.

A petition of Jno. Aldridge showed that whereas George Bunstone[?] of TA Co., dec'd. formerly pitched a crop both of corn and tobacco on the plant. of the petitioner but did not live to finish the same but the petitioner paid the said George's levy as will appear in court by receipt and did find and allow cask for to contain the crop of tobacco and was at the trouble of finding said B---stone in his sickness. Aldridge requests 500 lbs. of tobacco. Henry Coston, admin of George Bunston, to answer to this petitioner.

The petition of Mary Butler, wife of Wm. Butler, late of TA Co. was heard. She stated that her husband had gone away. It was ordered that the goods taken by the constable out of the house of Thomas Noricumb should be delivered into the hands of Mary Butler.

The petition of Capt. Henry Allexander was heard. He declared that Ralph Morly, his servant, had absented himself from service for 78 days and wished to be allowed runaway time according to the Act of Assembly; the court so approved.

It was presented that Wm. Norcum together with Tho. Norcum and Mary his wife at Bullingbrooke Hundred stole on 20 of 7 ber last, one turkey work rugg, one --- petticoat, one callico speckled handkerchief, one pair of --- strings, one remnant of crape being in all valued at 400 lbs. of tobacco, belonging to Christopher Batson. Wm. Nurcom was found guilty; corporal was remitted but he was required to restore 4 fold the amount. Thomas and Mary Nurcum and wife not guilty.

It was presented that Alexa. Deveraun of Mill Hundred on 3 Nov instant at Wye River stole a bridle and saddle of Michael Russell. He was ordered to receive 25 lashes.

It was presented that Bryant Kinnessey, Wm. Alleyn and Joan his wife of Mill Hundred on 23 July last stole a sheep of Antho. Mayle. Not guilty.

It was ordered that Robt. Macklin pay to Eliza. Reed 2000 lbs. of tobacco for the maintenance of her bastard child and also her freedom corn and clothes; and maintain the child for the future.

December Court 1688

Tho. Fisher was allowed 10,000 lbs. of tobacco for the building of Tuckahoe Bridge and his servant's labor.

Jeoffrey Mattershaw was allowed payment for 11 months accommodations of Jno. Lewis and his burial.

January Court 1688

Edward Colstock, servant to Tho. Yewell, was judged to be 16 years old.

The petition of Lewis Ferrell stated that he had served his full time of service to Richd. Jones, blacksmith, who refuses to give him his freedom corn and clothes. It was ordered that Isaac Winchester [sic] either pay Ferrell 1200 lbs. of tobacco or pay him his freedom corn and clothes.

The petition of Samuel Abbott was heard; he said he had due to him from the estate of John Younger, dec'd., 760 lbs. of tobacco (700 lbs. for keeping his child and 1 bushel of English meal). Wm. Welch confessed judgment of the above amount.

Hugh Byrns complained that he had served his full time of 4 years to Thomas Bridges as by his indenture. The court so ordered.

Olliver Millington stated that his woman servant named Eliza: Redish had had a bastard child. He craves additional service for his charge and trouble. She was ordered freed and Millington was ordered to pay her freedom corn and clothes.

The petition of Wm. Watts was heard in which he as for 55 days of runaway time of his servant Jno. Smote. It was so ordered.

Edmund O'Dwyer's request for renewal of a license was approved.

Recorded were gifts from Edward Man to his dau. Lucy Man, hogs, cows, sheep, including a cow and lamb given by Capt. George Cowley; a heifer given by Amey [Anney?] Bishopp, wife of James Bishopp; a Ewe given by Hennora Holland, wife of Richd. Holland.

March Court 1688

Richard Murphy, servant to Jno. Boram was judged to be 11 years old.

Micha: Blany, servant to Harmon Footoks[?] was judged to be 7 years old.

John Flanhawne, servant to Abraham Morgan, was judged to be 10 years old.

William Lewis, servant to Tho: Skillington, was judged to be 15 years old.

Miles Coming, servant to Ralph Dawson, was judged to be 15 years old.

Margrett Bryan, servant to John Law was judged to be 9 years old.

Edward Bryan, servant to John Lane was judged to be 7 years old.

Daniell Carrell, servant to Richd. Swetnam, was judged to be 15 years old.

Tho. Mackahawn, servant to Richd. Swetnam, was judged to be 11 years old.

It was presented that Mary Toaes bore a bastard child.

It was presented that Grace Willis, servant to Wm. Finney, bore a bastard child.

It was presented that Ann Ledman, housekeeper to John Davis, bore a bastard child.

It was presented that Timothy Dunavan, cooper, on 26 Dec 1688, killed a barrow hog of Jno. Newnam.

It was presented that Andrew Fanin counseled and encouraged two servants to run away, one belonging to Judith Hemsley and the other to Wm. Hemsley.

It was presented that John Dames and Jane his wife published and disposed a certain libel entitled the "Pigg and Garden Feast" contrary to the Peace and the Laws.

It was presented that the overseer of the highways between Chester Mill and the southeast branch of Chester River did not clear the road according to Act of Assembly.

It was presented that Edward Pond on 27 Nov 1688 stole property of Mary ---.

It was presented that Tho: Nurcum of DO Co. on 14 7ber 1688 stole a horse and 1 1/2 yard of crape --- of Mary Butler.

It was presented that Edward Pond of Treadhaven Hundred broke and opened a hogshead of tobacco after it was received.

It was presented that Richard Pindergrasse of Wye assaulted Edmd. O'Dwyer.

It was presented that Thomas Nurcum of DO Co. on 14 of 7ber 1688 stole and privately conveyed away Hannah[?], wife of Christopher Batson.

It was presented that Morgan Cooke of Island Hundred on 20 July last stole 2 new shirts of Isaac Winchester. Not guilty.

The petition of Richard Deardeon was heard in which he stated that he had fully served his time with Richd. Royston. He was ordered freed and Royston ordered to pay him his freedom corn and cloathes.

The petition of Richard Roberts was heard. He said that his father being boatswaine of the good shipp the *More the Delight* brought the petitioner along with him as his boy in the said ship into this Province being then 14 years of age and through the persuasion of Richd. Royston and his wife that his father lease him behind for one year and they would taken all the care of the petitioner but his father not returning he has now served them as a slave for these 8 years and 4 months. It was ordered that he be freed and paid his freedom corn and cloathes.

The petition of Thomas Kinesley was heard. He said that whereas he did sell to Natha. Cleave his father-in-law, 5 barrels of Indian corn and 1 bushel of beans in March last which his father-in-law, dec'd., but the execs. refuse to pay.

It was presented that John Dames and his wife Jane of Wye River on 20 Aug 1688 in Island Hundred at Wye River did published and dispose certain libel entitled The Pigg and Garden feast to make discord and strife to ---, Jno. Brown and his wife Eliza. and Jno. Hacker and Jno.[?] Thrift and Mary his wife. Not guilty.

It was presented that Andrew Fanine provoked and encouraged two servant men to run away, one from Wm. Hemsley and one from Judith Hemsley on 24 Feb 1688. Found guilty and required to pay Wm. Hemsley 3300 lbs. of tobacco damages.

It was presented that Morgan Cooke of Island Hundred on 20 July last at Wye River at the plant. of Isaac Winchester, stole two new shirts of Isaac Winchester. Not guilty.

It was presented that Tho. Nurcum of DO Co. on 14 7ber 1688 stole a horse and 1 1/2 yards of crape stuff valued at 999 lbs. of tobacco belonging to Mary Butler of Bullingbrooke. He was ordered to restore 4 fold the costs and receive 39 lashes.

It was presented that Richard Pendergrass of Mills Hundred, planter, on 1 Aug 1687 at the plant. of Richd. Royston in Treadhaven Creek stole a sheep. Not guilty. Whereas Richd. Roberts, John Nuttall, Richd. Dearden and Elliner Butler were presented as accessories, they were also discharged.

May Court 1689

Elliner Berry, servant to Samuell Abott, was judged to be 15 years old.

Wm. Wells, servant to Bowdell was judged to be 14 years old.

Henry Durbridge [Burbridge?], servant to John Coppins[?] was judged to be 16 years old.

June Court 1689

Richard Evans, orphant, was judged to be 12 years old and ordered to live with John Price, innholder, until 21 years of age.

John Evans, orphant, was judged to be 10 years old and ordered to live with Jno. Price, innholder, until age 21.

Jno. Proctor, having a wife and 2 small children, and in debt, agrees to serve Wm. Prisk from 1 March until last of Oct next for 900 lbs. of tobacco.

The petition of Mary Ferris was heard; she stated that George Watts, Jr., dec'd., had given her a yearling heifer with its increase. The calf is now grown to be a cow with calf and John Ayres, her father-in-law, killed the cow about 4 years ago and now refuses to make satisfaction for the cow and her increase. The petitioner is an orphan born and brought up in TA Co.

The petition of Thomas Earle, an orphant born and brought up in TA Co. was heard. He stated that he had a stock of cattle due him on the plant. belonging to him, now in the possession of John Ayres which did formerly marry the mother of the petitioner and since his father's death has imbezzled and made away with the petitioner's cattle. The court ordered John Ayres to deliver to Tho: Earle 2 cows with calf, a 3-year old heifer with calf and 2 two-year old heifers.

The petition of Wm. Jackson, son of Richd. Jackson, dec'd., was heard. He stated that his father d. with an estate valued at £100 and left children Richard, Thomas and William Jackson but made Richd. Miran and Thomas Thompson, execs. of his last will. The petitioner asked for an account of the estate so that the execs. might grant some of the estate to his guardian, Thomas Jackson, for the petitioner's maintenance.

Edmd. Bryant, servant to Tho. Bowdell, was judged to be 20 years old.

It was ordered that Christopher Batson and his wife Hannah find security for their good behaviour and appearance at the next court.

Grace Willis, servant to Wm. Finney, being presented for bearing a bastard child, the said Finney obliged himself to pay 500 lbs. of tobacco for her fine.

Mary Lawrence being presented for bearing a bastard child was ordered to receive 29 lashes. The court consented to take a fine of 500 lbs. of tobacco.

George Palmer of Bullingbrooke Hundred was indicted for that he did on 20 Oct 1688 stole several hogs from the woods not belonging to him the said George Palmer. Not guilty.

It was presented that Charles Ferris, planter on 26 Dec 1688 and several days since at the French [?] Woman's Branch near Chester in TA Co. stole from out of the woods several barrow hogs and a sow, not belonging to him. He was ordered to restore the value of the hogs fourfold and to stand in the pillory 1/2 hour.

It was presented that Edward Pond, Treadhaven Hundred, on 20 Nov 1688 at Choptank, Bullingbrook Hundred stole out of the house of Mary Butler of Bullingbrooke Hundred a bushel of Indian corn. He was found guilty.

September Court 1689

Tho. Fisher petitioned for runaway time of his servant, John Bishopp, as 8 days which was judged accordingly.

William Hemsley petitioned for runaway time of his servant, Tho. Thissellwood. Thomas was ordered to abide with his master until next court.

Tho. Broadhurst declared that he was in fear of his life of Robt. Harrison. Robert Harrison was required to give security and to appear at next court.

Margrett Robins, attorney for her husband Geo: Robins assigned to Timothy Wyett a mare in exchange for a cow and calf and 5 shillings.

A letter of attorney was proved.

Know all men by these presents that I Archbald Grier of Albermarle County of North Carolina being the true and lawful Attorney of Cuthbart Phelps I have received this 16th day of June 1690 of Robert Grundy merchant of Talbott County & Debora Grundy his wife being the executrix of the last will and testament of Thomas Impey deceased the full & just sum of 30391 lbs. of neat tobacco ...

16 Nov 1690:

William Copell of TA Co., planter gave to his grand child Jane Elly a cow called Lovely.

On 17 March 1690/1:

I Thomas Bowdell doe give to my son Thomas Bowdell & my son Lofftus Bowdell one maire called ... and one maire called ... Young Bonney when son Thomas comes to the age of 21.

On 15 April 1691:

Thomas Goffe and Sarah Goffe [Gosse?] relict of John Ingrum authorized and empowered George Smith to receive the rents of the plant. where John Ingrum did live wherein Edmond Willcock is a tennant for 5 years yet to come and after that time empower said Smith to let or otherwise dispose of the plant. and to receive the profits of the plant. until John Ingrum, son of John Ingrum arrives at the age of 21.

15 May 1689

Cicilly Alford gave all her right, title and interest of her daster Elinor Walker to Izebill Whittinton for the term of 20 years.

June Court 1692

Margery Strong and Maurice Davis, servants to Robert Grundy were judged to be of age.

James Ryley, servant to Ralph Fishbourne, was judged to be 20 years old.

Terrence Floyd, servant to Ralph Fishbourne, was judged to be 17 years old.

Thomas Loveley, an orphan child, was bound an apprentice to George Bowes until he comes of age, to learn the trade of taylor.

Dennis Maccartee, servant to John Poore, was judged to be 16 years old.

Patrick Powell, servant to Dennis Hopkins, was judged to be 17 years old.

Elizabeth Abrams, widow, was granted a letter of administration on the estate of Jacob Abrams, her late husband.

It was presented by the Orphans Jury that James Clayland, clerk, detained

Alice Taylor, dau. to George Taylor, being of lawful age.

It was presented by the Orphans Jury that Anne Mitchell als. Aldridge, extx. of George Aldridge, dec'd., for detaining and not delivering unto William Garey who m. Grace Aldridge, the dau. of the said George, 4 cows.

William Cooper, one of the orphans of John Cooper, dec'd., now coming to full age, requested his portion of his father's estate. The court ordered that Rice Evans to deliver his estate.

James Dalton and Martha Paine, wife of John Paine, appeared with their sureties: John Chase and John Paine.

It was presented that Joane Crowley bore a bastard child. She was ordered to receive 15 lashes.

William Martine, servant to Isaac Winchester, was judged to be 19 years old.

William Riche, son of Alice Riche, dec'd. was granted a letter of administration to her estate.

In the petition of Philemon and Vincent Hemsley, execs. of the last will of Judith Hemsley, it was stated that their mother had brought up a young girl from her infancy being now 8 years old and in 1687 it was ordered that the child serve their mother until age 21 but it was never recorded. The court ordered that the girl, Elizabeth Ford, serve the petitioners until age 18.

A motion of John Gurley and his wife Jane concerning their dau. Elizabeth, late servant to Thomas Bruffe, Jr. to examine the indenture. Bruffe was ordered to attend the next court and bring her indenture.

Robert Harrison, guardian of the orphans of George Taylor, dec'd., complained that Richard Royston who had some of the orphans and a great part of the estate of the dec'd., had abused the said orphans and should be accountable for the estate.

Robert Rattcliffe complained that he had a former order of the court against Mr. Richard Sweatnam for his crop of Indian corn made upon the plant. of Mr. Richard Sweatnam in Chester and in pursuance of the sd. order he has often demanded the same but cannot get it to the damage of the petitioner, his wife and child. The court agreed.

August Court 1692
Owen Macarter, servant to Judith Numann, was judged to be 19 years old.

Mathuslah Vauhan was ordered to serve his master Richard Hall 37 days.

September Court 1692
Richard Lawrence was bound by the court to serve William Hackett until age 20.

It was presented that Margarett Griffin, servant to Edward Mann, had born a bastard child. She was ordered to receive 20 lashes.

It was presented that Samuell Paine, John Tooton and Bryan Mounticue, on 20 Dec 1691 on the sabbath day in Island Hundred, killed and bore away several hogs, owners unknown. Not guilty.

It was presented that William Mounticue, planter and Samuell Paine, weaver, in Mill Hundred, on 30 July 1691, stole goods and chattels of John Coppin. Acquitted.

It was presented that John Price of Bullinbrooke Hundred, musitian, on 17 Jan 1691, killed and bore away a boar hog belonging to Richard White in Bullingbrook Hundred. He was ordered to receive 7 lashes and pay four fold the value of the hogs. At his petition his corporal punishment was remitted.

William Clayton had judged 60 days of runaway time against his servant George Eves.

Came into court George Hurlock and Elizabeth Davison, wife of Peter Davison, being presented for living together in common fame. She was ordered to receive 11 lashes.

November Court 1692

At the petition of Matthew Tomlin he was granted runaway from his servant Sarah Floyd who had absented herself 27 days.

Richard Dawson in his petition stated he had become bound and security for Roger Burras unto John Salter in the sum of 700 lbs. of tobacco and said Roger died poor without wherewithal for a funeral and since the petitioner was related to said Roger by marriage did bestow a decent funeral for him. Roger has left being only one gun and one old chest and a ---? which the petitioner desire to be given to him. Approved.

Mary Butler, wife of William Butler who had absconded, petitions to receive some of her husband's cloathes which had been taken by Edward Mann in payment for debt.

Jonathan Livermore, late servant to Peter Sayer petitioned for his freedom corn and cloathes, he having fully served his master. Sayer was ordered to give Livermore 3 barrels of Indian corn.

It was presented that Michaell Earle, innholder, on 26 March 1690 at Worrell Hundred, forged and invented the name and sale of Francis Butler, late of TA Co., dec'd., and forged a deed.

It was presented that John Hanner on 20 April last at the plant. of Richard Sweatnam at the fork of Coursegall [Corsica] Creek in Chester River stole a hhd. of tobacco of Robert Smith. He was ordered to stand in the pillory for 2 hours and pay Robert Smith four fold the cost. At his petition the corporal punishment was remitted.

It was presented that Thomas Johnings packed seconds into hhds. He was cleared by proclamation.

Elizabeth Story brought into court John Storey who was judged to be 4 years old and prayed that he might be bound to Seth Garret until of age. The court ordered that he be bound and that he be taught the trade of a carpenter.

It was presented that William Hollinsworth, Jr., on 26 March 1692 at Chester Hundred, stole, killed and bore away a barrow hog of Thomas Smith. He was ordered to receive 11 lashes and to pay four fold the cost.

At the end upside down:
Sarah Impey, dau. of Thomas Impey, b. 5 Dec ---- April following.
Mary Impey, dau. of Mr. Thomas Impey, b. 25 ---, bapt. 26 of same month 1686.
Thomas Impey d. 9 Oct 1686.

TALBOT COUNTY JUDGMENT RECORDS
Liber LL7 (1692-1696)

November Court 1692
William Hatfield acknowledged himself guilty of breach of peace and was fined 100 lbs. of tobacco.

Charles Chambers stated in his petition, having served William Dixon 9 3/4 years according to the indenture which time was expired last Sep yet is still detained in service. Ordered freed.

William Hemsley presented runaway time of his servant Essabell Clemans.

August Court 1696
Mary Dabey[?], servant of Phillip Connyers judged to be 20 years old.

Enrick Imbertson was brought before the court and it appearing that he was drunk he was ordered to be put in the stocks for one hour.

It was presented that Jane Tomlinson, servant to Dr. James Benson, was guilty of having a bastard child. Ordered to received 30 lashes and to serve her master an additional 6 months.

John Pitts brought Roger Summers, son of Roger Summers, dec'd., and with the consent of his mother he was judged to serve him until of age 21, he judged to be 8 years old on 22 Oct next.

John Lane against his servant Margarett Barr requested and received additional time of servitude for the time sustained by her in running away for 25 days.

It was ordered that Danll. Walker serve Catherine Finney until 1 Nov next.

Jacob Gibson was fined 500 lbs. of tobacco for refusing to serve as constable of Island Hundred.

It was ordered that the sheriff give notice to the Justices of the several Counties in August Court next that they issue their strict order and charge forthwith to the constables of each hundred within their respective counties thereby commanding them to go to every individual house of the said hundred in which they officiate and there demand and take an accompt from the master, mistress or dame of every such house in writing under such master, mistress or dames own hand what number of taxables they have which said list so taken they are to close, seal up after copy thereof made for the county court and transmit the same unto his Excellency. at the port of Annapolis by the 16th day of September next if the Assembly then sits otherwise by the first day of the next Provincial Court under pain of being prosecuted to the utmost severity of the law for contempt. Signed per order Hen: Denton, clerk of court.

John Duckworth of TA Co., carpenter, stood attached to answer James Crowley and Jane his wife of a pleas of trespass.

Griffith Jones of Philadelphia stood attached to answer unto John Edmondson of a plea of trespass. Edmondson complained that said Griffith in 1695 was indebted to him for 8000 lbs. of tobacco.

September Court 1696

At September Court 1696, Nicholas Poore appearing drunk before the court was ordered put in the stocks for half an hour.

TALBOT COUNTY JUDGMENT RECORDS
Liber AB 8 (1696-1698)

November Court 1696

p. 1. The Grand Jury: Thomas Martin, Joseph James, Sam. Abbott, Thomas Ball, Joshua Atkins, Wm. Skinner, Natha. Grace, John Games, Robt. Goff, Robt. Harrison, Richard Skinner, John Thrift, John Pooley, Tho: Roe, Robert Blunt, Michael Earle, Walter Kirby, John Downes, Wm. Elbournd, Wm. Dowlin, and Robert Broadway.

It was agreed that Henry Carter was permitted to keep a public ferry at the wading place at the north end; he was to proved a sufficient boat. He was to received 3500 lbs. of tobacco per year.

p. 2. William Hemsley was allowed runaway time for the absence (27 days) of his servant Albon Lloyd.

The petition of Edward Mecan was heard; he stated he had served Peter Sydes in his lifetime and since his death John Sides and has completed his time although John Sides refused to set him free. The court ordered John Sides to set him free and pay his corn and clothes.

p. 5. Thomas Hopkins, Sr., was allowed a levy for keeping Susana Collins for the ensuing year.

Nicholas Lowe was allowed a levy for keeping John Roberts, a poor lame man for the ensuing year.

p. 6. Thomas Bowdle was allowed a levy for keeping and clothing Robert Million, a very poor decrepid man.

Katherine Winchester, widow, was allowed 2400 lbs. of tobacco for taking care and looking after Mary Cartwright and finding cloathes for her, Mary being a poor decrepid girl.

Richard Sweatnam was granted a license to keep an ordinary at the towne of York in TA Co.

Richard Sweatnam was granted runaway time against his servant, Katherine Poor who had absented herself 119 days.

p. 7. Thomas Collins, servant to Mrs. Finney, chose John Jones, brazier and Richard Daniel to be his guardians to look after his estate.

It was presented that John Burnam and his wife Katherine on 30 Aug 1696, profaned the Sabbath by scolding, quarreling and fighting. John Burnam was fined 100 lbs. of tobacco.

p. 8. It was presented that Elizabeth Davis on 30 Aug 1696 profaned the sabbath by scolding, quarrelling and fighting. Fined 100 lbs. of tobacco.

It was presented that John Murphey of Bullingbrook, planter, on 13 Sep 1696 profaned the sabbath by swearing, drinking and being drunk. Fined 100 lbs. of tobacco.

It was presented that Warner and his wife Elizabeth on 14 June 1696 profaned the Lord's day by quarrelling and scolding. Fined 100 lbs. of tobacco.

p. 9. It was presented that Johannis Deheniossa of Tuckahoe Hundred, planter, on 27 Sep 1695, failed to meeting to mend and rectify the King's highway, being an overseer thereunto. The indictment was quashed by the jury.

p. 10. It was presented that Mary Crockers, servant to Richard Feedeman, had born a bastard child; she named Thomas Jobson as the father. She was ordered to receive 21 lashes. Richard Feedeman asked the court that he pay a fine instead and the court agreed to a fine of 500 lbs. of tobacco. He also agreed to keep the child. Mary Crockers came into court and bound her children: Thomas Crockers and Mary Crockers to Richard Feedeman until age 21.

p. 83. It was presented that Thomas Bruff had not delivered at March Court Elizabeth Gurley, dau. of John Gurley as commanded. The Jury was unable to reach a verdict and sent out again at which time they acquitted Bruff. The case was then appealed to the Provincial Court.

p. 121. Mary Whitticar, widow of John Whitticar was given an allowance for keeping a ferry at William Stadt.

Rodger Gill was given an allowance for keeping Tobias Kelley, a poor man for 4 months and burying him.

January Court 1696

p. 129. It was presented that Jane (Jennett) MackClain, servant to Elizabeth Oakley, had born a bastard child. She named Gilbert Tate as the father, he being another servant of Elizabeth Oakley. The child was born on 22 Dec 1695. Jennett was ordered to receive 15 lashes. Both Jennett and Gilbert Tate were ordered to serve Elizabeth Oakley an additional year. The child was to be maintained by Elizabeth Oakley.

p. 130. It was presented that Katherine White, servant to Edward Elliott (having about 3 years to serve), had born a bastard child. She said that William [Smith] (having about 2 years to serve), servant to Edward Elliott, was the father. Katherine was ordered to receive 20 lashes. She and William Smith were ordered to serve an additional 6 months.

March Court 1696

p. 195. The petition of Richard Lloyd was heard. He had bound himself an apprentice to John Seaton of TA Co. to learn the trade of ship carpenter and if said Seaton died before the petitioner's time was expired then the petitioner was to be free. Contrary to this the exec. of John Seaton, dec'd., sold him to Robert Edgar Webb who has abused him. Richard Lloyd was overruled.

p. 196. The petition of Margarett Griffin was heard. She said that she and her child being afflicted with the distemper called the yawes, for the cure of which she had bound herself to Sarah Bartlett, widow, for 2 years in return for meat, drink, washing, lodging and apparel. After 1 1/2 years Margarett, in view of the severity of her treatment by Sarah Bartlett, asked that she be disposed to someone else in consideration of additional service. The court ordered her freed and ordered John Bartlett to deliver her child to her.

Jacob Pride, being committed to prison for fighting and quarreling, and making his escape; it was presented that he be apprehended brought to court. Later pardoned.

It was presented that Robert Fellow had breached the sabbath. Fined 100 lbs. of tobacco.

It was presented that Hannah Bryon had born a bastard child; she declared that William Hatfield was the father. She was ordered to receive 20 lashes. Wm. Alderne offered to pay her fine in lieu of corporal punishment. The punishment was remitted and a fine of 500 lbs. of tobacco imposed.

p. 197. The petition of Morris Davis was heard. He stated that he had completed his term of servitude to Robert Grundy, being 5 years on 15 March instant. Grundy was ordered to pay him his freedom dues: corn and his clothes.

It was presented that Bryon Seney breached the peace. Fined 100 lbs. of tobacco.

Charles Murphey was found guilty of being drunk and fined 5 shillings or to be set in the stocks for 1/2 hour.

p. 198. It was presented that Elizabeth Mackdowell, servant to Andrew Price, has born a bastard child. She named Dr. Peter Jolly as the father. She was order to receive 10 lashes. At the motion of Andrew Price her corporal punishment was remitted in lieu of a fine of 500 lbs. of tobacco. Dr. Jolly was to be brought into court to give security to keep the county harmless from the maintenance of the child. At June Court 1697 he appeared and gave security.

The petition of John Pope and Dominick Kirwan was heard. They were designed, God willing, to erect an ordinary at the Port of William Stadt. A license was granted.

It was presented that John Burdon had stolen several items. Ordered to receive 30 lashes.

p. 199. It was presented that William Sacheverill, blacksmith at the dwelling house of Darby Tool upon the plant. of Col. Peter Sayer, had counterfeited money.

p. 200. It was presented that Thomas Earle of Miles Creek on 4 March 1696, killed and bore a way a sow of William Anderson. Not guilty.

p. 201. It was presented that John Nuttall and his wife Susanah on 10 May 1696 at Miles River, did seize a bay mare of Robert Gouldesborough, then in the pasture, and drove a 4 penny nail into the frog of one of the fore feet of the mare and did lame and utterly spoil the mare.

June Court 1697
p. 267. Martha Stoakes, servant to Thomas Baxter, was judged to be 16 years old.

p. 268. It was presented that Elizabeth Smithson had born a bastard child; she named Dominick Kirwan as the father. She said that the sd. child was got in Nov last was 12 months (sic) and that Dominick promised her marriage and that the child was got about 22 Nov last was a 12 month. Fined 20 shillings or 400 lbs. of tobacco. Her fine was paid by Patrick Dannelly. He was ordered to give security to keep the county harmless.

It was presented that Margrett Walker had born a bastard. She was ordered to receive 25 lashes.

It was presented that Mary Davis had born a bastard child; she named Edward Willkinson as the father. She was ordered to receive 25 lashes.

It was presented that Katherine Crockett, servant to John Pemberton, had born a bastard child. She was ordered to receive 25 lashes and serve her master an additional 8 months.

p. 269. It was presented that Margrett Nailer, servant to John Pemberton, has born a bastard child. She named William Ellson als. Dict. William Nellson as the father. She was ordered to receive 25 lashes.

The Orphan Jury presented Richard Harrington of St. Michaell's Parish for selling of a orphan boy named Thomas Cooper to Henry Frith of the same parish. it was judged that Harrington had possession of him by his father's last will. The presentment was quashed.

The Orphan Jury presented Richard Jones, Jr., of St. Paul's Parish and Thomas Tannor of Christs Parish for burning and spoiling of the houses, fencing and orchard of the orphans of Thomas Cooper, late of Kent Island. The court ordered them to be discharged.

The Orphan Jury presented John Wrightson of St. Michaell's Parish for keeping of an orphan boy of William Aryes called William Arye at making of tobacco and not brought up to what is required in the law.

The Orphan Jury presented Jesse Holten of St. Peter's Parish for wasting and embezzling the estate of the orphans of Cornelius Mulraynes of afsd. parish.

The Orphan Jury presented Robert Sides the orphant of Peter Sides, St. Paul's Parish, for running up and down the country like a vagabond and not settling himself where he ought to do.

The Orphan Jury found no cause that the orphan of Joseph Wickett called Henry Wickett should go from under the tuition of William Carr of St. Peter's Parish but only his own desire that he might chose his tutor.

It was presented that Mary Corverwell, a free woman, had born a bastard child. Fined 20 shillings.

It was presented that Isabell Coleman, a free woman, had born a bastard child. Fined 20 shillings

It was presented that John Lewis threatened the undersheriff, Richd. Jones. Discharged.

Robert Broadaway was appointed constable of Worrill Hundred in place of John Jones.

Robert Noble and Frances Noble chose as the guardians Coll. George Robotham and John Pemberton.

Morriss Sleany and Elizabeth his wife, admins. of the estate of Morriss Walahand of KE Co., presented the account. Morriss Slany was ordered to find security for the amount due to the orphans of Morris Wollahand (Thomas, Mary and Morriss Wollahand).

John Pursells was fined for being drunk and swearing oaths.

p. 272. It was presented that James Benney and his wife Katherine on 14 June 1696 profaned the Lord's day by quarrelling and scolding. James Benney was fined 100 lbs. of tobacco.

p. 284. Katherine Poor, servant to Ralph Dawson, Jr., was judged to be 17 years old.

p. 285. A petition of Richard James and Samuel Midgeley showed that they imported the persons underwritten on design of building a ship in this county at the plant. of Thomas Skillington on Tredhaven and arrived there about the beginning of June and are immediately taken into the constables list by which they are likely to become liable to pay the publick and county levies and taxes. They are but seafaring men not yet settled in country. They asked that these persons be taken off the list [of taxables]. Listed were the following persons: Nicho. Clark, Geo: Walton, James Garnett, Richd. Tasker, Wm. Cornett, Edwd. Case, Wm. Younger, --- Pendleton, Richd. Hindley, Arthr. Rigby, Gilbt. Coughin, Anto. Dennison, John Platt, Tho: Osborn, Nico. Boon, Robt. Letheland, Richd. Ball and Jno. Speakman and one Negro man - 21 in all. The court ordered that they ought to pay the levies.

It was presented that William Webb and Richard Clarke, giving security to keep the county harmless from the two bastard children begotten of the body of Ann Coaltman by George Phipps of the county.

Mrs. Katherine Finney proved a bill past by Stephen Willson to her dec'd. husband, Wm. Finney; also a bill past by John Kenneday.

p. 288. The petition of Thomas Knight and Thomas Bowdle was heard. It stated that they about 7 years ago were brought from their friends and relations out of England by Mr. Thomas Bowdle, the uncle of the petitioners, into this county and during his life did detain the petitioners as servants who are still detaining as servants by Mrs. Bowdle, relict of the said Mr. Bowdle. The conceive they ought to have served five years according to custom of the country and they pray for freedom. The court ordered them to be freed.

Francis Bullin was fined for being drunk.

Edward Jeffreys, servant of Daniel Glover, was ordered freed, his time of servitude being recomputed.

Thomas Silvester, aged 6 years next Jan was bound by the court with the consent of his mother, Eliza: Silvester, to Coll. George Robotham, until age 21.

p. 290. Richard Williams came into open court and made oath that he was in the towne of Foye in the west of England in the county of Cornwall and that about 14 years ago affirms if the ship called the *Mercy of Foye*, Wm. Lugger Master, arrived in the sd. harbour about the time afsd. laded with tobacco from Maryland and further the deponent saith that he came in a passenger in the same ship.

The petition of Sarah Yewell, widow, was heard. She stated that whereas John Worner, son to John Worner, late of this county, dec'd., was bound by the mother and father-in-law of the sd. orphant unto Thomas Yewell of the county, dec'd., who was husband to the petitioner. John Worner was appraised as worth £4; however the indenture had been lost. As admx. of her husband's estate she requested a new indenture be written. John Worner was judged by the court to be 10 years old last April and ordered to serve until age 21, Sarah Yewell to teach him to read.

Margrett Dehorty bound her son Joseph Blackwell, age 2 years, to William Haddon until age 21, to be taught to read and the trade of a tailer.

September Court 1697

p. 344. It was presented that Mary Whitehead, servant to Capt. James Murphey, has born a bastard child. Fined 20 shillings and ordered to serve James Murphey 9 additional months.

Sarah Davis, an orphant girl of Charles Davis, late of Kent Island, dec'd., now 8 years old, was ordered by the court to serve William Scott 8 years.

William Scott asked for runaway time from his servant, Robert Hackett, who had absented himself 106 days.

p. 345. It was presented that Mary Pearce, servant to Matthew Eareckson, had born a bastard child; she named Dennis Kelley, servant to Matthew Eareckson, as the father. She was ordered to receive 15 lashes. Each was ordered to serve Matthew Eareckson an additional 8 months.

It was presented that Margrett Small, servant to Edward James, had born a bastard child; she refused to name the father. She was fined 20 shillings which was paid by Edward James along with security to keep the county harmless of the child's maintenance.

The petition of the orphans of Wm. Anderson was heard. It was stated that the orphans had been very much abused by the widow and relict of their father. It was stated that their mother-in-law had beat them unreasonably and failed to give them food on which to subsist. The court ordered that John Anderson, one of the orphans, 12 years old next March, serve David Mills until age 20; William Anderson, one of the orphans afsd. to go to Robert Felowes, joyner and remain there until next court; Ann Anderson was ordered to serve David Mills until of age.

p. 346. Eziah Parrott, orphan of Henry Parrott, dec'd., was ordered to serve

William Sharpe until age 21, being now 12 years old.

Daniel Walker who keeps a ferry over the St. Michaell's River, asked for a license to keep an ordinary; it was granted.

The petition of Jane Burdon was heard. She stated that she had been brought into this country by Capt. Thomas Hedger of Ireland on 1 May 1686 and by him sold to George Robins, dec'd., and since the death of George Robins had served his relict and heir and is still detained by her contrary to law. The court ordered that Jane serve Thomas Robins, Jr. 3 more years.

p. 347. Charles Powell asked the court for runaway time against his servant Arthur Jones for absenting himself 30 days. Approved.

October Court 1697

p. 440. Richard Macklin was appointed clerk of the indictments, in place of Saml. Withers who had died.

It was presented that Ann Miller, servant to John Downes, had born a bastard child. Fined.

p. 441. Thomas Bale acknowledged to serve 2 years from the present under Wm. Hemsley in consideration Wm. Hemsley admits him to marry with his servant Margrett Dehorty who had five years to serve, whom Thomas Bale had got with child. Wm. Hemsley agreed to set them both free after the sd. two years and to keep the child.

James Lloyd and Margrett chose Phillemon Lloyd for their guardian.

It was presented by Kenelmne Skillington, constable of Tredhaven Hundred, that Ann Gasling had born a bastard child in Oct 1697.

It was presented by Thomas Fisher, constable of Tuckahoe Hundred that Hannah Nealle, wife of Morris Neale, and Mary Cooper, wife of William Cooper, were guilty of breach of the Lord's day by fighting on 27 June 1697.

Thomas Fisher, constable of Tuckahoe Hundred, presented John Lane for a common swearer.

The Grand Jury presented Jacob Pride for entertaining of a servant boy of Andrew Skinner, Sr., named Wm. Forbess on 1 June 1687.

The Grand Jury presented Joseph Vickers and his wife Mary for hog stealing on 12 Oct 1697.

Henry Carter who kept a ferry on Kent Island requested an increase in allowance. The court allowed him an additional 500 lbs. of tobacco per year.

Lawrence Knowles was granted a license to keep an ordinary at the towne of Doncaster for the year ensuing.

It was presented that Dominick Kirwan had committed several misdemeanors; it was ordered that his license to keep an ordinary be suspended.

January Court 1697

p. 469. Richard Wells chose John Hamor as his guardian.

p. 469 and 575. The petition of John Alexander was heard. In his petition he stated that Henry Alexander, by his last will bequeathed to his youngest dau. Katherine Alexander [John's sister] the plant. whereon he then lived, only reserving his wife's life thereon. Since the death of sd. Henry Alexander, his widow m. Timothy Lane and since the marriage has died but before her death she bequeathed a Negro and furniture to Katherine. The petition [which seems vague and not specific to the compiler] was quashed. However the court ordered that Timothy lane give good security for the orphant's estate. The court later ordered him to pay the orphan rent of her plant. when she came of age.

Thomas Bennett refusing to keep the ferry at William Stadts when he ought to have kept it according to his contract was fined 200 lbs. of tobacco for his contempt and ordered to enter into recognizance that the ferry be well kept until November next, the remainder of his time. He was given a license to keep an ordinary at his dwelling plant. on the west side of Tredhaven Creek.

p. 470. William Turloe was granted runaway time against his servant Thomas Prestridge being absent 24 days.

Ralph Moone renewed his license to keep an ordinary in the town and port of William Stadt.

It was presented that Quashe, a Negro slave of Richard Tilghman, had stolen several goods and merchandize from the execs. of Richard Sweatnam. He was ordered to stand in the pillory for one hour and receive 30 lashes.

p. 471. John Pride was fined 100 lbs. of tobacco for breach of the peace, fighting and quarrelling.

At January Court 1697, Michael Deane, behaving irreverently before the court was place in the stocks for one hour.

It was presented that Michael Deane stole goods from several persons.

p. 472. The license to keep an ordinary at Deep Water Point was renewed for James Auld was granted.

John Thrift was granted runaway time against his servant Michael Gerrim[?] who had absented himself 44 days.

The license for Thomas Bruff to keep an ordinary at the town of Doncaster was renewed.

p. 473. John Lane was presented for swearing and fined 5 shillings

It was presented that Joseph Vickars and his wife Mary killed and bore away a hogg of persons unknown.

February Court 1697

p. 520. Richard Chambers, servant to Volentine Carter, was judged to be 12 years old.

John Reed, servant to Volentine Carter, was judged to be 10 years old.

John Miller, servant to William Dixon, was judged to be 13 years old.

p. 521. Thomas D'lahay asked for runaway time against his servant, Gilbert Mahar who absented himself 29 days. Approved.

Rachell Bexley chose John Swift as her guardian.

James Reyley claimed to have served his time to Ralph Fishburne and requested to be set free to which the court approved, ordering that he be paid his corn and clothes.

p. 522. It was presented that Richard Belvin appeared to be a vagabond person and had stolen several goods of Nicho. Milburne, and was enticing several man servants to run away. Ordered to receive 15 lashes.

p. 523. John Berwick requested runaway time against his servant Elizabeth Adeson who had absented herself 211 days. Approved.

p. 524. Thomas Sockwell, cooper, and Mary Fortune, wife of Robert Fortune, were presented for keeping ill conversation with one another.

It was presented that Madm. Elizabeth Coursey, widow of Coll. Henry Coursey, detained a parcel of geese and ganders which did not properly belong to her which number is 8. The geese are supposed to be Andrew Price's.

It was presented that Grinedge Hormerly, Negro of Thomas Marcher now living on Kent Island and Jane Shoare of the same hundred and dau. of William Shoare had carnal copulation with one another last Oct 1697.

It was presented that Robert Hopkins, shoemaker, and Elizabeth Howard, wife of David Howard, had kept ill conversation with one another by common fame. Witnesses were John Newnam, Sr., Ralph Swift and John Swift.

It was presented that Ann Coulton had delivered a bastard child c29 July last.

Robert Broadaway, constable of Worrill Hundred, presented Elinor Conah, servant of Madam Elizabeth Coursey for having a bastard child c20 Jan last past.

It was presented that Susanah Merchant of Mill Hundred, at the house of Edwd. Fuller, had a bastard child Jan last past.

p. 525. Anthony Workeman was presented for a breach of the Sabbath day. Fined 100 lbs. of tobacco.

Morriss Neall and wife and William Cooper and wife were presented for a breach of the Sabbath. Each fined 100 lbs. of tobacco.

June Court 1698

p. 573. John Green, servant to Michael Russell, was judged to be 14 years old.

Giles Dining, servant to Mathew Reed, was judged to be 16 years old.

Alexander Scursington, servant to John Dawson, judged to be 10 years old.

Elizabeth Hewett, servant to John Dawson, was judged to be 8 years old.

Bryon Sweny, servant to David Blany, was judged to be 13 years old.

James Winder, servant to Thomas Thomas, was judged to be 13 years old.

Daniel Conder, servant to Sarah Godard was judged to be 14 years old.

Owen Sullivant, servant to William Gwin, was judged to be 17 years old.

John Murphey, servant to William Steevens, Jr., was judged to be 16 years old.

Ann Mackcollow, servant to Thomas Skillington, was judged to be 14 years old.

Thomas Boyce, servant to James Berry, was judged to be 14 years old.

Dennis Rork, servant to Edward Elliott, Jr., was judged to be 19 years old.

James Harvy, servant to John King, was judged to be 11 years old.

Daniel Grey, servant to Edward James, was judged to be 11 years old.

Thomas Macknamar, servant to John Downes, was judged to be 14 years old.

Elinor Carte, servant to Dennis Hopkins, was judged to be 17 years old.

William Bryon, servant to Lewis Derochburne was judged to be 18 years old.

William Tobe, servant to Edmund Goodman, was judged to be 17 years old.

Cornelius Worloe, servant to Mary Baggs, was judged to be 16 years old.

William Smith, servant to John King, was judged to be 9 years old.

p. 574. John Mill, servant to Joseph Rodgers, was judged to be 10 years old.

Ellinor Fennin, servant to John Wells, was judged to be 15 years old.

Dennis Collohan, servant to Benja. Peck, was judged to be 14 years old.

David Berry, servant to William Scott, was judged to be 13 years old.

Cornelius Shehan, servant to Thomas Robins, Jr., was judged to be 14 years old.

Mary Satchwell, servant to David Fairbanck, was judged to be 16 years old.

Thomas Agbester, servant to William Troath, was judged to be 19 years old.

Thomas Browne, servant to William Harrison, was judged to be 15 years old.

James Brey, servant to Mathew Eareckson, was judged to be 14 years old.

William Waland, servant to Mrs. Catherine Winchester, was judged to be 13 years old.

Edward Peace, servant to Ambros Kinnimon, was judged to be 13 years old.

Timothy Mahane, servant to William Hemsley, was judged to be 13 years old.

Owen Kelley, servant to William Hemsley, was judged to be 13 years old.

James FitzGerrell, servant to William Bell, planter, was judged to be 14 years old.

Alexander Lowrey, servant to Thomas Hopkins, Sr., was judged to be 14 years old.

Lawrence Karron, servant to Francis Steevens, was judged to be 14 years old.

John Painter, servant to Mary Sergant, was judged to be 16 years old.

John O'Daley, servant to Mrs. Phebe Bowdle, was judged to be 17 years old.

Patrick Heyhead, servant to Richard Skinner, was judged to be 17 years old.

John Cooper and Susana Cooper chose William Cooper as their guardian.

John Cooper, bound by the court an apprentice to William Curtis to learn the trade of a taylor until age 21, he being 16 years old last Feb.

p. 575. Robt. Noble, an orphan not yet to full age, prayed to be admitted to choose as his guardian, Edward Lloyd for his guardian, Coll. Robotham, one of his guardians being dead. Admitted.

It was presented that Ann Huse of Bullingbrooke, had abused an orphan girl known as Ann Huse being 13 years old.

At the petition of Ralph Swift, an orphan, to be bound to the trade of cordwainer, he was ordered to serve Arthur Emery, Jr., until age 21, he being 18 years old.

p. 576. Thomas Wallis, an orphan bound to David Arey until age 21, was judged to be 10 years old, to learn the trade of a cordwainer.

John Allen, orphant, ordered to serve Thomas Hawkins until age 21, was judged to be 16 years old, to learn the trade of cordwainer.

p. 577. John Meriday who was placed as a boy by John Meriday to live with Benja. Pride, now dec'd., until age 18, now being age 18 April last, the petition of John Meriday requests that sd. child be placed in his custody [relationship not given].

p. 579. Upon the petition of Margarett Johnson she was to served William Watts for 12 months. William Watts acknowledged owing her 2000 lbs. of tobacco.

Upon Richard Swift's petition, he was ordered to serve Robert Hopkins until age 21, he being 15 years old, to learn the craft of a cordwainer.

p. 580. It was ordered that the orphan Phillip Griffin live with David Rodgers until September Court next when he would be bound out.

Charles Hemsley was granted a license to keep an ordinary at the town of York.

At June Court 1698, because of his committing several misdemeanors, Charles Powell was expulsed from practicing any long in the court except for pending cases.

It was presented that Joseph Rodgers, given a warrant by Nicholas Lowe, High Sheriff, directed to Nathaniel Tuckar, constable of Chester Hundred, which said Joseph Rodgers refused to carry and burned it. Acquitted.

p. 581. It was presented that John Lankester, servant to Edward James of Kent Island, on 24 Nov 1697, stole, killed and bore a hog of Christopher Goodhand. He was ordered to receive 25 lashes and pay four fold the cost of the hog.

p. 582. It was presented that James Bampton on 10 Feb 1697 in Bullinbrooke Hundred, under the pretence of searching for stolen goods, not having a warrant, did break down the fencing and broke into the tobacco house of Peter Watts and other damage. Not guilty.

p. 583. It was presented that John King on 20 Jan 1697 at Island Hundred obstructed and blocked up the highway. Fined 100 lbs. of tobacco.

It was presented that John Seney on 10 Feb 1697 in Bullinbrooke Hundred under the pretense of searching for stolen goods broke down the fencing and broke into the tobacco house of Peter Watts. Fined 1000 lbs. of tobacco.

August Court 1698

David Laton, servant to Wm. Dikinson, was judged to be 16 years old.

Samuell Pratt, orphan bound by the court as an apprentice to Clause Dutititery to learn the trade of a taylor, to serve him until age 21, he being 8 years old on 15 Sep next.

Richard Chase ordered to give security to keep the county harmless from a bastard child begotten of Jane Jones, servant to John Nabb. Also fined 20 s.

Jane Mackgerven, servant to Wm. Carr, was judged to be 13 years old.

Wm. Gwin asked for runaway time against his servant

Gilbert Maha who absented himself 39 days. Approved.

John Wright, a lame orphan, was bound to John Copidge until the age of 21, he being 14 years old.

Richard Steevens chose Michll. as his guardian.

It was ordered that Robert Broadaway take into custody the estate of Alice Sides and give security for same.

John Oldgates and his wife Hannah entered a pleas of trespass against David Mills.

TALBOT COUNTY JUDGMENT RECORDS
Liber RF10 (1705-1706)

June Court 1705

The petition of John Griffin showed that James Christinson, son and orphan of John Chrisinson, dec'd., was in 1699 was bound to John Holland until he came of age and the said Howland soon after runaway out of the parts and left the said orphan at the petitioner's house who has kept him. And the petitioner has kept John Davis the son of Peter [?], signed the year 1698 who was given by the said Peter[?] Davis's wife to the petitioner. Both boys were bound by the court to John Griffin until age 21.

Anna --- showed that Benjamin Kininmont at court on 20 Sep 1698 acknowledged a conveyance for 100 a., part ---.

Joseph Lee, an orphan boy was bound to Daniell Sherwood until age 21.

Sarah Cartwright chose as her guardian Robert Harrison.

John Morgan asked for runaway time against his servant Dennis Cussoon for absenting himself 54 days. Approved.

John Morgan asked for runaway time against his servant Dutatis Hardin for absenting himself 47 days. Approved.

Mary Willis, an orphan girl was bound to Henry Harris until age 18.

The petition of Thomas Taylor of Kings Creek was heard. He stated that about 4 or 5 Dec last a distempered lame woman named Mary Barnes was brought and set down at his door. She was ordered to be transferred to the house of Daniell Sherwood.

John Worley, overseer of the highways was allowed at the next laying of the levy 1000 lbs. of tobacco for the erecting of a bridge between the plant. where John Pemberton, dec'd., dwelt and the plant. of Collo. George Robotham, dec'd.

Charity Mattux, orphan and dau. of Charles Mattux, was bound to Andrew Skinner until age 21, she being 2 years old.

Elizabeth Mattux, orphan dau. and twin of Charles Mattux was bound to James Auld until age 21.

Sarah Mattux, orphan and dau. of Charles Mattux was bound to Richard Feddeman until age 21.

Henry Mands [Meends?], son and orphan of James Mands was bound to John Randall until age 21.

James Meends, son and orphan of James Meends, was bound to Thomas Emerson until age 21.

John Steward and his wife Bridgett were bound by the court to Vincent

Hemsley in satisfaction for fees owned the county.

Dennis Connoly asked for runaway time against his servant Cornelius Flinn for absenting himself 10 days.

It was presented that Margarett Benfield on 20 Oct 1704 at Treadhaven Hundred was delivered of a bastard child. She named William Harriss as the father. She was ordered to receive 25 lashes.

It was presented that Rachel Knight, servant to John Simons on 20 Oct 1704 at Warrell Hundred was delivered of a bastard child. She was ordered to receive 25 lashes.

It was presented that Robert Small, ship carpenter, on 1 Nov 1704 at Mill Hundred, when warned to attend by Thomas Bennett, overseer of the roads from Thomas Bennett to John Dawson, in order to assist in clearing and grubbing of the roads, refused to obey and serve Thomas Bennett. Fined.

It was presented that Margarett Black alias Dictus Margaret Black, servant to Robert Grundy, Gent., on 30 Aug 1704, at Tuckahoe Hundred, was delivered of a bastard child. She was ordered to receive 25 lashes. Punishment was suspended since she was big with child.

September Court 1705

William Fitzgarrill, servant to Katherine Alderne was judged to be 11[?] years old.

Lawrence Roach, servant to Richard Bennett, was judged to be 14 years old.

Mary Small, illegitimate girl bound by the court to serve Lawrence Everett until age 21, she being 8 years old last June[?].

Margarett Pope claimed runaway time against her servant John Cooper who absented himself 6 days. Approved.

Thomas Hetherington, orphan boy, was bound to Foster Turbutt until age 21.

William Webb, son and orphan of William Webb, dec'd., chose George Haddaway as his guardian.

William Kempstead complained that Thomas Johnings and George Jackson did enter his house and beat his wife.

It was ordered that Daniel Shahan be issued a summons to appear in order to be bound over to the next Provincial Court.

It was presented that Elizabeth Dry otherwise called Elizabeth Luney of Kent Island, late servant of John Copedge, on 10 Feb 1704 at Lower Hundred on Kent Island was delivered of a bastard child. She named Nicholas Pooley as the father. Fined.

It was presented that Kathrine Harriss alias Dictus Katherine Harris, servant to Thomas Baxter, on 4 May 1705 in Lower Hundred of Kent Island was delivered of a bastard child. Thomas Baxter paid the fine and gave security for keeping the county harmless from the maintenance of the child. Kathrine was ordered to servant Baxter another 12 months for the damage and trouble he sustained.

It was presented that Jane Mishar alias Dictus Jane Mishar of Kent Island, servant to Erreckson [sic]. on 30 March 1705 at Lower Hundred on Kent Island was delivered of a bastard child. She refused to name the father. She was ordered to receive 25 lashes.

It was presented that Margarett Reaning alias Dictus Margarett Reaning, servant to Lawrence Everett, on 4 Nov 1704 in the Lower Hundred of Kent Island was delivered of a bastard child. She refused to name the father. She was ordered to receive 25 lashes.

It was presented that Ellinor Sullivane alias Dictus Elinor Sullivane, spinster, on 30[?] May 1704 in Bay Hundred was delivered of a bastard child at the house of William Webb. She was ordered to receive 25 lashes.

It was presented that Jane Fey, spinster, servant to Richard Tilghman, on 12 Dec 1704 at Worrell Hundred was delivered of a bastard child. Fined and ordered to serve Richard Tilghman an additional 6 months.

It was presented that Thomas Greenhough, servant to Robt. Ungle, at Mill Hundred on 17 June 1704 killed and bore away a lamb, five poultry, one gander and one sow, all belonging to Robert Ungle. Ordered to receive 15 lashes and to pay Robert Ungle four fold.

It was presented that William Wilson, servant to Robert Ungle, at Mill Hundred on 17 June 1704 killed and bore away a lamb, five poultry, one gander and one sow, all belonging to Robert Ungle. Ordered to receive 15 lashes and to pay Robert Ungle four fold.

It was presented that Mary Rowles, servant to Robert Ungle at Mill Hundred on 17 June 1704 killed and bore away a lamb, five poultry, one gander and one sow, all belonging to Robert Ungle. Ordered to receive -- lashes and to pay Robert Ungle four fold.

It was presented that William Loutch, planter, on 1 Oct 1704 at Island Hundred committed fornication with Kathrine Hawkins. Fined 30 shillings. At November Court 1705 it was ordered that he serve an additional 6 months.

It was presented that Kathrine Hawkins on 1 Oct 1704 was delivered of a bastard child. She was ordered to receive 25 lashes.

November Court 1705

Mary Frone, orphan girl, was bound to serve John Coppedge until age 18.

Dennis Hopkins, Jr. acknowledged receiving 10 bushels of Indian corn from Jane Hemsley widow of William Hemsley, after the decease of William Hemsley, having paid him before his death.

Elizabeth Murphey, orphan girl, was bound to serve Thomas Williamson until age 21.

Christopher Higgs asked for runaway time against his servant William Lull, having absented himself 52 days. Approved.

William Martin prayed for runaway time against his servant John Gurlington who absented himself 79 days. Approved.

Mary Mattox, orphan girl, was bound to Robert Robertson until age 21.

Sarah Murphey, orphan girl, was bound to Mathew Griffith until age 19, she being 12 years old next March.

James Wolahane, servant to Isaac Harriss was judged to be 12 years old.

John Fitzgarrill, servant of Robert Ungle, was judged to be 10 years old.

Judith Bennett was granted a license to keep the ferry from her now dwelling plantation to the port of William Stadt.

It was presented that a lame Negro named Mingo, a slave of Vincent Hemsley, was set free by the said Vincent Hemsley. The Negro is ordered returned to said Hemsley who is ordered to see that he is provided for.

The petition of John Cooper was heard. He claimed he had served his full time of service with Mrs. Margarett Pope. Mrs. Pope was ordered to pay sd. Cooper for an overplus of time.

William Dixon, the glover, prayed for runaway time against John Anderson.

It was presented by William Warner that Kathrine ---, servant of William Warner, had delivered a bastard child, the father being Thomas Elsberry. She was ordered to serve an additional year.

Robert Finley prayed for damages against his servant Kathrine Hawkins who had born a bastard child. She was ordered to serve an additional 6 months.

Several complaints were made against William Mitchell, an innholder, "for keeping evil rules and orders in his house ... ." He was ordered to be suppressed from keeping an ordinary.

It was presented that Elinor Cartee, on 3 May 1705, at Lower Hundred on Kent Island, was delivered of a bastard child. She refused to name the father.

It was presented that Margarett Bishop, of Chester Hundred, spinster, servant to John Skillington, on 20 -- 1705 at Chester River, was delivered of a bastard child. She named Charles Warner as the father. Fined.

It was presented that Mary Ridley, servant to Col. Edward Loyd of Island Hundred, on 20 Aug 1705, at Island Hundred, was delivered of a bastard child. She refused to name the father. She was ordered to receive 30 lashes and to serve her master an additional year.

It was presented that Anne Johnson, servant to John Pitt, on 15 Aug 1705 at Kings Creeke at Tuckahoe Hundred, was delivered of a bastard child. She refused to name the father. She was ordered to receive 30 lashes and to serve her master an additional year.

It was presented that Margarett Croatee of Mill Hundred, servant to Peter Harwood, on 10 June 1705, at Mill Hundred was delivered of a bastard child. She named Robert Carr as the father. She was ordered to receive 15 lashes.

It was presented that Magarett Black, servant to Robert Grundy, had born a bastard child. She was ordered to receive 25 lashes and to serve her master an additional year.

It was presented that Mary Carter was delivered of a bastard child. She named the father as John Burk. She was fined.

It was presented that James Abernetha, planter, on 20 June --- committed fornication with Elizabeth Salisbury. He was fined and entered into recognizance with good sureties to save the county harmless from the bastard child.

It was presented that Dorothy Toppin of Chester Hundred, now servant to Andrew King, on 30 Nov 1704, at Chester Hundred, was delivered of a bastard child. She named the father as Henry Gold.

It was presented that Sarah Urling of Chester, servant to Andrew King, on 10 March 1704 at Chester Hundred, was delivered of a bastard child. Fined.

It was presented that Manuel, a Negro, and Monseiur, a Negro, slaves of John Salter of KE Co., on 2 Nov in 1705, at Mills Hundred, stole a rug, a blanket, one pari of britches, a muslin neck cloth, being of the value of 200 lbs. of tobacco, belonging to John Martin [Marlin?]. They were each ordered to receive 30 lashes.

It was presented that Aron Warner, planter, at Worrall Hundred on 30 Aug 1704 stole a sheep of Charles Blake. Ordered to receive 30 lashes and stand in the pillory one hour.

It was presented that James Price in Bullingbrook Hundred on 3 May 1705 stole a hog of person unknown. Acquitted.

It was presented that Patrick Laughall, planter, on 1 Nov 1704 in Mill Hundred being by Thomas Bennett, overseer of the roads that lead from Thomas Bennett to John Dawson, being summoned or warned to attend the said overseer to assist him in the clearing and grubbing, did refuse to obey and serve the said Thomas Bennett as overseer. Fined.

It was presented that Nathaniel Condin, taylor, at Wye River on 3 May 1705, stole one yard of material of Thomas Emerson worth 3 shillngs and 6 pence. Not guilty.

It was presented that Thomas Kelly of Kent Island on 20 Nov 170- at Kent Island committed fornication with Gillion Mackdwyer. Not guilty.

It was presented that James Kirkham on the last day of June 1705 at Choptank River in TA Co. assaulted John Lane the younger.

An allowance was given to Denial Sherwood for keeping Eliz. Haddock 3 months and burying her.

January Court 1705

A complaint was made by John Vaine, servant of Edward Williams.

Cornelius Flinn, servant to Dennis Conelly requested his freedom dues. Cornelius was ordered to return to his master and serve for 10 days runaway time. His master is to use his utmost endeavour to cure the leg of said Cornelius Flinn.

David Mills assigned over to William Dixon, John Anderson to serve Dixon.

Thomas Greenaway, orphan boy, was bound by the court to James Coursey until age 21, he being now 5 years old.

Thomas Jackson was ordered to pay the freedom dues of Margarett Costagin.

John Anderson was ordered to receive 20 lashes for stealing goods of William Dixon, his master, and absenting himself.

Samuel Davis asked the court for 4 days runaway time from his servant John Clarke. Approved.

It was presented that Mary Marshall, servant to Moses Harriss on 18 March 1704 was delivered of a bastard child. She named Henry Richardson as the father. She was fined.

March Court 1705

It was presented that John Anderson, servant to William Dixon, had stolen a horse from George Jackson.

Joane Linshaw, servant of Richard Cooper, was judged to be 22 years old.

John Vaine, servant to Edward Williams, prayed for freedom dues and payment for 5 months service over the agreement. Approved.

The petition of Moses Tonnard was heard. He said he was imported into the province a servant and had an indenture given to him by the person that kept him, to serve 7 years according to the terms of the indenture but his master, Richard Feddeman refused to discharge him. He was ordered to serve his master the time that he was formerly judged as a servant without indenture.

Isaac Abrams chose Mr. Vinct. Hemsley as guardian.

Alce Welsh swore that Charles Neale was the father of --- ?

Came into March Court 1705 Elizabeth Mackclanahan, wife of Thomas Mackclanahan and proved two instruments of writing from the said Thomas Mackclanahan.

The petition of Gerrard Keneday was heard. He stated he had served Thomas Robins 7 years according to his indenture and prayed to be discharged.

William Tippins asked the court for 10 days runaway time against his servant, John Congery. Approved.

The petition of John Barnes was heard. He said he had married the relict of William Viney, dec'd., and David Arey retains Godfrey Viney, son of sd. William Viney, dec'd. in his service and refuses to deliver him to the petitioner and his mother. Ordered discharged.

William Diamond, illegitimate child, was bound by the court to serve Thomas Beswicks until of age.

Richard Alderne, orphan boy, was bound by the court to serve --- Loyd until age 21.

Jane Blackwell prayed judgment for runaway time against her servant, Margarett Agon, having absented herself 20 days.

The petition of Bryan Brother requested that he be given freedom from his master Henry Coursey. His master was summoned to appear at next court.

The petition of James Flood[?] was heard. He stated he was imported into the province and sold as a servant to William Green and was adjudged by the court and his time is now completed and James Auld in whose custody the petitioner is now.

William Garey, son and orphan of William Garey, chose Tristram Thomas as his guardian. William Garey was bound to Tristram Thomas for 4 years; he was to learn the trade of a cordwainer.

Katharine Wells, orphan and dau. of Zorobabell Wells chose her bro. Humprey Wells as her guardian. She was bound to John Coursey and his wife Mary until age 20, a term of 6 years.

Jacob Gibson complained that he had a saddle and bridle stolen from him at the court about a year earlier and nos has found the said saddle in the custody of Samuel Hambleton, who when examined by the court states he bought it from Edward Slater.

It was presented that Murtough Harrow, planter, otherwise called Murtough Roe, planter, on 20 Aug 1705, did deal, buy and sell with the servants and slaves of Robert Gouldsborough, in goods which had been stolen from their master, valued at 500 lbs. of tobacco. Fined 1000 lbs. of tobacco.

It was presented that Elizabeth Diamond, spinster and servant to Thomas Beswick, on 7 Feb 1704, committed fornication with William Welsh and bore a bastard child. She was ordered to receive 20 lashes and serve her master an additional 9 months.

It was presented that William Willson, planter, David Collwell, cordwainer and Thomas Downham, cordwainer, on 14 Nov 1705, stole one gun, two pewter dishes, one large looking glass, one back sword, three tinn pans, one feather bed tick, one skillet, some plates, 3 books of physick and chyrurgery, two Bibles, 3 yards of red bayes, a chest, one tin kettle, a pair of bellowes, a pair of fire tongues, one brass mortar and a pestle and other household goods and materials being of the value of 800 lbs. of tobacco, belonging to Thomas McCh---. David Collwell was acquitted.

It was presented that John Cornine[?], Negro, on 20 Oct 1704 at Tuckahoe Hundred killed and bore away a hog of John Barnes. Not guilty.

It was presented that John Cornine[?] and Mary Barnes on 10 Oct 1704 at Tuckahoe Hundred cohabit together. He was fined.

It was presented that Hannah Neale, wife of Morris Neale of Island Hundred, planter, on 20 July 1704, stole cloth worth 12 s. from Mary Harris. Acquitted.

It was presented that William Willson, planter, David Collwell, cordwainer and Thomas Downham, cordwainer, on 14 Nov --- in Chester Hundred, stole property of Thomas Mackclanahan. Thomas Downham was acquitted.

It was presented that William Welch, servant to Thomas Beswick, planter, on 7 Feb 1704, committed fornication with Elizabeth Diamond. He was ordered to receive 20 lashes.

It was presented that Mary Jones, servant to James Auld, spinster, on 10 Aug 1705, committed fornication with Michaob Maughan, also a servant to James Auld, and bore a bastard child. Each was ordered to receive 20 lashes and to serve their masters an addition 6 months.

Katharine Sherwood, having born a bastard child, named the father as John Leeds. Fined.

Robert Roberts of PA, glover, was summoned to answer unto James Coursey of TA Co.

TALBOT COUNTY JUDGMENT RECORDS
1706-1708 (Microfilm CR6399)

June Court 1706
John Coppedge brought an orphan boy named Samuell Mosely, son of Joseph Mosely and prayed that he be bound to him. Approved.

Henry Burgess, servant to Vincent Hemsley and Timothy Mahan, servant to Robert Finley, ordered into the custody of the sheriff.

Thomas Williams stated he has a son aged about 14 who under the delusions and persuasions of Richard Kempston has bound himself a servant to the said Richard until he comes of age unknown and now seeing his folly is unwilling to serve said Richard. The court ordered him to be free.

James Spencer brings before the court an orphan boy named Joseph Bell, son of James Bell, dec'd., and prayed that he may be bound to him; to learn the trade of sawyer. Approved.

Trustrum Thomas, master and guardian of Wm. Gary, son and orphan of Wm. Gary, dec'd., asked that the orphan's portion of the estate be delivered to him by the execs. Approved.

John Staple[?], servant to Thomas Baxter, was judged to be 20 years old.

It was ordered that Henry Moone, son and orphan of Ralph Moone, live and abide with Robert Grundy until he comes of age to choose his guardian.

John Gilgore on Kent Island, states his wife died about two years earlier and had a child by him, the petitioner, and a daughter by her first husband named Mary Pondder [Peadder?], then about 8 1/2 years old. The dau. to go to her aunt Griffin to live when or if the petitioner married. The petitioner accused Matthew Griffin of molesting and disturbing the petitioner in an attempt to get the girl into his custody. It was ordered that the girl live with said Griffin until old enough to choose her guardian.

It was ordered that Peter Sharpe, overseer of the highways, clear the road through the White Marsh by the church and to go from Samll. Abbett's bridge on the back of Wm. Fray's plantation and by James Bishopp's and then to Peach Blossom road.

William Harrison prayed judgment against his servant, Richard Linton for 66 days runaway time.

William Troth petitioned to resurvey a tract of 300 a. called *Acton* whose bounds depend on another tract called *Jordans Hill* containing 100 a. A warrant was ordered.

Robert Small brought Charles, son of Jacob Seth, dec'd. and prayed that he be bound to him, to learn the trade of ship carpenter. Approved.

Nicholas Gouldesborough, son and orphan of Nicholas Gouldesborough, dec'd. ...?

Nathaniell Teagle prayed for judgment against his servant named John Hunnikin for 38 days of runaway time.

Thomas Collins brought Alexander Kinninmont, son and orphan of Ambros Kinninmont, and prayed that he bound to him until age 21, he being then age 16 on 7th of this instant, to learn the trade of shoemaker. Approved.

John Randall brought Ambros Kinninmont, son and orphan of Ambros Kinnimont, dec'd., and prayed he be bound to him until age 21, he being age 12 on 22 Nov last past, to teach him to cypher and the trade of a millwright. Approved.

Mary Procter shewed that Joan Moore before she married John Alteen gave her a feather (bed) and furniture and a cow and calf, but the said John Alteen refused to deliver same.

John Commee a poor old Negro to be allowed at the next laying of the levy the sum of 600 lbs. of tobacco for his payment of a fine.

Theodorus Bonner admitted to practice as an attorney in the court.

Richard Cumberland, servant to John Lane prayed for his freedom for having completed his time. Freed.

Mary Burgess petitioned that by duress of imprisonment she was in Oct last in DO Co. by the means and procurement of Wm. Jones, Patrick Ewan and John Finch was induced to sign and seal an indenture by which she became bound to the said Finch for 4 years upon a pretended consideration and she has been sold several times until sold to Robert Smith. Freed.

Charles Warner admitted committing fornication with Margaret Bishopp. Fined.

Rebecca Green of TA Co., spinster, was charged with committing fornication on 20 June 1705 at Kent Island of TA Co. She declared that Mark Barden was the father. Fined with sureties to save the county harmless of the bastard child and to serve Caleb Cockerill 4 years for his maintaining the child.

It was presented that Henry Richardson on 20 Aug had carnal knowledge of the body of Mary Marshall. Fined 600 lbs. of tobacco.

It was presented that Mary Nightingale, servant of George Mathar, on 10 Sep 1705 committed fornication with George Mathar, begetting a bastard child. Ordered to receive 25 lashes. He was fined 600 lbs. of tobacco.

It was presented that John Leeds on 10 June 1705 had carnal knowledge of Catharine Sherwood with her consent and begot a bastard child. Fined.

It was presented that Mary Burk, servant to John Lyon, on 10 Sep 1705 committed fornication with Edward Jones and begot a bastard child. Ordered to receive 25 lashes.

Edward Jones was presented for committing fornication with Mary Burk on 10 Sep 1705. Ordered to receive 25 lashes and to serve John Lyon 6 months.

It was presented that Gillian Fling, spinster, servant to William Pratt, on 10 June 1705 committed fornication with William Hatfield. Ordered to receive 25 lashes. William Pratt to receive 21 days runaway time and for his costs after the expiration of her normal servitude.

It was presented that William Jones, taylor, on 2 June 1705 assaulted Margaret Walker. Fined 500 lbs. of tobacco.

It was presented that Andrew Imbert, physician, with his two servants and David Puyett, John Rugg, John Oeak, Thomas Donoly, Henry Savage, Dennis Rodman and Phillip Hambleton, on 25 March last past entered the plantation of David Ambross of Worrell Hundred and took a parcel of fence rails. Fined 100 lbs.

of tobacco each.

It was presented that Francis Rochester, servant to Robert Gouldsborough, on 10 May --- in Miles Hundred stole 3 bushels of wheat, 3 turkeys, 10 lbs. of sheep wool and other, worth 500 lbs. of tobacco, belonging to Robert Gouldesborough. Not guilty.

It was presented that Timothy Mahanny, on 4 March 1705, stole a silver seal used by the county clerk. Ordered to receive 39 lashes and stand in the pillory for 2 hours.

It was presented that Henry Burgess, servant to Vinct. Hemsley, on 5 March 1705, sole a silver seal of the county clerk. Ordered to receive 30 lashes and stand in the pillory for 2 hours. He also receive 93 days additional servitude as runaway time.

It was presented that Anne Highmuss[?], spinster, on 10 May 1705, stole a shirt, a linen sheet, a pair of stockings, pair of gloves, in the dwelling house of Vincent Hemsley. Ordered to receive 10 lashes and stand in the pillory 1/2 hour and pay 4 times the value of the stolen goods.

Edward Chetham, chyrurgeon, complained that John Elmes, labourer, at Chester River on 29 July 1704 retained the said Edward Chetham, but has not paid his debt for which said Chetham seeks to attach the property of said Elmes.

Peter Webb, formerly constable of Bullingbrooke Hundred and refusing to serve, was fined for contempt 500 lbs. of tobacco.

August Court 1706

Brian Brother, having served Henry Coursey 4 years, demanded his freedom. Ordered freed and freedom dues paid.

Sarah Sango stated that during her time of service with Thomas Bowdle, she delivered of two children, and she not being free, said Bowdle detains the children, notwithstanding that the begetter of the children gave said Thomas a servant with 5 years to serve, in satisfaction of keeping the children. It was ordered that the petitioner's children be free from service of Thomas Bowdle.

Richard Bruffe requested to renew his lycence to keep an ordinary in the town of Doncester for the ensuing year. Approved. Mary Jones, servant to James Auld, in respect to her bearing of a bastard child, was ordered to serve an additional 6 months for damages and 2 additional months for maintenance of the child.

James Flood, servant to Robert Harrison, ordered to be free.

It was presented that Catharine Douglass, spinster, servant to Joan Gough, on 20 June 1705, in Mill Hundred, committed fornication with James Powell. Ordered to receive 35 lashes and serve Joan Gough for damages 18 months additional time.

It was presented that Bridget Crestiell, spinster, on 20 June 1705 at Kent Island committed fornication with Maurice Kiney. Fined.

It was presented that Arthur Connar on 10 Jan 1705 committed fornication with Mary Moore, servant to Wm. Shanahan. Fined.

It was presented that Anna Maria Crotchawoodlan, spinster, servant to Eliza. Gouldesborough, widow, committed fornication with Thomas Bowdle and begot a bastard child. Ordered to receive 20 lashes, serve her master 15 additional months, and the child to serve James Laws until she attains the age of 21.

It was presented that Mary Moore, spinster, on 10 Jan 1705, committed fornication with Arthur Connar. Fined.

It was ordered that Francis Bickham and his wife Jane be discharged from their recognizances.

Philemon Hemsley prayed judgment against his servant, David Plimon, for 40 days of runaway time.

Isaac Browne to serve his master, Robert Robertson, additional 15 days runaway time.

William Cooper appointed overseer of the new road from Wye Mill to Tuckahoe Bridge for the ensuing year.

Richard Kellan shewing that he having been imported into the Province a servant and having served his time with Henry Coursey; yet he was not set free. Ordered freed with runaway time of 6 days and 54 days served over his time, with Henry Coursey to pay him 250 lbs. of tobacco.

It was presented that Charles Neale in 1705 committed adultery with Alice Welch, his servant. Acquitted.

November Court 1706

Cisly Manders, widow, prayed judgment against her servant, Eliza. Anniss for 29 days of runaway time. Cisley named Thomas Pearce, another of her servants, who had absented himself with the said Elizabeth, and requested 7 days runaway time plus 4 months for costs.

William Catrupp prayed judgment for 14 days runaway time from his servant, John Smith.

Matthew Griffith appointed guardian of Mary, orphan and dau. of Lazarus Pether, dec'd.

Richard Hopkins prayed judgment against his servant Patrick Towle for 16 days of runaway time.

Edmund Fitzjarrell, shewed that he had lived with John Mullikin with whom his parents had left him at their decease.

It was ordered that William Hempstead, overseer of the highways, clear the road from Thomas Jackson to the place where Henry Carter formerly kept ferry.

It was ordered that Enon Williams, overseer of highways, clear a road from the head of Harriss's Creek to Matthew Tilghman's woods and from the little meeting house to the said Wardes.

John Oldson of Kent Island shewed that whereas Thomas Jackson keeps the wading place ferry and he being very negligent in his charge as appears by the complaints; ordered that Oldson have leave and lycence to keep the ferry.

Ordered that John Buly, a poor lame man, to given board at the house of Daniell Sherwood who would be allowed payment after the laying of the levy.

It was ordered by a motion and request of Benjamin Pecke on behalf of Judith Bennett that the said Judeth have leave and lycence to keep the ferry at her dwelling plant. the ensuing year and be allowed the same as before.

The following overseers of the highways to be summoned: John Roe, Wm. Haddon and Andrew Skinner.

Thomas Jackson requested to have the lycense for his ordinary (at his new dwelling place) renewed. Approved.

Ralph Stevenson requested to have a lycense to keep an ordinary at the town and port of Oxford for the ensuing year. Approved.

Daniell Sherwood to keep --- Burrell, a poor antient decrepid woman, for the next year at the county's expense.

It was presented that Vallentine Fustein, planter, on 24 March 1705 at Island Hundred stole one pair of shoes and a pair of stockings belonging to William Tarlow [Turlow]. Ordered to receive 15 lashes and stand in the pillory one hour.

Hannah Osbourne, widow of William Osbourne, and admx. of Edward Owens plaintiff against Robert Smith assignee of George Martin.

To Geffery Mattershaw, a poor old man, clothing to be provided to him and his wife.

George Ensley, a poor old man was given some relief.

Thomas Bullen, a poor old blind man was given some relief.

Wm. Leeds, a poor decrepid person was given relief toward clothing.

Richard Arrington, Sr., a poor object of charity was given relief.

Wm. Walker was paid for keeping Miles River Ferry.

Edward Pond, a poor old man, received some relief.

Wm. Naylor, a poor old man, received some relief.

Alexander Larramore, a poor old man, received some relief.

January Court 1706

Richard Hynson requested a lycense to keep an ordinary at Chester Mill.

Approved.

Edmund Shehan in his petition shewed he was a servant to Phillip Copedge of Kent Island for 7 years and completed his servitude but said Phillip Copedge refuses to give him his freedom dues. The court ordered that Shehan be satisfy the claim.

Richard Dudley was appointed constable of Tuckahoe Hundred for the ensuing year in the stead of Walter Trotter.

It was presented that Eliz. Cooke, spinster, otherwise called Elizabeth Parvis, on 10 July 1705 committed fornication. Fined.

It was presented that William White of Kent Island on 2 Feb 1702 stole a barrow hog of Alexander Ferbes worth 200 lbs. of tobacco. Acquitted.

It was presented that Walter Quinton on 30 Aug 1706 at St. Peters Parish assaulted James Whitney. Fined 500 lbs. of tobacco.

It was presented that Walter Quinton on 10 Nov 1706 on a Sunday at Williamstadt in TA Co. was very drunken and did profane the Lords day. Fined 100 lbs. of tobacco.

It was presented that Richard Cumberland on 4 Oct 1706, at Tuckahoe Hundred, stole a hog of John Lane. Ordered to receive 25 lashes and stand in the pillory for 2 hours.

It was presented that George Draherty, planter, on 20 Jan 1704 at Tuckahoe Hundred stole 3 barrels of Indian corn belonging to John Lane. Ordered to receive 25 lashes and stand in the pillory for two hours.

It was presented that William Morrison, dec'd., stood indebted to the Queen for 250 lbs. of tobacco for a fine.

March Court 1706

John Moore, son and orphan of Francis Moore, dec'd., was bound to Richard Tilghman until age 21, he being 10 years old sometime May following.

Christopher Santee appointed constable of Island Hundred.

Thomas Alexander appointed constable of Third Haven Hundred.

Richard Cooper, constable of Third Haven, not appearing in court as ordered; fine was remitted when he explained he could not catch his horse.

Ann Lewis entered a petition saying that she came into the country as a servant and was sold to Thomas Thomas, now dec'd. and served her complete time. She not seeks her freedom dues from her mistress. Elizabeth Thomas was ordered to pay the remaining part of the freedom dues, namely, 2 barrels of Indian corn and a cap of white linen.

Richard Bruff asked for a judgment against his servant, James Cosley, for 8 days runaway time. Approved.

Isaac Winchester asked for judgment against his servant, Daniell Cawhalles for 221 days runaway time. He was a runaway for various times in every year from 1699 through 1705.

Anne Fling, an illegitimate child of Gillian Fling, was bound by the court to serve William Pratt until she reached age 21, she being one year old on 5 May following.

Richard Cumberland petitioned that he had served his full time of servitude with John Lane and now requested his freedom dues. The court so ordered.

It was presented that Jane Read, spinster, servant to Isaac Winchester, on 10 May 1706 at Kent Island committed fornication and begot a bastard child; she named Daniell Haley [Huley?] as the father. Fined and ordered to serve an additional year and one-half to Isaac Winchester, considering maintenance of the child and her master's payment of the fine.

It was presented that Margaret Black, spinster, servant to David Arey on 10 May 1706 in Tuckahoe Hundred committed fornication and begot a child by Alexander Day. Fined (paid by her master) and to serve her master an additional 10 months.

It was presented that Mary Witheridge, spinster, otherwise called Mary Fitzgarrell, on 20 June 1705 in St. Peter's Parish committed fornication at various times with Edmund Fitzgarrell to beget her with child. Ordered to receive 12 lashes.

June Court 1707

David Fitzgerall claimed that he was detained illegally by Walter Quinton; the court ruled that he was held as a servant by indenture and not illegally; to serve 52 days of runaway time.

James Higgins claimed that Ralph Stevenson had misused his son who was a servant to said Ralph.

Elizabeth Johnson, servant to James Hopkins, stated she was bound by her parents as a servant to John Hopkins, for 15 years and 2 months, which time expired about middle of April last past but she was not set free. John Hopkins d. May 1692. She was freed and it was ordered that James Hopkins pay her for the overplus of time, 170 lbs. of tobacco.

Joseph Gough brought his servant William Davis, who was judged to be 13 years old.

William Donnelly, son and orphan of James Donnelly, dec'd., was bound as an apprentice to William Gother until 21 years old, he being 14 years old next Valentine's day; to learn the trade of turner.

William Dixon, glover, claimed that at his house was Eliza. Horney, dau. of a Geoffry Horney, a poor decrepid woman who can neither stand nor go since about 4 years ago and her said father being gone and her mother dead was left helpless until he the petitioner took charge of her; she being deluded by some wicked person has delivered of a bastard child and is unable to care for it. Samuel Hambleton, the alleged father of the child, to appear at the next court.

Edward Clarke proved his account against John Jadwin, dec'd. by the testimony of his son Henry Clarke.

Robert Finley prayed judgment against his servant Margaret Barr for 150 days of runaway time; approved.

Daniel Sherwood took the oath as Sheriff of TA Co. His undersheriffs were John Sherwood, Philip Sherwood and Charles Ungle.

John Rodgers and Joseph Rodgers, sons and orphan of David Rodgers, dec'd., were bound by the court to serve William Turner until age 21. David Rodgers, son and orphan of David Rodgers, dec'd. chose Wm. Turner as his guardian.

It was presented that Mary Jones of Bay Hundred, spinster, on 20 March 1705 committed fornication and begot a child. She named the father as Michaell Mahane, servant to James Auld. Ordered to receive 25 lashes.

It was presented that Catharine Noble, servant to John Emerson, on 4 June 1705 and other times committed fornication with John Rathell, taylor, and begot a child. Ordered to receive 25 lashes.

It was presented that William Welsh, servant to Thomas Beswick, on 4 Aug 1706 and at other times, committed fornication with Elizabeth Diamond and by her begot a child. Ordered to receive 25 lashes.

Noting that Timothy Mahany and Henry Burgess were convicted for stealing the county seal, and had received corporal punishment, they are still liable to pay 4 fold the value of the seal.

A transcript from the DO Co. court was recorded concerning Anne Matthews, a woman of evil fame, who came into the county to be delivered of a bastard child; her whereabouts were being sought. She was found at the house of Francis Faulkner in the freshes of Great Choptank River on 6 Jan 1702. She was fined 400 lbs. of tobacco.

It was noted that on 4 Dec 1705 James Parke, labourer, was convicted of breaking into the dwelling of James Busby on 13 July 1705 and stealing 30 --- of linen, 3 Indian stuff neck cloths, 1 piece of kenting linen, a pair of shoes and other goods - for which he received sentence of death, to be hanged. He is not pardoned.

August Court 1707

Arthur Rigby had his servant James M'Cartee judged at 19 years of age.

A letter of attorney was proved from William Willson to his wife Mary Willson.

David Fitzgrrell complained that his master, Joseph Earle, did not allow him sufficient victuals or clothes to support life. Earle was fined 100 lbs. of tobacco. David was ordered to serve an additional 24 days of runaway time.

Judeth Bennett, widow, requested that she have a lycense to keep an ordinary. Approved.

Richard Bruff renewed his license to keep an ordinary in the town of Donchaster.

Edward Stevenson renewed his license to keep an ordinary in the town of Oxford.

Laughlan M'kdaniell brought an orphan girl named Winifred Dennis and had her bound to him until of age 18, she being 7 years old in Feb next.

George Cowley and his wife Mary, extx. of Ralph Dawson, Sr., dec'd., having been presented for not learning Nathaniel Hawke, an orphan who was formerly bound to said Ralph to learn the trade of cooper; now bound to said Cowley to learn the trade of sawyer.

Walter Trotter and Joseph Bruscupp, brought into court for fighting and quarreling in the presence of one of the Justices during the sitting of the court; they to find sureties for their behavior.

Henry Harriss asked that his fine be remitted, he being a taylor and newly come on shore and not knowing that Mr. Vincent Hemsley was one of her majesty's justices of the peace.

Appeared Edmund Fish who m. Eliza. Worgan, admx. of Wm. Worgan, dec'd., he giving security to the orphans, Rachel Worgan, £10.8.8, Mary Worgan, £10.8.8 and Phebe Worgan, 10.8.8, the remainder of the payments due them.

Thomas Hopkins and his wife Anna, extx. of the last will of Alexander Ray, dec'd., appeared to give security to the orphans of said Ray, namely, Alexander Ray to the amount of £6.6.6, Mary Ray to the amount of £6.6.6, John Ray to the amount of £6.6.6 and Anna Ray, to the amount of £6.6.6.

Arthur Rigby and Peter Anderton were bound to pay each of the orphans of Andrew Orem, £4.76, namely: Maurice Orem, Susanna Orem, Thomas Orem, Margarett Orem and Andrew Orem.

William Troth, who m. Sarah Pratt, admx. of George Pratt, dec'd., was bound to pay the orphans of George Pratt: Thomas Pratt, £3.15 and Anne Pratt, £3.15.

John Lyon, admx. of Samuell Abbott, Jr., dec'd., was bound to the orphans of said Samuell Abbott: Thomas Abbott, Samuell Abbott and John Abbott, to the amount of £6.4.1 each.

Walter Quinton, who m. Sarah Gwinn, admx. of William Anderson, dec'd., was bound to the orphan of William Anderson: John Anderson to the amount of

£12.18.7.

William Hadden who m. Margarett Burt, admx. of Henry Burt, dec'd., gave security to the orphans of said Burt: Mary Burt, Henry Burt and Mabel Burt, to the amount of £4.15.5.

Elizabeth Gorsuch, widow and admx. of Richard Gorsuch, dec'd., with her sureties, John Lyon and Wm. Martin, gave security to the orphan of said Gorsuch, son Richard Gorsuch, £19.12.6.

John Mullikin who m. Sarah Mitchell, admx. of John Mitchell, dec'd., gave security to the orphans of said Mitchell: John Mitchell, Alice Mitchell and Sarah Mitchell, to the amount of £12.8.2.

Christian Hunt, extx. of John Hunt, along with her sureties, Robert Harrison and John Hunt, gave security to the orphan Peter Hunt, for the amount of £5.18.1 1/2.

It was presented that John Rathell, taylor, on 4 June 1705 and at other times, committed fornication with Catharine Noble and begot a child. Fined 600 lbs. of tobacco.

It was presented that Margarett Griffin, admx. of John Griffin, dec'd., did not learn James Phisinson an orphan to the trade of a sawyer. Acquitted.

It was presented that Edward Lee did not learn the orphan boy named Richard Marshall, son of Wm. Marshall, dec'd., to read and the trade of shoemaker. Acquitted.

John Oldham, a resident of the town and port of Oxford for 12 years or more, requests to keep the Standard of Weights and Measures for the county. Approved.

Patrick Cavan was appointed overseer of the following roads: from Abbotts Mill to the lower end of Banbury Neck and all the road between Miles Creeke and the Beaver Damm Branch and from the Cross Road at the head of the Beaver Damm Branch until it fall to the road that leads to Bullinbrook White Marsh.

September Court 1707

Matt: Tilghman brought judgment against his servant Henry Hart for an additional 8 days runaway time.

John Kemp and Ennion Williams, execs. of the last will of Robert Kemp, gave security to the orphans of Robert Kemp: Edmund Kemp, William Kemp, Sarah Kemp, each to receive £10.17.3.

Eliza. Martin and Francis Martin, execs. of the last will of Francis Martin, dec'd., gave security to the orphans of Francis Martin: Jacob Martin and Charles Martin, each to receive £17.2.

Elizabeth Thrift, extx. of the last will of John Browne, dec'd., gave security to the orphans of John Browne: Nicholas Browne, Elizabeth Browne and James

Browne, each to receive £9.10.10.

John Tibbels, admin. of John Tibbells, dec'd., his father, gave security to the orphans of John Tibbells, dec'd.: Robert Tibbells and Susanna Tibbels, each to receive £28.12.6.

Joseph Earle received a judgment of 21 days runaway time against his servant, David Fitzgarrell.

John Anderson, servant to Wm. Dixon, glover, prayed to be set free; to serve 4 more years.

It was presented that Johanna Neale, single woman, at St. Peters Parish, on 11 Oct 1705 committed fornication and begot a child. Fined 600 lbs. of tobacco.

It was presented that Mary Gorman, single woman, servant to Tho: Martin, on 10 Jan 1705 and at other times, in Tredhaven Hundred committed fornication with a Negro and begot a child. She declared the father was Tobe a slave of Thomas Martin. Ordered to receive 30 lashes. And on 20 Feb 1706 Mary Gorman committed fornication with a Negro and begot a child, the father of whom she said was Tobe, slave of Thomas Martin. She was ordered to receive 30 lashes and to serve one additional year; the child to be sold to Thomas Martin for 700 lbs. of tobacco.

It was presented that Francis Shry on 10 March 1706 committed fornication with Sarah Voss, widow. Fined 600 lbs. of tobacco.

It was presented that William Hatfield on 10 June 1705 committed adultery with Gillian Fling. Fined 1200 lbs. of tobacco.

November Court 1707

Wm. Hadden requested runaway time against his servant, Henry Betts

John Morgan prayed for judgment against his servant, Dennis Casheen for 23 days of runaway time; approved.

John Morgan prayed for judgment against his servant named Dictatis Hardin for 76 days or runaway time.

Absalom Thrift, son and orphan of John Thrift chose as his guardian John Browne.

Jane Blackwell, extx. of John Blackwell, dec'd. gave security to the orphans of said John Blackwell: John Blackwell, 2 cows and calves, a young mare and a pair of silver shoe buckles when of age; Abednigo Blackwell, to be given 2 cows and calves, a young mare, a hat and a pair of silver shirt buttons.

Ralph Dawson, exec. of William Jones, taylor, along with John Tibbells and James Dawson, gave security for the payment to the orphans of dec'd.: son William Jones, £17.9.3; dau. --- Jones, same sum.

Joane Kinnimont, admx. of Ambros Kinnimont, along with Andrew Skinner and Thomas Collins, gave security for the payment to the orphans of dec'd.: dau. Margaret Kinnimont, £15.5.6; son Alexander Kinnimont.

Joseph Hardin, son and orphan of Robert Hardin, dec'd., prayed to be set free from any service to Elizabeth Hardin his mother in law, alleging that he is 21 years old; the court ruled that he would be 21 on Oct next and would be free at that time.

It was ordered that if Ralph Dawson keep James Farrell, a poor distempered boy the ensuing year, the said Ralph Dawson would be allowed 1000 lbs. of tobacco.

Henry Matthews, son of Anne Matthews was bound to Thomas Robins until age 21, he being 7 years of age Feb next.

It was presented that Sarah Voss on 10 March 1706 committed fornication with Francis Shry and begot a child. Fined.

It was presented that Ann Matthews on 20 Nov 1706 committed fornication and begot a child. Fined.

It was presented that Joseph Earle on 20 Feb 1706 at Bullinbrooke in TA Co., bargained and bought from Negroes, slaves and servants of Nicholas Lowe, goods that were stolen from Nicholas Lowe worth 500 lbs. of tobacco. Fined 1000 lbs. of tobacco and ordered to pay Nicholas Lowe 1000 lbs. of tobacco.

It was presented that Isaac Johnson, planter, servant to Dennis Hopkins, on 6 Nov 1707 at Tred Haven Hundred, stole a barrow hog of Dennis Hopkins. Not guilty.

It was presented that Michael Baldwin, servant to Dennis Hopkins, on 6 Nov 1707 at Tred Haven Hundred, stole a barrow hog of Dennis Hopkins. Not guilty.

Payment was made to Wm. Dixon, glover, for keeping Eliz. Horney, a poor lame woman and her child, and for burying sd. Eliz.

January Court 1707

It was presented that Eliza. Gerald Fitzgerald, spinster, servant to Richard White, on 10 May 1707, committed fornication and begot a child; she named Wm. Lehe as father. Ordered to serve Richard White an additional year and receive 21 lashes.

It was presented that Elizabeth Mason, spinster, on 10 May 1706 committed fornication with John Cooper, planter, and begot a child. Fined 600 lbs. of tobacco.

It was presented that Samuell Hambleton on 18 Dec 1706 committed fornication with Elizabeth Horney, a lewd woman, and begot a child.

Robert Grundy and his wife Margarett, extx. of John Pemberton commenced action against James Benny.

March Court 1707

John Arrington shewed that his sister on her death bed left one of her daus. named Jane Dius[?] to live with him and has kept her since infancy. His brother, Richard Arrington attempts to entice the orphan away; the petitioner requests that the girl be bound to him until she comes of age. Because Richard offered security to learn her to read and John Arrington offered no security, the girl was ordered into the custody of Richard Arrington.

Richard Cooper brought an illegitimate child named Anne Truloe, dau. of Susannah Truloe, and asked that she be bound to him until she came of age 21, she being 4 years old on 15 Aug next. Approved.

John Allexander argued that there is a road marked and made through his corn field by some of the sect of the Quakers in no wise convenient for the mill or other publick place but purposely marked out as a ready road to a private meeting house of the Quakers. He asked to be allowed to grubb and make clear a road around his corn field fence.

Michaell Commins brought an orphan girl named Mary Loyden, dau. and orphan of John Loyden to be bound to him until age 21, she being 6 years old on 15 Dec last past; he also had bound to him, Richard Loyden, orphan of John Loyden, dec'd., until age 21, he being 4 years old 15 Aug next; Richard to learn the trade of weaver.

Robert Martin, son and orphan of Thomas Martin, chose his brother William Martin as his guardian.

Richard Cooper asked for a payment of 600 lbs. of tobacco for keeping a bastard child of his servant, Katharine Laughton from Jan last until June Court next.

It was presented that Catharine Laughton, spinster, servant to John Barker, on 10 May 1707 committed fornication and begot a child by Negro Paul, a slave of the said John Barker. She declared that Hugh Hutchins was the father. Ordered to receive 30 lashes.

It was presented that Negro Tobey, slave to Thomas Martine, on 10 June 1705 committed fornication with Mary Gorman, a lewd woman, and begot a child. Ordered to receive 25 lashes.

It was presented that Mary Bullock, single woman, at St. Peters Parish, on 20 Aug 1706 committed fornication and begot a child, naming Marke Noble as the father. Fined.

It was presented that John Cooper, planter, on 10 May 1706 committed fornication with Elizabeth Mason and begot a child. Fined 600 lbs. of tobacco.

It was presented that Owen Sulivan of St. Peters Parish on 10 Oct 1707 committed fornication with Catharine Farrell, servant to William Carey, being a lewd woman, and begot a child. Fined 600 lbs. of tobacco.

It was presented that Walter Quinton, planter, of St. Peters Parish on 4 Nov 1707 erected fence and thereby stopped up the common road called the Queens highway. Fined 100 lbs. of tobacco.

William Clayton and his wife Joan complained against Edward Combes, stating that Joan when she was known as Joan Gough on 19 Nov 1706 at Tredhaven Creeke, sold to said Edward Combes, an ox, for which he has not adequate paid.

June Court 1708
Jane Dius, an orphan girl, was bound unto James Benson until age 18, she now 11 year sold.

Nathaniell Teagle had his servant, Catharine Hughs, judged to be 21 years of age, to serve according to law.

Samuel Abbott, son of Samuell Abbott, Jr., chose as his guardian, John Lyon.

Edward Colwell, son of Hannah Colwell, was bound with the consent of his mother, to William Skinner until age 21, and if said William Skinner died before the term ended then Edward was to serve William's son [named not given].

It was ordered that Mary Bowers, wife of John Bowers, be allowed 1000 lbs. of tobacco for keeping an illegitimate child named Susannah Reed, for the ensuing year.

Martin Kenny, servant to John Long, complained that he had served 1 1/2 years over his time; ordered freed and John Long to pay for the overplus of time, 700 lbs. of tobacco.

Susannah Johnson entered a plea on behalf of her son, John Benstead, against William Anderson to said John Benstead was bound, complaining of want of necessaries and unkind usage.

It was presented that Ellinor Ballafield, spinster, servant to Michaell Kerby of St. Peters Parish, on 10 Sep 1707 committed fornication with George Roe and begot a child. Fined.

It was presented that Joseph Kennemont, painter, on 29 June 1707 in St. Michaell's Parish married Margaret Ray, dau. of Alexander Ray and Anna his wife; and Anna Ray is the natural sister of the afsd. Joseph Kennemont, to which he confessed and was acquitted, paying his fees [sic].

It was presented that Christiana Jones, widow, no 20 Sep 1707 at St. Paul's Parish in TA Co., committed fornication and begot a child; she declared that John Randall was the father. Fined.

It was presented that Catharine Farrell, servant to William Carey, planter, of

St. Peters Parish, on 10 Oct 1707 committed fornication with Owen Sullivan and begot a child. Ordered to receive 25 lashes.

It was presented that Robert Morton on 6 March 1707 assaulted James Hunter. Fined 100 lbs. of tobacco.

It was presented that Marke Noble, planter, on 20 Aug 1706 committed fornication with Mary Bullock and begot a child to which he confessed.

It was presented that Hugh Hutchins otherwise called Hugh Hutson, of St. Peters Parish, on 10 April 1707 committed fornication with Catharine Laughton and begot a child. Ordered to receive 25 lashes.

It was presented that Henry Smith, planter, on 20 Aug 1707 at St. Paul's Parish, TA Co., committed fornication with Frances Reed, servant to Catharine Aldern, and begot a child. Acquitted.

It was presented that Frances Reed, servant to Catharine Alderne, on 20 Aug 1707 in St. Paul's Parish, TA Co., committed fornication with Henry Smith and begot a child. She refused to name the father. Ordered to receive 39 lashes and to serve an additional year of servitude.

It was presented that Walter Trotter, Gent., on 20 April 1708 erected a fence blocking the highway from Kings Creek bridge towards the plantation of John Needells. Fined 100 lbs. of tobacco.

September Court 1708

A petition of Elizabeth Fleming stated that she was an indented servant who had been sold to Nathll. Teagle and his wife Agnes, and had served them the full term; however they still detained her. Freed.

It was presented that Catharine Duglass, servant to William Clayton, had borne a bastard child and that James Powell was the father. Ordered to receive 25 lashes

It was presented that James Powell had begot a bastard child on the body of Catharine Duglass, servant to William Clayton. Fined and required to give security for the maintenance of the child.

Mary White, orphan girl, was bound to David Fairbanck until age 18, she being 12 years old.

It was presented that William Buckley, Jr., begot a bastard child on the body of Sarah Hawke. Fined.

Richard Bennett had the age of his servant, Michaell Bryan judged to be 14

Agnes Teagle brought her servant, Katharine Hues, to have her age judged; but Katharine objected, saying that she was to serve but a term of 4 years [regardless of age]. The court agreed.

November Court 1708

John Glover, son and orphan of John Glover, dec'd., chose John Henricks as his guardian.

It was presented that Catharine Noble had born a bastard child; the father being Valentine Santee, her master. Surety for Valentine Santee was his mother Anne Santee. The case to be heard next March Court.

Joseph Simmons, a poor orphan son of Richard Simmons, dec'd., was bound by the court to Daniell Sherwood until he comes of age, he being 7 years old.

It was ordered that James Lloyd agree with Doctr. John Brown towards the cure of Barthomew Berry, a poor old man being distempered.

Payment was made to Richard Arrington, Sr., a poor old man, upon petition.

Payment was authorized to Daniel Sherwood for interring Richard Burke.

TALBOT COUNTY JUDGMENT RECORDS
Liber FT1 (1714-1717)

March Court 1714

Francis, orphan son of Richard Hazeldine to bound to Richard Danill[?] until ---, being 4 years old on 6 June last.

Evan Price appeared who m. the widow of Robert --- , gave security to guarantee the residue of the dec'd. estate to [children]: John Booker, when at full age, £1.16.1/2; Lambert Booker, £1.16.1/2; Margaret, £1.16.1/2; [name obliterated].

Elizabeth Mansfield, admx. of Richard Mansfield, dec'd., along with her sureties, Richard Mansfield and Edward Prine[?] gave security to pay the heirs: William, £1.18.4 1/2; and Thomas, £1.18.4.

It was presented that Jane Edwards, servant to Sophia Scott, widow, on 20 May and other times committed fornication with --- , and begot a child. Ordered to receive --- lashes.

It was presented that John Rathel committed fornication with Bridget Penny[?] and begot a child.

It was presented that Sarah Burroughs, spinster, on 26 Oct --- in St. Peters Parish stole a broad green bonnet of John Oldham. Not guilty.

Robert Hopkins brought a boy named Nehemiah Higgins whose mother being --- and father gone out of the country, to be bound to him until of age.

John Whaley refuses to maintain Ralph Attoe, an illegitimate; Marke Noble offers to take the child.

It was presented that Mary Heath, servant to Thos. Prince has borne a bastard child; she named the father as Joseph[?] Broom. Ordered to receive 25 lashes.

Catherine Crissell, an illegitimate child, was bound to Edmond Fish until of age.

August Court 1715

Jacob Gibson brought his servant named John Wilton to have 20 days runaway time added to his servitude.

November Court 1715

Samuel Broadway appointed constable of Tuckahoe Hundred.

James Hogell[?] brought his servant boy named John Perry [Percy?] and had his age judged as 14.

Thomas Higgins, son of Michll. Higgins of DO Co., being 5 years old, was bound to Dr. Francis Rolle.

Elizabeth Feddeman, widow, brought an old Negro man called Tony, aged and blind, to be exempt from taxables.

Elizabeth Herrington, servant to George Bowes petitioned against her master, stating she was put to serve a term of 18 years; he argued she was to serve until age 21; ordered to serve until age 21.

Thomas Sevill was bound to Edward Roe till age ---, he being 18 years old 22 Sep last.

Lambert Clements petitioned to keep a ferry at his dwell. plant. to DO Co., to be allowed 2500 lbs. of tobacco per annum.

It was presented that Judith Wells, servant to Peter Anderton had given birth to a bastard child. Ordered to receive 31 lashes.

It was presented that Agnus Fanar, servant to Peter Anderton had given birth to a bastard child. Ordered to receive 31 lashes.

It was presented that Catharine Crookshanks has given birth to a bastard child. Fined 30 shillings.

It was presented that Rowland Johnson, servant to Richd. Bruff, committed fornication with Catherine Crookshanks, servant to his master and begot a bastard child. Fined 600 lbs. of tobacco.

It was presented that Elianor Brittain, servant to Thomas Edmondson gave birth to a bastard child. Fined.

It was presented that John Bexley begot a bastard child by Elianor Brittain. Fined 30 shillings and ordered to give security for the maintenance of the child

It was presented that Sarah Harwood gave birth to a bastard child. She named Oliver Kranivett as the father. Fine paid by Peter Harwood.

It was presented that Elisha Manwearing on 10 March 1714 in St. Peters Parish, committed adultery with Mary Turner, servant to Robert ---, cordwainer, and had carnal knowledge of her body. The charge appears to have been dropped

June Court 1716

Mary Bruff, servant to William Martin, petitioned against her master for her freedom and freedom dues. Approved.

----annah Mahany petitioned against Wm. Finney for detaining her dau., Frances Neale, as a servant.

Joseph Blackwell, servant to William Walker, petitioned against his master for not keeping him to his trade.

---ah Emerson brought Richard Jones, son and orphan of Richard Jones, dec'd., to appoint a guardian, the orphan being 11 years of age in April last.

Ann Watts, widow brought an orphan girl named Sarah Summers[?], age 11 on 13 March last past, to serve Ann Watts until age 18.

Peter Webb brought his servant boy named Edward Davis who was adjudged to be 14 years old.

It was presented that Hezekiah Mekotter, carpenter, in Bullingbrook had misused Thomas Hues who was bound to him in not keeping him to his trade. Dismissed in that the orphan was almost free.

It was presented that William Danielin had begotten a child on the body of Margaret Wright, servant to Henry Sutton.

It was presented that Christopher Fields, planter, on 18 June 1715 in St. Michael's Parish, assaulted James Anthony. Fined 50 lbs. of tobacco.

It was presented that Susana Moulton, servant to John Bedfield on 30 June 1715 committed fornication with Evan Evans. Ordered to receive 21 lashes.

It was presented that Sarah Barrows, spinster, on 30 June 1715 committed fornication and begot a bastard child. Ordered to receive 31 lashes.

It was presented that Margarett Higgins, spinster, on 10 Aug 1713 in St. Peters Parish committed fornication. Not guilty.

Richard Bennet made complaint against Jacob Loockerman of TA Co., Gent., and Magdalen his wife lately called Magdalen Edmondson in a plea for £1.11.

November Court 1716

Hannah Neale, orphan girl, was bound to Timothy Mahany until she arrives at the age of 18.

Martha Neale, orphan girl, was bound to Timothy Mahany until age 18.

Frances Neale, servant to Catherine Finney, was set free at the petition of said Frances.

At the petition of George Johnson, late servant to Thomas Johnson, Liverpool, merchant, having served his full time, requests his freedom dues. Approved.

Charles Stevens brought Hope Mason, dau. and orphan of John Mason, dec'd., to be bound to him until age 18.

John Mason, son and orphan of John Mason, was bound to Edward Hurd[?] until age 21.

Andrew Orum presented a petition against his step-father, Arthur Rigby, stating that he was a bound to his step-father for 7 years in order to learn a trade and whereas he has served 5 years without any instruction in a trade. Set free.

A mulatto girl called Betty born to a servant woman belonging to Ann Davis called Elizabeth M--- was by the court bound to Thomas Price until age 21, she now being 5 months old.

William Heath, a mulatto boy born of Mary Heath, was bound by the court to Thomas Price until age 31, he being 10 months old.

Mary Turner, a mulatto girl born to Mary Turner, servant to Robert Hoskins, was bound to William Clayland until age 31, she being a year old Sep last. Also another mulatto girl born of the same woman, age 2 months old, was bound to William Clayland.

Margaritt Huesdale als. Wright swore that William Dannelin was the father of her child.

It was presented that Mary Davis, spinster, on 30 June 1715 at St. Michael's Parish committed fornication with Edward Perkins, cooper, and begot a child. Deferred until next court.

It was presented that Mary Huggins, servant to Jane Finley, widow, on 30 Jan ---, committed fornication. Ordered to receive 20 lashes.presented   that the same Mary Huggins on 30 Aug 1715 committed fornication and now bears 2 children. She was ordered to serve an additional 18 months.

It was presented that Mary Stanton on 10 April 1716 in St. Peter's Parish committed fornication and begot a child; she named Thomas Bryan as the father. Fined 30 s.

It was presented that Catherine Roberts, servant to Arthur Connar, on 1 May 1716, committed fornication with Thomas Donellan. Ordered to received 21 lashes and ordered to serve an addition year of servitude.

It was presented that Margaret Partlet, spinster, on 30 June 1715, in St. Paul's Parish, committed fornication. Fined 30 shillings.

It was presented that Adam Fareow, servant to Arthur Rigby, on 4 Nov 1716 in St. Michael's Parish, stole a hogg of Job Cornish. Acquitted. Not guilty.

It was presented that Thomas Rathol, servant to Arthur Rigby on 4 Nov 1716 stole a hog of Job Cornish. Not guilty.

It was presented that Mary Turner, spinster, on 20 June 1714, committed fornication with a Negro called Jo and begot a child. Ordered to receive 31 lashes, but she being very sick the punishment was suspended until next court,

It was presented that Mary Turner, servant to Robert Hopkins, cordwainer, on 10 May 1716 committed fornication with a Negro slave and begot a child. Ordered to receive 31 lashes, but she being very sick the punishment was suspended until next court when the punishment was carried out.

It was presented that Mary Heath, servant to Thomas Price, planter, on 13 June 1715 in St. Michael's Parish, committed fornication with a Negro slave and begot a child. Ordered to receive 31 lashes, and she being very sick the punishment was suspended until next court.

It was presented that John Lace, servant to Edwd. Martland, on 5 Oct 1716, stole a pair of women's shoes belonging to Francis Armstrong. Not guilty.

March Court 1716

It was presented that Catherine Jones, servant to Francis Neale, lately dec'd., on 10 Aug 1716, committed fornication with Thomas Mills. Ordered to receive 31 lashes.

It was presented that Jane Edwards, servant to Sophia Scott, on 10 April 17--, committed fornication. Ordered to receive 31 lashes.

It was presented that William Dannelley on 10 Jan 1715 in St. Peter's Parish committed fornication with Margaret Wright, servant to Henry Sutton. Fined 30 shillings.

It was presented that Mary Thunderman, on 10 Aug 1716, committed fornication. Fined 30 shillings.

It was presented that William Barwick on 10 Aug 1716 committed fornication with Mary Thunderman, servant to Robert Noble. Not guilty.

It was presented that Mary Unahann, servant to Richard White, on 10 -- 1715 in St. Peters Parish committed fornication. Ordered to receive 31 lashes.

It was presented that Elizabeth Mace [Maco?], servant to Ann Davis, on 10 Jan 1715, committed fornication with a Negro called Jack and begot a child. Ordered to receive 21 lashes and to serve an additional year of servitude.

It was presented that Hannah Hewet, servant to John Kerns[?] on 13 May 1715 in St. Michaels Parish committed fornication. Not guilty.

It was presented that Anthony Jacob, planter, on 10 Sep 1715 in St. Paul's Parish in TA Co. stole some clothing material worth 3 shillings. Ordered to receive 10 lashes and stand in the pillory for 1/2 hour.

It was presented that Edward Perkins, cooper, on 30 June 1715 committed fornication with Mary Davis, spinster, and begot a child. Fined 600 lbs. of tobacco.

It was presented that Catherine Buckley on 20 June 1715 at the town of Oxford in St. Peters Parish stole 2 gallons of rum from the house of Thomas Planner, the value of 10 shillings. Not guilty.

June Court 1717

--- Valliant brought his servant boy, John Dent and had his age judged to be 14 years old.

--- brought his servant named John Stubbs and proved 10 days of runaway time.

William Skinner brought illegitimate child named Lewis Mathewson, to be bound to him until age 21.

Major Thomas Emerson was appointed guardian to Richard Jones, orphan of Richard Jones, late of QA Co., dec'd.

Robert Harrison, Sr., petitioned on behalf of his grandchildren, John and James Harrison, the sons of James Harrison, lately dec'd. *[partially obliterated; apparently the grandfather was attempting to remove custody of the estate of the orphans from their step-father who had married their mother and had cut down much of the timber of the land.]*

It was presented that Frances Read, servant to William[?] Matthews, planter, on 10 April 1716 in St. Paul's Parish, committed fornication. She named Robert Ratcliff as the father. Fined 30 shillings.

It was presented that Margaret Wright, spinster, servant to Henry Sutton, on 10 July 1716 in St. Peter's Parish committed fornication with John Danelly. Ordered to receive 31 lashes.

It was presented that Ann Farnworth, servant to Walter Quinton, innholder, on 10 May 1716, in St. Peter's Parish, committed fornication. She declared the father to be --- Shepherd, a sailor of the ship *Eliza. of Liverpool*. Fined 30 shillings.

It was presented that John Herbert, planter, on 10 Jan 1715 in St. Peter's Parish committed fornication with Mary Hains, servant to Richard White of TA Co. Not guilty.

It was presented that Margaret Taylor, spinster, on 10 April [no year given], in St. Michael's Parish, committed fornication. Ordered to receive 21 lashes.

It was presented that Sarah Hardman, spinster, on 10 July 1716 in St. Michael's Parish, committed fornication. Ordered to receive 35 lashes.

It was presented that Thomas Mills, planter, on 10 Aug 1716 in St. Peter's Parish committed fornication with Catherine Jones, servant to --- Neale, dec'd. Acquitted.

... [Very faint] ...

August Court 1717

Peter Bennett who m. the widow of Benjamin Peck was summoned with Thomas Hopkins, Sr., and John Peck his sureties to guarantees the orphan, Benjamin Peck, one of the orphans of afsd. Benjamin Peck, £24.

It was presented that Margaret Higgins, spinster, on 10 Aug 1716 in St. Peter's Parish, committed fornication with William Gorman. Ordered to receive 21 lashes

It was presented that Thomas Maid in St. Paul's Parish, TA Co., on 10 Aug 1716, committed fornication with Catherine Mackdaniel. Fined 30 shillings.

It was presented that Catherine Mackdaniel on 10 Aug 1716, in St. Paul's Parish, committed fornication with Thomas Mayd, planter. Fined 30 shillings.

INDEX

John, 114, 115
BALDWIN
Michael, 158
BALE
Thomas, 133
BALL
Benjamin, 25, 78, 82,
100
Richard, 131
Susannah, 78
Thomas, 126
BALLAFIELD
Ellinor, 160
BAMPTON
James, 138
BARDEN
Mark, 148
BARKER
John, 159
BARKHURST
George, 101
BARKS
Elizabeth, 115
BARNERS
Charles, 18
BARNES
Ann, 107
Charles, 42
Francis, 69, 90
James, 42
John, 18, 31, 42, 145,
146
Mary, 139, 146
BARNETT
William, 21
BARNEY
Francis, 45
John, 29, 43
BARNOTO
Francis, 18
BARNS
Ann, 107

Francis, 69
John, 42, 50
BARR
Margaret, 154
Margarett, 125
BARROWS
Sarah, 164
BARTLETT
John, 128
Sarah, 128
BARTON
John, 4
BARUNDY
John, 39
BARWICK
William, 166
BASLEY
Joane, 3
BASSY
Jeane, 3
Michaell, 3
BATCHERLY
Richard, 19
BATSON
Christopher, 108, 117,
119, 121
Hannah, 108, 119,
121
BAXTER
John, 25, 47, 49, 52,
59
Roger, 69
Thomas, 93, 129, 140,
141, 147
BAYLEY
Thomas, 102
BAYNARD
Francis, 28
Robert, 94
Sarah, 94
Thomas, 90
Williamander, 91

BEARD
John, 59
BECK
Solomon, 29
BECKET
James, 26
BECKINGHAM
William, 22
BECKLESS, 36
BECKWITH
Frances, 20, 22
Henry, 1, 5, 28
Nehemiah, 12
BECKWORTH
Charles, 20
BEDFIELD
John, 164
BEDWICKS
Thomas, 145
BELFORD
William, 110
BELL
Edward, 114
James, 146
Joseph, 146
William, 137
BELVIN
Richard, 135
BENFIELD
Margarett, 140
BENHAM
Benjamin, 75
BENNET
Richard, 164
BENNETT
John, 98
Judeth, 155
Judith, 142, 151
Mr., 65, 73, 92
Peter, 168
Richard, 90, 94, 140,
161

BUSIK
  Rebecca/Rebenna/
  Robena, 12, 13, 14
BUSWICK
  James, 8
BUTCHER
  Robert, 10
BUTCHERLY
  Hannah, 12
  Robert, 12
BUTLER
  Elizabeth, 110
  Elliner, 120
  Francis, 124
  James, 95
  Margaret, 95
  Mary, 117, 119, 120,
    121, 124
  Susanna, 62
  William, 95, 108, 117,
    124
BUTTLER
  Susannah, 86
BUTTON
  John, 4, 9, 79
  Peter, 45
BYAS
  William, 50
BYRNS
  Hugh, 118
BYUS
  William, 49
CAFFEY
  Michel, 43
  Rachel, 43
CAMMEE
  John, 148
CAMPBELL
  Walker, 23
  Walter, 10
CAMPBLE
  Walter, 19

CAMPERSON
  Stephen, 64
CANERLY
  William, 7
CANLIN
  John, 86
CANNELY
  Joseph, 50
CANNON
  Edward, 41
  Elizabeth, 16
  Henry, 27, 46
  James, 13, 15, 25, 26,
    42
  Joshua, 13
  Mary, 13
  Matthew, 13
  William, 28, 36
CANNOR, Thomas, 16
CANTIN
  John, 75
CANTWELL
  Richard, 54
CARAWIN
  Elizabeth, 56
  Patrick, 56
CAREY
  William, 160
CARLTON
  John, 90
CARMAN
  Thomas, 76
  William, 70
CARR
  Francis, 55
  Hannah, 33
  Robert, 143
  William, 130, 138
CARRADYNE
  John, 96
CARRARY
  Margaret, 75

CARRELL
  Daniell, 119
CARRORY
  Margaret, 75
CARRY
  Mathew, 1
  Matthew, 2
CARSEY
  James, 72
CARSH
  Edward, 72
CARTE
  Elinor, 136
CARTEE
  Elinor, 142
CARTER
  Elizabeth, 98
  Henry, 126, 133, 150
  James, 15, 51
  Jeremiah, 51
  John, 51, 90
  Mary, 51, 64, 71, 81,
    143
  Peter, 36
  Richard, 98, 109
  Robert, 6
  Val., 90
  Valentine, 99
  Volentine, 135
CARTWRIGHT
  Mary, 127
  Sarah, 139
CARVIN
  Morris, 36
CARWIN
  Elizabeth, 59
CASDEY
  Rose, 19
CASE
  Edward, 131
CASHEEN
  Dennis, 157

William, 70, 89, 124, 160, 161
CLEAVE
Nathaniel, 120
CLEMANS
Essabell, 125
CLEMENT
John, 103
CLEMENTS
Lambert, 163
CLIFT
Joseph, 85, 90
CLIFTON
Jonathan, 27
Sarah, 46
Thomas, 33, 46
CLIFTS
Joseph, 63
CLOCK
Morris, 71
CLOUDES
Nicholas, 102
CLOUDS
Nicholas, 91
COAL
Diane, 58
John, 58
COALTMAN
Ann, 131
COARNER
Magdalin, 6
COARSON
Sarah, 21
COBHAM
Elizabeth, 5, 11
COBURN
Ann, 60
COCKAYNE
Betty, 19
Elizabeth, 19
Mary, 19

COCKCRAFT
Thomas William, 33
COCKERILL
Caleb, 148
COCKLEY
Thomas, 29
COCKRAINE
Edward, 106
COCKRUN
Jane, 62
COFFIN
John, 43
COLE
Issabell, 106
John, 43, 51, 58
COLEMAN
Isabell, 130
COLLIER
Matthew, 97, 99
COLLINOR
Jane, 112
COLLINS
Francis, 113
Mary, 114
Mathew, 70
Patrick, 16
Rachell, 21
Sarah, 111
Susana, 127
Thomas, 112, 113, 127, 147, 158
Ursula, 70
COLLOHAN
Dennis, 136
COLLWELL
David, 145, 146
COLSON
Marmaduke, 113
Robert, 113
COLSTOCK
Edward, 118

COLT
Robert, 73
COLTMAN
Ann, 103
COLTON
Thomas, 6
COLWELL
Edward, 160
Hannah, 160
COMBES
Edward, 160
William, 103
COMBS
John, 44
William, 106
COMEGYS
Nathaniel, 90, 96
COMING
Miles, 118
COMMINS
Michaell, 159
COMPERSON
Stephen, 90
CONAH
Elinor, 135
CONDER
Daniel, 136
CONDIN
Nathaniel, 143
CONELLY
Dennis, 144
CONGERY
John, 145
CONLEY
Stephen, 19
CONNALLY
Bryan, 80
CONNAR
Arthur, 150, 165
CONNELLY
Bryan, 63, 72, 85, 92, 94

CONNER
Charles, 69
Nathaniel, 71
Philip, 71, 79
CONNERLY
John, 35, 46
Owen, 35, 46, 47
CONNOLY
Dennis, 140
CONNOR
Charles, 84, 85, 90
John, 69
Nathaniel, 90
Philip, 90
Phillip, 78
Thomas, 16
CONNYERS
Phillip, 125
CONWAY
Sarah, 114
COOK
Ann, 35, 40
Francis, 88
John, 38, 46, 59
Mary, 18, 24, 35
Thomas, 3, 8, 30, 35,
46
William, 104
COOKE
Edward, 1, 2, 7
Elizabeth, 152
James, 59
Morgan, 119, 120
Rebeckah, 108
Thomas, 1, 5, 9, 10
William, 108
COOPER
(N), 27
John, 123, 137, 140,
142, 158, 159
Mary, 133

Richard, 27, 47, 52,
59, 144, 152, 159
Susana, 137
Thomas, 88, 94, 95,
97, 130
William, 68, 123, 133,
135, 137, 150
COPEDGE
John, 140
Phillip, 152
COPELL
William, 122
COPIDGE
John, 138
COPPEDGE
John, 141, 146
COPPIN
John, 105, 124
Sarah, 105
COPPINS
John, 120
CORBUT
Thomas, 61
CORBUTT
Garrett, 40
Thomas, 40, 46
CORNELINSON
Andrew, 65
CORNELIUSON
Andrew, 65
Mary, 85
CORNER
Magdalin, 6
William, 6
CORNETT
William, 131
CORNINE
John, 146
CORNISH
Job, 165
Sidney, 56

CORREY
Thomas, 117
CORSON
Thomas, 21
CORVERWELL
Mary, 130
COSLEY
James, 152
COSTAGIN
Margarett, 144
COSTIGIN
Margaret, 68
COSTON
Henry, 117
COTTER
John, 28
COTTON
Richard, 64
COUGHIN
Gilbert, 131
COULTON
Ann, 135
COURSEY
Coll., 76
Colo., 88
Elizabeth, 72, 135
Henry, 117, 135, 145,
149, 150
James, 84, 144, 146
John, 62, 73, 82, 83,
145
Mary, 87, 145
William, 67
COURSON
Elizabeth, 60
John, 21
Mary, 59
Sarah, 21
Thomas, 59, 60
COVEY
Richard, 36
William, 3, 5, 12

Edward, 164
Elizabeth, 58, 127
Henry, 22, 26
James, 101
John, 12, 105, 119,
139
Mary, 130, 165, 166
Maurice, 122
Morris, 129
Peter, 139
Samuel, 144
Sarah, 52, 132
William, 153
DAVISE
William, 5
DAVISON
Elizabeth, 124
John, 12
Peter, 124
DAWSON
Hannah, 37
James, 157
John, 8, 136, 140, 143
Obadiah, 58
Obbediah, 35
Ralph, 118, 131, 155,
157, 158
Richard, 27, 36, 49,
53, 60, 124
Thomas, 36
William, 49, 60
DAY
Alexander, 153
DAZEY
Anne, 97
DE---
Allexander, 116
DEACON
John, 110
DEALE
Catharine, 71
John, 71

DEAN
Dorothy, 44
Eizabeth, 44
Francis, 52
John, 22, 30, 44, 47
Mary, 44
William, 30, 94
DEANE
Michael, 134
William, 12
DEARDEN
Richard, 120
DEARDEON
Richard, 119
DEHENIOSSA
Johannes, 75
Johannis, 127
DEHENOYOSSA
Johannis, 94
DEHINEYOSSA
Johannes, 83
DEHINEYOSTA
Johannes, 79
DEHINOYOSSA
Johannis, 98
DEHORTY
John, 33
Margrett, 132, 133
DELIMSYOSTA
Johannes, 75
DELINEY
Johannes, 69
DELL
Thomas, 24, 39
DENHAM
Robert, 111
DENNIS
John, 77
Peter, 113
Winifred, 155
DENNISON
Antony, 131

DENNUM
Robert, 109
DENNY
Christopher, 94, 101
DENT
James, 27, 35
John, 167
DENTON
Mr., 5
Vachel, 20
DENWOOD
Levin, 56
DEROACHBURN
Mary, 65
DEROCHBURNE
Lewis, 136
DEVERAUN
Alexander, 117
DIAMOND
Elizabeth, 145, 146,
154
William, 145
DICKINSON
Charles, 31
William, 104, 105,
112
DICKS
Elizabeth, 10
Robert, 10
DIKINSON
William, 138
DINING
Giles, 136
DIUS
Jane, 159, 160
DIXON
Geoffry, 153
William, 102, 110,
125, 135, 142,
144, 157, 158
D'LAHAY
Thomas, 135

T., 90
FALLEN
  Daniel, 58
  John, 34
FALLIN
  Barnaby, 58
FALLON
  Barnaby, 15
  John, 32
FANAR
  Agnus, 163
FANIN
  Andrew, 119
FANINE
  Andrew, 120
FAREOW
  Adam, 165
FARGASON
  James, 55
  Thomas, 42
FARGUSON
  Alexander, 18, 50
FARMER
  Samuell, 105
FARNWORTH
  Ann, 167
FARRELL
  Catharine, 160
  James, 158
FAULKNER
  Francis, 154
FE---
  Andrew, 99
FEDDEMAN
  Elizabeth, 163
  Philip, 68
  Richard, 139, 144
  Shadrack, 22
FEDDMAN
  Shaddrack, 17
FEEDEMAN
  Richard, 127

FELLOW
  Robert, 128
FENNIN
  Ellinor, 136
FERBES
  Alexander, 152
FERRELL
  Lewis, 118
FERRIS
  Charles, 121
  Mary, 120
FEY
  Jane, 141
FIELDING
  James, 1, 11
  Katharine, 7
  Katherin, 6
  Katherine, 1, 2, 11
FIELDS
  Christopher, 164
  Matthew, 16
FINCH
  John, 35, 46, 148
FINLEY
  Jane, 165
  Robert, 142, 146, 154
FINNEY
  Catherine, 126, 164
  Katherine, 131
  Mrs., 127
  William, 113, 119,
    121, 131, 164
FISH
  Edmond, 163
  Edmund, 111, 115,
    155
FISHBOURNE
  Ralph, 111, 122
FISHBURN
  William, 51
FISHBURNE
  Ralph, 135

FISHER
  Flower, 59
  John Pritchet, 55
  Thomas, 64, 72, 76,
    81, 85, 90, 91, 92,
    118, 121, 133
  William, 3, 12
FISHING CREEK
  POINT, 48
FITZGARRALD
  Garrett, 107
FITZGARRELL
  David, 157
  Edmund, 153
  Mary, 153
FITZGARRILL
  John, 142
  William, 140
FITZGERALD
  Elinor, 43
  Elizabeth Gerald, 158
  Honour, 9, 10
FITZGERALL
  David, 153
FITZGERRALD
  Eleanor, 100
FITZGERRELL
  James, 137
FITZGRRELL
  David, 155
FITZHUGH
  Catharine, 85
FITZJARRELL
  Edmund, 150
FITZPATRICK
  Bryan, 9
FLANHAWNE
  John, 118
FLEAHARTY
  John, 4
FLEHARTY
  Ann, 34

HETHERINGTON
Thomas, 140
HEWET
Hannah, 166
HEWETT
Elizabeth, 136
HEWS
Mary, 56, 57
HEYATT
Edward, 98
HEYHEARD
Patrick, 137
HICKMAN
James, 33, 46
Sarah, 33
Thomas, 38
HICKS
Henry, 51
James, 84
Levin, 50
Thomas, 5, 8, 9, 12
HIDE
Phinehas, 102
HIGGINS
James, 153
margaret, 168
Margarett, 164
Michaell, 163
Nehemiah, 162
Thomas, 163
HIGGS
Christopher, 142
HIGHMUSS
Anne, 149
HIGLEY
Edward, 117
HIGMAN
Mary, 20
HILL
Arthur, 76
Henry, 31
Isaac, 11

Penelopy, 41
Richard, 64
Thomas, 66, 68
William, 1, 2
HINDLEY
Richard, 131
HINDMAN
Jacob, 49
James, 73, 79, 84, 86, 88
Mrs., 88
HINDS
Elizabeth, 16
Mary, 55
HINES
Elizabeth, 14, 16
HOBBS
Mary, 73, 82, 82, 93
Robert, 55
HOCKEN
John, 87, 88
HODSON
James, 30
John, 8, 19, 20, 28, 44, 46, 50, 59
Levin, 35
Roger, 50
Rosannah, 28
Vienna, 24
HOG QUARTER, 59
HOGE
Elizabeth, 71
HOGELL
James, 163
HOGYARD, 56
HOKOS
Peter, 18
HOLDBROOK
William, 49
HOLDING
Richard, 65, 78

HOLLAND
Hennora, 118
John, 86, 139
Mary, 29, 48
Richard, 4, 9, 12, 111, 112, 118
Robert, 101
Susannah, 112
HOLLINGSWORTH
Charles, 97
John, 103, 105
Thomas, 89
William, 66, 73, 74
HOLLINGWORTH
Robert, 92, 97
HOLLINSWORTH
Charles, 62, 117
Isaac, 72
Thomas, 81, 82, 86
William, 72, 85, 92, 125
HOLLOWAY
William, 32
HOLT
John, 67
HOLTEN
Jesse, 130
HOLTON
Anne, 25
William, 25
HONEY
Thomas, 81, 91
HONY
Thomas, 71, 72, 85
HOOPER
Col., 48
Enn., 50, 54
Ennalls, 30, 48
Henry, 19, 21, 33, 53, 57
James, 18, 50, 54
Richard, 5

Alice, 73
Edward, 63, 137, 142
Elizabeth, 82, 85, 103
Henrietta Maria, 103
James, 133, 162
Margrett, 133
Philemon, 72, 97, 98
Phillemon, 133
Richard, 114, 128
LOADEN
Anne, 41
LOCERMAN
Thomas, 18
LOCKERMAN
Jacob, 8
LOCKSLY
Elizabeth, 56
LOLLER
Elizabeth, 102
LONDON
Ann, 31
James, 87
LONG
Elizabeth, 22
John, 59, 86, 160
Mary, 11
Samuel, 14, 16
Thomas, 11, 59
LOOCERMAN
Jacob, 18
LOOCKERMAN
Dorothy, 52
Govert, 19
Jacob, 19, 52, 164
Magdalen, 164
Rosannah, 36, 47, 52
Thomas, 30, 43, 49, 60
LOOCKERMANN
Jacob, 5
LOUDS
Thomas, 75

LOUTCH
William, 141
LOVELEY
Thomas, 122
LOWDER
Charles, 77, 84
LOWE
Colo., 79, 92
Jacob, 52
John, 35, 44
Mary, 35
Nicholas, 64, 72, 78, 81, 86, 127, 138, 158
William, 4
LOWREY
Alexander, 137
LOWTHER
Charles, 62, 68
LOYDEN
John, 159
Mary, 159
Richard, 159
LUCK BY CHANCE, 51
LUDMAN
Edward, 36
LUGGER
William, 132
LULL
William, 142
LUNEY
Elizabeth, 140
LUNN
John, 12
LUXS
Thomas, 19
LYON
John, 148, 155, 156, 160
M---
Elizabeth, 165

MABBOT
Kymton, 103
MABBOTT
Kempton, 106, 107
MACARTER
Owen, 123
MCATT
Edward, 127
MCCALLUM
Neil, 40
MACCALLUM
Neil, 53
MACCARTEE
Dennis, 122
M'CARTEE
James, 154
MCCH---
Thomas, 146
MCCOLLISTER
David, 20
Patrick, 44
MCCORMACK
John, 24
Michel, 24
MCCOTTER
Alexander, 38, 47
MCDANIEL
(MacDaniel)
Johann, 60
Johannah, 60
Walter, 50
MACE
Elizabeth, 166
John, 56
Nicholas, 44
Thomas, 44
MCGRAW/
MACGRAW
Godfry, 50
John, 17
MCHILL
Ann, 40

Lucy, 118
Sarah, 109
MANARTHY
C., 36
Charles, 45
MANDERS
Cisly, 150
MANDIDER
John, 19
MANDS
Henry, 139
James, 139
MANER
Tedy, 110
MANN
Edward, 124
MANNING
Nathaniel, 35
Richard, 18
MANSFIELD
Elizabeth, 162
Richard, 162
Thomas, 162
William, 162
MANSHIP
Nathan, 35
MANWEARING
Elisha, 163
MAP...
Daniel, 39
MARCHANT
Will, 8
MARCHER
Thomas, 135
MARGARETS
FNACY, 53
MARINE
Jonathan, 35
William, 27
MARKFAR
Dunken, 18

MARKHAMS
DESIRE, 48, 54
MARLIN
John, 143
MARLOW
Patrick, 8
MARRETT
John, 27
MARSH
Mary, 113
Sarah, 115
Thomas, 69, 72, 81,
85, 91, 92, 113,
115
MARSHALL
Charles, 62, 79, 85
James, 45
John, 17
Mary, 144, 148
MARSHALL
Richard, 156
William, 156
MARSHALLS
OUTLETT, 62
MARTIN
Charles, 156
Elizabeth, 156
Francis, 156
George, 151
Jacob, 156
John, 143
Mary, 10
Phebe, 66
Robert, 159
Susannah, 52
Thomas, 126, 157,
159
William, 66, 94, 142,
156, 159, 164
MARTINE
Thomas, 159
William, 123

MARTLAND
Edward, 166
MARVEL
Elizabeth, 47
MASON
Elizabeth, 158, 159
Hope, 165
John, 165
Mathew, 68, 73, 77
Sebastian, 4, 5
MASSEY
Nicholas, 6, 75, 78,
114
Peter, 75
Thomas, 75
MATHAR
George, 148
MATHER
William, 45
MATHERS
George, 69
MATHEWS
Anne, 68
Moris, 7
William, 45
MATHEWSON
Lewis, 167
MATTERSHAW
Geffery, 151
MATTERSHAW
Jeoffrey, 118
MATTHEWS
Ann, 158
Anne, 154, 158
Henry, 158
William, 167
MATTOX
Mary, 142
MATTUX
Charity, 139
Charles, 139
Elizabeth, 139

MISHEW
  William, 5
MITCHEL
  Levin, 55
  Mary, 54
MITCHELL
  Alice, 156
  Anne, 123
  John, 113, 156
  Rebeccah, 108
  Rebeckah, 113
  Rosannah, 32
  Sarah, 156
  William, 142
MOASLEYS ANGLE,
  45
MOFFET
  William, 61
MOHON
  Anne, 26
  Esther, 26
  John, 26
  Margaret, 26
  Priscilla, 26
MOODY
  Ann, 106
MOONE
  Henry, 147
  Ralph, 134, 147
MOOR
  George, 97, 99
  Mary, 97, 99
  Michael, 96
  Richard, 93, 97
MOORE
  Francis, 152
  Joan, 147
  John, 152
  Mary, 150
  Michael, 84
  Richard, 64, 82, 90

MOORS
  Thomas, 17
MORDICK
  Anne, 63
MORECOCK
  Anne, 81
  Mary, 85
MORGAN
  Abraham, 118
  Elizabeth, 61
  James, 52
  John, 45, 139, 157
  Margret, 114
  Owen, 5
MORLY
  Ralph, 117
MORRELL
  Thomas, 88
MORRIS
  Ann, 36
  George, 37
  John, 82
MORRISON
  William, 152
MORTON
  Robert, 161
MOSELY
  Joseph, 146
  Samuell, 146
MOUBREY
  William, 39
MOULD
  Humphery, 7
  Humphry, 8
MOULTON
  Susana, 164
MOUNSIER
  Thomas, 84
MOUNT SILLEY, 42
MOUNTFORT
  Thomas, 102

MOUNTICUE
  Bryan, 124
  William, 124
MOVALL
  David, 13
MUIR
  J., 50
MULATTO
  Agnis, 35
  Betty, 165
  Judy, 35
  Sarah, 32
MULGRAVE, 34
MULLIKIN
  John, 150, 156
MULRAIGNE
  Cornelius, 106
MULRAYNES
  Cornelius, 130
MUNDAY
  John, 48
MUNROE
  duncan, 89
MURFEY
  John, 97
MURPHEY
  Charles, 129
  Elizabeth, 142
  James, 112, 132
  John, 80, 127, 136
  Sarah, 142
  Thomas, 93
MURPHY
  David, 6
  James, 42, 111
  Richard, 118
  William, 18, 106
MURRAY
  Elizabeth, 16
MUSE
  John, 30

Frances, 28
Henry, 1, 12, 19, 22,
  31, 35, 37
John, 28, 30, 33, 37,
  40, 44, 50
Major, 9
William, 28, 44
TROATH
William, 136
TROTH
Sarah, 155
William, 147, 155
TROTTER
Walter, 152, 155, 161
William, 9
TRQAVERS
Henry, 18
TRULOE
Anne, 159
Susannah, 159
TRUNDLE
Elizabeth, 73, 75, 77,
  78, 86
TRYALL
Elizabeth, 99
TUBMAN
Richard, 41
TUCKAR
Nathaniel, 138
TUCKER
Nathaniel, 63, 67, 71,
  89
TULL
Richard, 20
TUNES
Aaron, 1
TUNISEY
Aron, 6
TURBOTT
Michaell, 101
TURBUTT
Foster, 140

Michael, 113
Michaell, 108
William, 94, 98
TURLE
William, 63, 64, 67,
  70
TURLO
Major, 81, 92
William, 51, 72, 81,
  84, 85, 89, 91
TURLOE
William, 134
TURNER
Henry, 60
Mary, 163, 165, 166
William, 154
TWIGG
John, 30
TWYFORD
Francis, 1
William, 26, 53
TYPINS
William, 92
UNAHANN
Mary, 166
UNDERWOOD
Mary, 63, 64, 72, 80,
  85, 91
UNGLE
Charles, 154
Robert, 141, 142
URLING
Sarah, 143
VAINE
John, 144
VALLIANT
(N), 167
VANDERFORD
Charles, 74, 80
VASS
Robert, 56

VAUGHAN
Thomas, 104, 107
William, 94
VAUHAN
Mathuslah, 123
VAULX
James, 2, 36, 50
VAUS
Robert, 110
VEACH
Thomas, 51
VICARS
Isaac, 14
John, 14
VICERS
John, 44
VICKARS
Joseph, 134
Mary, 134
Thomas, 8
VICKERS
John, 44
Joseph, 133
Mary, 133
Thomas, 44, 50
VICTOR
Thomas, 5
VIETCH
Thomas, 7
VINCENT
Barbarah, 110
Elizabeth, 110
John, 3
VINEY
Godfrey, 145
William, 145
VINSON
Bruffitt, 39
James, 31
VOSS
James, 49
Sarah, 157, 158

WILLOBY
  Martha, 25
  William, 1
WILLOWBY
  Edward, 2
  Hannah, 2
  Martin, 59
  William, 2
WILLSON
  Jane, 105
  John, 5, 90
  Joseph, 34
  Mary, 154
  Stephen, 131
  William, 70, 145, 146,
    154
WILLY
  John, 16
WILSON
  Charles, 109
  Ephraim, 18
  Ruth, 102
  William, 114, 141
WILTON
  John, 163
WINCHESTER
  Catherine, 136
  Isaac, 99, 118, 119,
    120, 123, 153
  John, 91
  Katherine, 127
WINDER
  James, 136
WINDOES
  Henry, 44
WINFEILDS
    TROUBLE, 47
WING
  Ann, 45, 47
  Thomas, 55, 60
WINGATE
  Anglow, 30

John, 30
Phillip, 30, 38, 51
WINLOCK
  Edward, 71, 81, 92
WINN
  Ephraim, 76
WINNE
  Ephraim, 79
WINSMORE
  John, 5, 9
WINSTANLY
  Edith, 39
  Elizabeth, 58
WINSTON
  George, 105
WINTERSELL
  Jane, 112
  William, 111, 112
WITHERIDGE
  Mary, 153
WITHERS
  Samuel, 133
WOLAHANE
  James, 142
WOLFE
  Thomas, 87
WOLLAHAND
  Mary, 131
  Morriss, 131
  Thomas, 131
WOLLMAN
  Mr., 102
WOOD
  Elizabeth, 99
  John, 99
WOODGATE
  John, 30, 33
WOODLAN
  Richard, 30
WOODLAND
  Richard, 53, 58

WOODWARD
  Benjamin, 44
  Martha, 8
  Mrs., 1
WOOLEN
  Oliver, 18
WOOLFORD
  Elizabeth, 19
  James, 13, 14, 19, 23
  John, 18, 19, 32, 50
  Roger, 19
  Thomas, 15, 19, 57
WOOLLEN
  Edward, 42
  John, 42
  William, 42
WOOLMAN
  Mr., 104
  Richard, 108
WORGAN
  Elizabeth, 155
  Mary, 155
  Phebe, 155
  Rachel, 155
  William, 155
WORKEMAN
  Anthony, 135
WORLDLEY
  John, 65
WORLEY
  John, 68, 139
WORLOE
  Cornelius, 136
WORNER
  John, 132
WRAUGHTON
  Thomas, 12
  William, 12
WRENCH
  William, 70, 89, 94
WRIGHT
  Charles, 95, 98

David, 37, 61
Edward, 44, 78, 79,
  83, 98
John, 37, 61, 98, 99
Margaret, 164, 166,
  167
Margarett, 106
Margaritt, 165
Nathaniel, 63, 90, 111
Samuel, 72
Solomon, 63, 64, 72,
  80, 81, 85, 87, 89,
  91, 92, 98
Thomas, 85, 89
Thomas Hynson, 94,
  96

WRIGHTSON
  John, 130
WROTTEN
  Ambros, 30
  Thomas, 57
WYAETT
  Thomas, 65
WYASS
  William Perry, 39
WYATT
  William, 86
WYETT
  Timothy, 122
WYNN
  Jane, 107

YEWELL
  Sarah, 132
  Thomas, 62, 73, 86,
    89, 118, 132
YONGE
  John, 6
YOUNG
  Charles, 93, 97
  Edward, 99
  John, 22
  Levi, 26
  Mathew, 26
  Rachel, 26
YOUNGER
  John, 118
  William, 131

Heritage Books by F. Edward Wright:

18th Century Records of the German Lutheran Church at Philadelphia, Pennsylvania (St. Michael's and Zion): Volume 1, Baptisms, 1745–1769
Robert L. Hess and F. Edward Wright

18th Century Records of the German Lutheran Church at Philadelphia, Pennsylvania (St. Michael's and Zion): Volume 2, Baptisms, 1770–1786
Translated by Robert L. Hess, Ph.D. Edited by F. Edward Wright

18th Century Records of the German Lutheran Church of Philadelphia, Pennsylvania (St. Michael's and Zion): Volume 3, Baptisms, 1787–1800
Translated by Robert L. Hess, Ph.D. Edited by F. Edward Wright

18th Century Records of the German Lutheran Church at Philadelphia, Pennsylvania (St. Michael's and Zion): Volume 4, Marriages and Confirmations
Robert L. Hess and F. Edward Wright

18th Century Records of the German Lutheran Church at Philadelphia, Pennsylvania (St. Michael's and Zion): Volume 5, Burials
Robert L. Hess and F. Edward Wright

Abstracts of Bucks County, Pennsylvania, Wills, 1685–1785

Abstracts of Cumberland County, Pennsylvania, Wills, 1750–1785

Abstracts of Cumberland County, Pennsylvania, Wills, 1785–1825

Abstracts of Philadelphia County, Pennsylvania, Wills:
Volumes: 1682–1726; 1726–1747; 1748–1763; 1763–1784; 1777–1790; 1790–1802; 1802–1809; 1810–1815; 1815–1819; and 1820–1825

Abstracts of South Central Pennsylvania, Newspapers, Volume 1, 1785–1790

Abstracts of South Central Pennsylvania, Newspapers, Volume 3, 1796–1800

Abstracts of the Newspapers of Georgetown and the Federal City, 1789–99

Abstracts of York County, Pennsylvania, Wills, 1749–1819

Adams County [Pennsylvania] Church Records of the 18th Century

Baltimore Directory of 1807

Berks County, Pennsylvania, Church Records of the 18th Century, Volumes 1–4

Bible Records of Washington County, Maryland

Bucks County, Pennsylvania, Church Records of the 17th and 18th Centuries, Volume 1: German Church Records

Bucks County, Pennsylvania, Church Records of the 17th and 18th Centuries, Volume 2: Quaker Records: Falls and Middletown Monthly Meetings
Anna Miller Watring and F. Edward Wright

Bucks County, Pennsylvania, Church Records of the 17th and 18th Centuries, Volume 4

Caroline County, Maryland, Marriages, Births and Deaths, 1850–1880

Citizens of the Eastern Shore of Maryland, 1659–1750

Colonial Families of Cape May County, New Jersey, Revised 2nd Edition

Colonial Families of Delaware:
Volumes: Volume 1; Volume 2: Kent and Sussex Counties;
Volume 3 (2nd Edition): Kent and Sussex Counties;
Volume 4: Sussex County; Volume 5: New Castle; Volume 6: Kent County

www.ingramcontent.com/pod-product-compliance
Lightning Source LLC
Chambersburg PA
CBHW062217270326
41930CB00009B/1769

* 9 7 8 1 6 8 0 3 4 4 8 5 1 *